The American Soul

Jeremy P. Tarcher / Putnam

A member of Penguin Group (USA) Inc.

New York

Rediscovering

the Wisdom of

the Founders

The American Soul

JACOB NEEDLEMAN

Most Tarcher/Putnam books are available at special quantity discounts
for bulk purchase for sales promotions, premiums, fund-raising, and
educational needs. Special books or book excerpts also can be created
to fit specific needs. For details, write Penguin Group (USA) Inc. Special Markets,
375 Hudson Street, New York, NY 10014.

Jeremy P. Tarcher/Putnam
a member of
Penguin Group (USA) Inc.
375 Hudson Street
New York, NY 10014
www.penguin.com

Grateful acknowledgment is made to Random House, Inc., for permission to
quote in Chapter 3 excerpts from *Lao Tsu: Tao Te Ching,* translated by Gia-Fu Feng
and Jane English (Vintage Books, 1989), and to Clear Light Publishers, Santa Fe,
New Mexico, for permission to quote in Chapter 6 excerpts from
White Roots of Peace by Paul Wallace.

The Library of Congress Catalogued the hardcover edition as follows:

Needleman, Jacob.
The American soul / by Jacob Needleman.
p.   cm.
ISBN 1-58542-138-3
1. National characteristics, American.   2. United States—History.   3. United
States—Moral conditions.   4. Social values—United States.   5. Spirituality—
United States.   I. Title.

E169.1 .N43   2002   2001046311
973—dc21
ISBN 1-58542-226-6 (Paperback edition)

Printed in the United States of America
1   3   5   7   9   10   8   6   4   2

Book design by Janet Parker

Where there is no vision, the people perish.

PROVERBS 29:18

To my teachers

ACKNOWLEDGMENTS

My first thanks are to the Fetzer Institute for the understanding and support that helped me to complete this book, and for the warmth and idealism of the whole Fetzer community.

I owe a great debt of gratitude to friends and colleagues who read this book at various stages of completion and offered much-needed criticism and encouragement. Roger Lipsey took on this task in a far more rigorous and loving way than I had a right to expect even from such a valued friend. In the same spirit, I wish to thank Angeles Arrien, George Baker, Sharon Ball, Steven Brown, Carlo Brumat, John Hunt, Nancy Larson, Rob Lehman, John Miller, John Oliver, John Piazza, Judy Shelton and Alison Tierney.

I have been very fortunate in the editors who have worked with me. Mitch Horowitz at Tarcher was everything an editor should be, both down-to-earth and practical when necessary, bringing his own visionary insight into the questions that I was trying to confront. I am also deeply grateful to Harriet Rubin for the editorial commitment, energy and intelligence that helped me to undertake the writing of this book. Roger Scholl also offered valuable observations and support.

I wish to thank my agent, Michael Katz, for his unfailing professionalism, his keen insights and his friendship over the years.

My thanks also to Ashala Gabriel for her help, her encouragement and her continuing faith in my work.

I am especially grateful to Maril Rianna Blanchard for allowing me to make extensive use of her superb unpublished retelling of the Iroquois creation story and for her generous help at any time of the day or night when I was defeated by the computer.

My personal assistant, Shivanii Singh, together with her husband, Frank

Cordes, helped me in ways too numerous to mention—with an extraordinary combination of intelligence, efficiency and pure open-heartedness.

Likewise, I am grateful to Noelle Cafagna for all the ways she helped during the preparation of the early drafts.

I am deeply grateful to my friend Sidney Lanier for the spirited conversations that nourished my wish to understand the inner meaning of the idea of America.

I owe special thanks to Roger Weir for sharing with me his remarkable knowledge of American history and his insight into its metaphysical dimensions.

I wish also to thank Laurance Rockefeller for the generous support that enabled me to start this project.

Finally, my wife, Gail, brought me the incalculable support of understanding exactly what I was hoping to accomplish in this book, while tirelessly helping in every essential aspect of its writing with her keen critical mind, her eagle eye and, above all, her unwavering conscience and her love.

CONTENTS

II. In the Beginning

III: The Crimes of America

Conclusion: The America of Our Hopes 329

Preamble

He used to call himself "the last American." In fact, he seemed anything but American—with his commanding British accent, his aristocratic bearing and his bred-in-the-bone sense of form, always and in everything. I would smile to myself when he spoke like that. I was born here, after all. How could a foreigner, even a man as great-hearted as he was, lay such claim to America? Only now do I begin to understand what he meant, and only now do I see how deep his love for America really was.

It was the summer of 1974. The Vietnam War was tearing the country apart. The image of America's invincibility and goodness was crashing down around us. I had gathered a group to meet him at his summer house overlooking San Francisco Bay—about fifteen people, most of whom were my students, and a few like myself from the older generation, who could not accept the judgment against America that was rising into the world through the moral agony of the younger generation. I had been encountering this judgment every day in my classes at the university, but I continued to turn away from it, unwilling to question the fundamental goodness of my country.

I had brought some students and colleagues to meet this man, whom I had long considered remarkable for his wisdom and wide-ranging intelligence. I knew that although before World War II he had pursued a diplomatic career in Great Britain, his life had soon taken him in quite a different direction; and never once in all the years I had known him had I heard him say much about purely political questions. I never doubted that he was a shrewd observer of modern life, and his success in business was evidence of his worldly acumen. But with him, the main issue was always the path of self-knowledge, the need to awaken from the illusions about oneself that hold humanity in their grip and that prevent us from seeing reality and living according to conscience. I had never known anyone who could speak with more insight about the nature of this path, this way of seeking that lies at the root of all the great spiritual philosophies and traditions of the world. The quarrels of nations, the fervor of patriotism, the programs of social movements, the luster of heroic figures or partisan symbols: I was sure that all this was to him part of the sleep of the human race. And the task of waking up demanded, among other things, the struggle to free oneself from the falsehoods and attachments that gave these social and political phenomena their hypnotic power.

And so it astonished me when he suddenly interrupted one of the younger people who was once again speaking of America with contempt, condemning not only its war policy but the whole structure of its government, the injustice that they felt was built into its institutions and its laws and that had shaped its entire history. America was hypocritically betraying all that it claimed to stand for. American corporations were raping nature and the world. The media were under the thumb of American greed, blanketing the earth with a global consumerism that was destroying the values of simpler, nobler cultures.

Such views were not delivered in any systematic way, but rather crept in and out of my students' questions and conversation throughout the evening as they gave voice to their revulsion at what America offered them for their future and their present daily life.

We were sitting on the patio under a black, moonless sky, our faces lit by the flickering light of a few candles in the center of a large stone table. We all had iced drinks in our hands or in front of us. His interruption took the form of very slowly putting down the glass that was in his hand—so slowly and quietly, and with such a measured, even movement that at first it seemed like some kind of ritual gesture. Everyone suddenly became quiet and looked at him, waiting. I remember listening for a long time to the waves of the bay and watching the lights of San Francisco across the water. The wind was shifting and turning cool. People were putting their collars up and hugging themselves, but no one dared get up. Foghorns were answering each other like far-off, unseen sea creatures.

Just as slowly and evenly, he angled his long, lean body back in his chair and gazed at nothing in particular. Then he turned his head as though it were a gun turret and looked directly at the husky, bearded young man who had just been speaking about the crimes of America. In the flickering candlelight, his bony face seemed wondrously alive and menacing at the same time. What he said to the young man—and of course to all of us present—was only this:

"You don't know what you have here." Then, after an uncomfortable pause, "You simply don't know what you have."

I doubt if anyone really understood what he meant. He was obviously speaking about America and telling us we did not appreciate what it was. But apart from that, we—in any case, I—could be sure of nothing else. Had this remarkable man of the spirit suddenly descended into ordinary patriotism or some kind of political partisanship? Certainly not. It was not only that such an attitude would have utterly contradicted what I knew of his views about the human condition and the inner causes of war and violence; more than that, it was the *way* he had just spoken—with the sense of presence and weight that he always reserved for ideas that referred to what is sacred within us, which transcends all distinctions of nation, class or race.

A few days later, talking to my students about what he had said, I thought of all the historical events he must have witnessed in his life. In the early part of the century he had lived and traveled widely throughout Asia and Europe, emigrating to the United States in 1944. His business had brought him into contact with many of the governments and leaders that shaped history between the First and the Second World Wars, and he had seen, from within, the forces at work in the play of nations. As a trained engineer, he also had an insider's understanding of the power of modern science and technology. And as for his grasp of philosophical ideas, I frequently found myself shedding my professional "expertise" and bowing to his keen insight. In his presence, I often felt myself to be a "mere" American: raw, uneducated, awkward, naive—like a child. Yet that evening *he* was the American, "the last American," freezing us with the unfathomably powerful statement:

"You don't know what you have here."

I.

The Idea of America

ONE

OUR AMERICA

America was once the hope of the world.

But what kind of hope? More than the hope of material prosperity, although that was part of it; and more than the promise of equality and liberty, although that, too, was an important part of it. And more than safety and security, precious as these things are. The deeper hope of America was its vision of what humanity is and can become—individually and in community. It was through that vision that all the material and social promise of America took its fire and light and its voice that called to men and women within its own borders and throughout the world. America was once a great idea, and it is such ideas that move the world, that open the possibility of meaning in human life.

It has been said that any question can lead to truth if it is an aching question. For one person it may be the question of life after death, for another the problem of suffering, the causes of war and injustice. Or it may be something more personal and immediate—a profound ethical dilemma, a problem involving the whole direction of one's life. An aching question, a question that is not just a matter of curiosity or a fleeting burst of emotion, cannot be answered with old thought. Possessed by such a question, one is hungry for ideas of a very different order than the familiar categories that usually accompany us throughout our lives. One is both hungry and, at the same time, more discriminating, less susceptible to credulity and suggestibility. The intelligence of the heart begins to call to us in our sleep.

For many of us, such is now the question of the meaning of America. But it is also an elusive question. If we consider America only as a nation, that is, as a man-made construction, then it is hard to feel any ultimacy about the problem of America. Nations, as such, come and go: Persia, Rome, Byzantium have all sunk into the ocean of time. All the empires and national states of the past have come and gone in what seems like the twinkling of an eye, though in their time each appeared to itself and to the world as strong and real and enduring. And, of course, our era has witnessed the stunning disintegration of vast collectivities: the Third Reich, the Soviet Union, the political organization of Eastern Europe. Even the idea itself of "nation" may be disappearing or transmuting into what has been termed a "global web" of financial instrumentalities, electronic communication and advanced technological consumerism.

All my life I had been unable to understand or sympathize with people who seemed so passionately concerned about the preservation or enhancement of America. It had often seemed to me hypocrisy, a mask that covered the all-too-human fears for one's personal safety or comfort, sometimes mixed with the kind of self-righteousness that had turned me away from the religions of church and synagogue. But I was even more troubled by people who attacked America and who were always arguing about hidden conspiracies, intentional injustices that were built into "the system," and so forth. Why, I wondered, were they not just as concerned about the human condition itself? And about their own incomprehensible mortal life on earth? They made me feel that I was selfish to have such questions burning in me.

And so, I was astonished and strangely joyous when I finally turned directly to studying the history of America and found almost everywhere that the men and women who carved out the ideals of America were driven by the same transcendent questions that had always been my own as well. I began to see that for many of these men and women America meant the struggle for conditions of life under which these ultimate questions could be freely pursued.

This glimpse of the motive of the Founders was at first very fleeting and insubstantial. Time and again this perception of mine was overwhelmed by the "authority" of the accepted views about everything pertaining to America. Historical knowledge and theory, political and economic opinions about the meaning of past and present events—the old as well as the latest views about America—covered over that glimpse into the origin of the American experiment. Even the accepted views about the religious motivations of the Founders clouded the issue—in fact, these commonly accepted views were the most distracting of all. They equated the religious impulses of our forefathers with the religion I knew from my own childhood, a religion that was simply dull and oppressive.

A New Beginning

America is the fact, the symbol and the promise of a new beginning. And in human life, in our lives as they are, this possibility is among the most sacred aspects of existence. All that is old and already formed can continue to live only if it allows within itself the conditions for a new beginning. Life itself is the mysterious, incomprehensible blending of the new and the old, of what already is and what is coming into being. The question of America is there: if America loses the meaning of its existence and if, in fact, America is now the dominant cultural influence in the world, then what will become of the world? The question of America leads all of us directly into the question of the purpose and destiny of human life itself in this era.

America and the Teachings of Wisdom

THE WORLD OF IDEAS AND THE DISEASE OF MATERIALISM

Our world, so we see and hear on all sides, is drowning in materialism, commercialism, consumerism. But the problem is not really there. What we ordinarily speak of as materialism is a result, not a cause. The root of materialism is a poverty of ideas about the inner and the outer world. Less and less does our contemporary culture have, or even seek, commerce with great ideas, and it is that lack that is weakening the human spirit. This is the essence of materialism. Materialism is a disease of the mind starved for ideas.

Throughout history ideas of a certain kind and nature have been disseminated into the life of humanity in order to help human beings understand and feel the possibility of the deep inner change that would enable them to serve the purpose for which they were created, namely, to act in the world as conscious, individual instruments of God, the ultimate principle of reality and value. Ideas of this kind are formulated in order to have a specific range of action on the human psyche: to touch the heart as well as the intellect; to shock us into questioning our present understanding; to point us to the greatness around us in nature and the universe, and the potential greatness slumbering within ourselves; to open our eyes to the real needs of our neighbor; to confront us with our own profound ignorance and our criminal fears and egoism; to show us that we are not here for ourselves alone, but as necessary particles of divine love.

These are the contours of the ancient wisdom, considered as ideas embodied in religious and philosophical doctrines, works of sacred art, literature and music and, in a very fundamental way, in indications of practical methods by which a man or woman can work, as it is said, to become what he or she really is. Without feeling the full range of such ideas, or sensing even a modest, but pure, trace of them, we are bound to turn for meaning to the lawfully existing instinctive impulses within ourselves toward physical pleasure (impulses which are meant to serve and not lead) and to the artificially induced illusions of what the ancient wisdom calls pride or the ego with its attendant fears, hatred and servility, as well as to the ego's exploitation of the intellect in the form of a swollen overestimation of disconnected logic and purely mental knowing. *This* is the root of materialism, the cultural neurosis of an era that believes that only the external senses show us the real world and that only physical or social comfort is worth striving for. Simply put, the neurosis of materialism leads us to despair. Despair because the impulse of hope, which is implanted in human nature as part of our unique consciousness, finds nothing in the world or in our concept of ourselves that carries the mark of indubitable, enduring truth and goodness, those two ultimate principles toward which that impulse of hope is meant to lead us.

But no idea exists alone. Great ideas are always part of a living system of ideas, all of which are necessary for the full understanding of any one of them. When we speak of the idea of America, we are speaking of many interconnected ethical ideas, both metaphysical ideas that deal with ultimate reality, and ethical and social ideas, which *all together* offered hope to the world. The idea of America, with all that it contained within it about the moral law, nature, God and the human soul, once reflected to some extent the timeless, ancient wisdom that has guided human life since the dawn of history. America was a new and original expression, in the form of a social and political experiment, of ideas that have always been part of what may be called the great web of Truth. Explicitly and implicitly, the idea of America has resonated with this ancient, timeless wisdom and has allowed something of its power to touch the heart and mind of humanity. It is necessary to recover this resonance, this relationship, however tenuous and partial, between the teachings of wisdom and the idea of America.

What are these "teachings of wisdom"? The fact of the matter is that it is possible to discern a profound commonality at the heart and root of all the major religions and spiritual philosophies of the world. Differing in outer expression and emphasis, these age-old traditions are nourished by a single hidden current of interconnected ideas—like so many ancient trees of varied form and foliage watered by the same underground stream.

Between Two Worlds

Within this vast body of teachings about man in the universal world, several elements stand out as critical for our understanding of the idea of America. One of the most central of these elements is the idea of man as a being who exists between two worlds—an inner world of great spiritual vision and power, and an outer world of material realities and constraint. Both worlds call to us, and as long as we live, we are obliged to give each its due. Our task, our place in the scheme of creation, is to become conscious instruments of action on earth under the aegis of divine law and love. But, in order to fulfill this role, we must work to transcend the sense of self-identity that society thrusts upon us and that prevents us from recognizing our own inner self and its power to serve the good. In this ancient teaching, freedom is understood not as the license to obey one's desires but as obedient submission to a deep inner law; independence is understood as the discovery of one's own authentic self, which—although it may seem paradoxical—is also a mirror of the common cosmic Selfhood; equality is understood as every human being's right to seek the truth and to be allowed to give his or her light to the common welfare.

The idea of man's two natures, along with some of its ethical implications, was dramatically expressed in the teaching known as Stoicism, which flourished in the early Roman Empire and which served as inspiration to Washington, Adams, Jefferson and many other of the Founding Fathers of America.[1] The most politically powerful man of his time, the Emperor Marcus Aurelius, and one of the least powerful, the freed slave Epictetus, who was a mentor to the Emperor, both adhered to the Stoic philosophy. In this teaching, a human being is viewed as a being whose individual mind is meant to reflect and manifest the same all-universal and all-beneficent consciousness that creates and maintains the cosmos. At the same time, we are made to live for a finite time in a mortal body and are obliged by the true power of reason (which includes cosmic love) to care for our neighbor and to answer the moral requirements of family, society and culture—all of which are also part of the universal scheme. Although our inner nature is cosmic, our finite life is on earth; our duties are to both the immortal presence within and, while we live on earth, to our temporary role in the social order. Our task is simultaneous inner freedom and full outer engagement. In the words of Epictetus:

> It is difficult [and necessary] to unite and combine these qualities—the diligence of a man who devotes himself to material things, and the constancy of one who disregards them [i.e., who is not attached to them]—yet not impossible. Otherwise, it would be impossible to be happy.[2]

And in the words of the Emperor Marcus Aurelius, speaking of the need to accept the desires and sufferings attendant upon being obliged to live in a mortal body on earth and the simultaneous duty to act according to the dictates of one's own inner God: "Nothing will happen to me which is not in conformity with the Nature of the All. [But] it depends on me to do nothing which is contrary to my god and my *daimon* [inner spirit]."[3]

THE INNER MEANING OF DEMOCRACY

As for the idea of democracy, the Founding Fathers—Washington, Jefferson, Franklin and others—never conceived of it solely as an external form of government. The meaning of democracy was always rooted in a vision of human nature as both fallen and perfectible—inwardly fallen and inwardly perfectible. To a significant extent, democracy in its specifically American form was created to allow men and women to seek their own higher principle within themselves. Without that inner meaning, democracy becomes, as Plato and Aristotle pointed out twenty-five hundred years ago, a celebration of disorder and superficiality.

All the rights guaranteed by the Constitution were based on a vision of human nature that calls us to be responsible beings—responsible to something within ourselves that is higher than the all-too-human desires for personal gain and satisfaction; higher than the dictates of the purely theoretical or logical mind; higher than instinctive loyalties to family and tribe.

This higher reality within the self was called many things—reason, conscience, Nature's God. When this idea is left out, or treated as though its meaning were obvious, then the ideals of independence and liberty lose their power and truth. They become mere names that mask the ever-present tendency of nations and groups and individuals to seek only their own external and short-term advantages.

Great ideas, ideas that meaningfully reflect something of the world's ancient tradition of wisdom, have the power to bind people together and to bring unity under a goal and a vision that are stronger and deeper than all personal, short-term gain. This is the mark of great ideas: they unify people and they also act to *unify the disparate parts of the human being;* they speak of a social order that is possible *on the basis of an ordering within the individual self.* The idea of America once had something of this power of unification.

WHY WE NEED HEROES

It is the same with the heroes we learned about as children—Washington, Jefferson, Lincoln. Once they stood as symbols incarnating the idea of America. They lived their lives amid the same forces and obstructions within which every human being must find his or her way through life. But we regard them as heroes because they also lived and acted in relation to something that transcends and transforms the human condition. Each had his weaknesses, his defeats, his doubts; but in each of them another and greater force existed that expressed itself as the idea of America. In this, they were heroes in the ancient sense of the term: they were demi-gods.

THE IDEA OF MAN'S TWO NATURES

In many ancient mythic traditions, the hero is a demi-god, a symbol of man as a two-natured being. In Greek mythology, he is usually the offspring of an immortal god and a mortal mother—as were Achilles, Perseus, Hercules and many others. This juxtaposition of the eternal and the finite, the divine and the human in the hero's makeup gives the ancient legends their particular drama, poignancy and mystery. And, it might be added, their haunting sense of reality. No one who hears these tales with an open heart can fail to sense that, although the stories in them are in a literal sense impossible, in a deeper sense they are portraying the world and life as they really are—they are portraying the laws and forces that actually govern human life in the cosmos.

But it is difficult to hold these two opposing aspects of human nature together in one's mind; neither the logical mind nor the merely emotional mind can do it. The idea of our two natures, which is such an essential aspect of the ancient wisdom, requires great artistry and many other related ideas and conditions of life in order for it to remain a vital force in a culture or in one's individual approach to life. The idea in its many forms often decays through mistaken overemphasis on one or another of the two aspects of human nature. Either the hero begins to be regarded as purely superhuman and a god, or the transcendent aspect of the hero's nature is rejected and the all-too-human aspects emphasized. In the former case, the hero is regarded as an unattainable ideal with little or no relevance to our actual lives—as a kind of fantasy that promotes self-deception about our human weaknesses. In the latter case, through emphasizing only the human weaknesses of the hero, we lose the hope of transcendence and cynically, despairingly reduce our vision of man to that of a socially conditioned animal.

Our heroes have gone from being regarded as nonhuman gods who could do no wrong to being seen as mere mortals whose great deeds were only the result of chance external forces and whose great words were often hypocritical or motivated by the desire for personal gain. At the very most, such "realism" grants our heroes brilliant minds, shrewdness, or the kind of morality that is often betrayed by their actions. We swing between naive idealism and cynical "realism." We have lost the ability to understand that a hero is the representation of an idea.

MYTH AND THE MEANING OF AMERICA

We need to rediscover the deeper, mythic meaning of our heroes and our nation—a mythic meaning not for children, but for adults. Adults need mythic symbols just as much—or even more—than children. We need ideas; but we need ideas expressed in ways that touch not only our logical minds but also our feelings. It is one of the teachings of wisdom that the merely logical mind—when it is cut off from the intrinsically higher human feelings of wonder and the sense of the sacred—inevitably becomes a plaything of the external senses, convincing us that only what is perceived with these outward-directed senses is real. Ideas communicated through myth, on the other hand, show us a world that is perceived through the vision of wonder, love of truth and the sense of the sacred, the impulse to serve and to participate in a greater reality—what we may call the inner world.

Many of us may think of myth as something opposed to fact, as falsehood or superstition. But in the root meaning of the word, the great myths of mankind are representations of cosmic and spiritual ideas, expressed in a way that touches the deeper springs of the mind—the intelligence of the heart. This mythic world does not exclude the world of concrete, everyday reality, but includes it in a greater awareness of the paradox of human existence. Within this wider vision, when we see, for example, the flaws and compromises in the life and character of one of our heroes, these "facts" will be inseparably juxtaposed with his immense courage or moral vision or self-sacrifice for the good of the nation. The mythic vision will not treat these contradictory aspects of his nature as merely a sign of hypocrisy or inner disorder. On the contrary, it will regard that contradiction as a reflection of the mystery of the two levels within our human nature—the divinity within man joined to the all-too-human. We need to reclaim these symbols before they are destroyed by narrow "realism" or naive "idealism." We need to reclaim them in a way that corresponds to what is necessary for us now in our own era.

They are there, these symbols, or archetypes, in our hearts and minds; Lincoln is there, Jefferson is there, Washington is there, the Constitutional Convention is there, and, as we shall see, many other people and events are also there. They live in our subconscious, and we need to let them come forward and act again upon us. As it is, they are now being covered over by a foolish realism that sees only "facts" of the outer world and is blind to the laws of the inner world. Do we have so many symbols and sources of mythic power in our primal consciousness that we can afford to eviscerate these American meanings that are already there waiting to help us? *We need to remythologize the idea of America.*

THE WEB OF TRUTH AND THE TWO HISTORIES OF AMERICA

What I am saying is that the idea of America has brought a special kind of hope to the world because it has carried, to some extent, ideas rooted in an ancient, primordial wisdom. The idea of America has expressed enough of that wisdom to touch the hearts of men and women throughout the world who yearned not only for wealth or safety or comfort, but also for meaning and transcendence. This idea of America needs to be recovered—and it can be recovered by looking at our historical icons in the light of ancient wisdom. The aim is to build—or rebuild—a bridge between our contemporary American culture and the source of hope and meaning that has always existed behind the scenes of what we call history.

We need to consider that there are two histories of the world and that, correspondingly, there are also two histories of America. In the great sweep of world events over the centuries, what we call history is mainly, as one modern observer has termed it, "the history of crime." We measure our epochs and periods by wars, convulsions, revolutions, assassinations and violent usurpations; mass executions, oppressions of peoples, invasions, murders and enslavements. The wars of the Mediterranean basin—the wars between ancient Greece and Persia and Sparta, for example—define our view of antiquity; the career of the conquering Alexander the Great defines and names another whole period of history. And although we reckon time by a sacred reality, the birth of Christ or, as in the Hebraic tradition, the image of the sacred creation of the universe, everything that happens after the sacred beginning of historical time, everything we take as significant, is an event that exhibits one or another of the elements of human depravity or violence. Even such seemingly neutral historical designations as the "Industrial Revolution" or the "Enlightenment" or the "Scientific Revolution," when we examine their meaning, translate into names for periods of accelerated external change in human affairs and imply little real reference to the moral or conscious development of human beings.

One might object that wars and revolutions produce such dramatic changes in the life of cultures that they must stand out as historical markers, much in the way that mountain ranges and great rivers mark the spatial borders of a nation or people. But the marking of history as we know it is more than a matter of convenience and gross, external determinations. Little or nothing in our history books communicates the horror and insanity of war, even so-called "noble" wars. Little or nothing helps us to feel the significance of the cunning and egoism, the callousness and self-deception of those individuals and events that are called "history makers." And even if the reporters of history try to present this aspect of human action, it is almost left behind and covered by all the other aspects of civilization that are presented as valuable—such as art or science or religion or social or economic improvements. To give only a paragraph or a chapter to a war in which thousands or even millions have been brutally murdered, and then go on to discuss the social improvements brought about by the consequences of the event, would be, on an individual level, a little like treating the murder of one's parents, say, mainly as a biographical event that "ushered in" a new period of wealth or independence in one's life.

THE SECOND HISTORY

But there is another history of the world, a second history, that flows from the efforts of more inwardly developed men and women to introduce truth and wisdom into the life of humanity. The proper meaning of the word "civilization" refers to these efforts and their results. We could speak of these undertakings as the introduction of great ideas into the world, but we must also keep in mind that such ideas come into the world not only in the form of philosophical teachings, but also in the form of religions, science, art—music, painting, sculpture, dance, architecture, myth and story. The great cathedrals of Europe are examples of such "insertions" into the life of the world, especially when taken in conjunction with certain other expressions of the wisdom teaching of Christianity—certain aspects of medieval music, for example, as well as the dynamic infusion of new theological meaning and hope brought by the deepened mythos of the figure of Mary.

Examples are countless of these "insertions," although one must be careful of one's own subjective preferences in estimating their authenticity. One might cite, as further examples, the monuments of ancient Egypt, the Hebraic scriptures, the life and story of Christ, the philosophy and practice—also involving the science of music—of Pythagoras and his school and the life and example of Socrates, just to name a few of the most obvious. And, of course, if one turns to the East, there would also be an overwhelming number of examples from what we are beginning to understand about the cultures of India, Tibet, China . . .

NO IDEA EXISTS ALONE

Looking at the past from this perspective—namely, from the perspective of the idea of the two histories—one soon comes upon a particular difficulty in discrimination. Just as no great idea exists alone, but is related to a network of ideas that provide a sense of hope or direction to human life, so are art forms and images and scriptures—and manners and customs—embedded in a network of ideas and orientations that altogether comprise their message and benefit to the world. But what we see in history is that ideas and symbols are often broken off from the larger matrix of which they are a part. Such piecemeal ideas and symbols may then serve as influences toward degeneration and destruction. They may become allied with highly subjective and divisive views and be taken over by the passions and ambitions of unregenerate human nature. We could even say that in such cases the energy of great ideas and symbols fuels the very tendencies of human life that they, in their authentic context, were meant to oppose. Although it is true that great ideas are one of the main forces that move the human race forward, often, in their broken or subjectivized form, they in fact intensify human violence and self-deception.

Murder and bloody war under the banner of Christian love; devastation under the banner of submission to Allah—such examples abound in human history. Ideas of honor, self-respect, duty to one's heritage and gods, the sacredness of the tribe or king—ideas that may originally have been part of the second history of the world, influences inserted into the sweep of human life—when broken off from their context, have repeatedly sown despair instead of hope throughout the cycles of civilization. To be disillusioned with Christianity because of the Inquisition or the Crusades, or their less vivid counterparts in modern life, does not necessarily represent a judgment on the Christian teaching itself, but on how broken pieces of it have combined and been used in the course of human history. This fate has befallen most of the great religions of the world.

THE METAPHYSICAL FUNCTION OF CIVILIZATION

The second history of civilization is the record of the regenerative influences introduced into the world over the centuries and millennia and of their positive action on the quality of human life. More often than not, this positive action takes place in a quiet way and may not be entirely visible to our everyday perception. The action of great ideas or the artistic expressions of wisdom or authentic religious rituals and doctrines call people to an inner life or to a kind of communal relationship that does not and cannot call attention to itself in the same way as does the coarser and often negative action of isolated ideas and symbols. This second kind of influence is extremely powerful, but also extremely subtle and, in the course of human history, fragile—in the sense that it is easily misused or misperceived. But whether outwardly perceived or not, this influence forms a kind of underground current that runs within or alongside the great raging river of the history that we know. No civilization can long endure or justify itself unless it allows these two currents to exist—one that moves outward toward the life of action and reaction in the outer world, and one that flows inward toward the endless source of consciousness and being.

To speak of two histories of America is to assert that this second current, this influence of great wisdom, has flowed through the life of this country from the very beginning. Alongside the tumultuous, twisting-and-turning, dangerous and phenomenally powerful river of the American history that we know, there has also flowed, forming quiet, backward-gliding eddies along the banks, the current of the ancient wisdom.

THE PROMISE AND THE CRIME OF AMERICA

The real hope of America has always been that at the heart of its promises of liberty, equality and social opportunity there has sounded the call and the possibility of the search for the sacred within one's self—whatever name of whatever god or power of mind or consciousness has been chosen to designate that sacred reality.

But even the distant, but real, reflection of wisdom throws dazzling light on the disappointments, the mistakes, the failures and even the crimes of America, helping to free us from naive expectations and equally naive resentments concerning the first history of America or of any other human enterprise on this earth. Wisdom teaches, and ordinary experience easily confirms, that the train of events in human history brings forward violence, injustice and the betrayal of truth—just as much as it may bring forth great external achievements. Wisdom teaches us to be neither foolishly discouraged by America's failings nor foolishly enthusiastic about its stated ideals, and the accidents of geography and natural resources that have contributed so much to its physical and economic strength over the past two centuries. In its outer life, its first history, America has murdered and cheated and broken its promises and betrayed its ideals in ways that are not so different from the first history of mankind as a whole. It is dangerously naive to imagine that because the current of wisdom may flow through a country that that country will, en masse, behave according to it. It is not so, just—so wisdom teaches us—as it is not so in the lives of individuals.

The teachings of wisdom prepare us for this fact, and fact it is, about our lives: individually and collectively, we betray our ideals in our acts and actions; but at the same time, it is possible in the midst of this life of self-betrayal for a transforming force to enter and to lead men and women toward a new kind of life. But this possibility demands the working together of communities of individuals who are intensely devoted to the work of studying and understanding the teachings of wisdom. And one of the forms of such communal life is what we call in this book "the second democracy," the democracy that actually tries to live inwardly according to the ideals of self-determination, liberty of thought and conscience, respect for the selfhood of one's neighbor—ideals whose expression in words is so familiar to us. The democracy we know speaks about these things and puts them into practice outwardly to a greater or lesser degree. But it is the second democracy that actually tries to understand these ideals in their fullest meaning and in so doing nourishes and sustains—invisibly, to be sure—the life of the democracy we know.

THE HOPE OF AMERICA

The hope of America lies in the fact that it has made room for the search that characterizes the second history of the world. The hope of the democracy we know is that it allows—and, to a certain extent, calls us all toward—the life of conscience, of respect for one's neighbor, that is rooted in the teachings of wisdom about the actual and potential selfhood of humanity.

The hope of America lies not in its first history, but in the reality of its second history.

The hope of America lies and has consisted in the fact that its political ideals and forms of government, its iconic actions and archetypal heroes, reflect in two directions at once—toward the external good of a life of liberty and equality and the reasonable search for a normal life of community and creative aspiration; and at the same time inwardly toward the search for inner development, the life of conscience and reason that defines the true nature of humanity and gives life its ultimate meaning. The hope of America lies in large measure in the extent to which its ideals and forms of action, and its main symbols of identity, point in two directions at once: to the outer and the inner simultaneously. But this capacity of an idea, a form, a heroic figure, to point us in these two directions is the very meaning of the word "myth." A mythic image, symbol or event contains just this unique power of inner and outer meaning, spiritual and material meaning. America needs to recover its mythic dimension. If not, if it begins to live only in its first history, only in the outer dimension, it will have lost all that really nourishes the life of a nation or an individual. It will be an outer empire alone, an empire only of money or military power or empty promises.

And such an empty empire will soon die. And to the extent that the world still places its hope in America, the world may die with us.

The American Virtues and Their Shadows

To reanimate the idea of America will demand more than moral or patriotic fervor, more than believing or rejecting fixed concepts about democracy and liberty. It will demand a new effort of thought, an effort to sound new depths of the idea of America.

Each aspect of the idea of America and much of what we can recognize as noble or hopeful in the American character draw strength from a hidden connection to the teachings of wisdom that have guided humanity throughout the millennia. And many of the distortions of the American vision and the American character can be seen as perversions of this timeless vision of human nature and its possibilities. By way of concluding this introduction, we need to look once again and a little more closely at the startling contrast between a more profound meaning of some of America's ideals and what they are now in danger of becoming. The names, the words, have remained the same over the centuries, but the meanings are slipping away and, often enough, turning into their own opposites.

LIBERTY: FREEDOM OF CONSCIENCE OR SELF-GRATIFICATION?

At the root of the American ideal of liberty is the right of every human being to search for and attend to the dictates of conscience. Political liberty means first and foremost the social conditions necessary to allow this search for one's own moral or spiritual light. But this ideal and right has been taken to mean merely the right to satisfy one's own subjective desires, whatever they may be, without any reference to the existence of the moral law within. In this way, the idea of liberty descends into the glorification of desire as such, which is an infantilization of its fundamental meaning.

INDEPENDENCE: INDIVIDUALITY OR INDIVIDUALISM?

Historically and intrinsically, the American ideal of independence has a political meaning that echoes a deeply internal and metaphysical meaning. Self-determination as an inner ideal means the voluntary submission of the physical and socially conditioned aspects of human nature to the interior power of conscious selfhood. It is this interior conscious power that, paradoxically, represents both the uniqueness of every human being and his or her fundamental independence from socially conditioned personality. Paradoxically, authentic individuality means freedom from individualism. Or, to put it in language that more closely resembles the language of the ancient wisdom: The true *I am* is independent of the ego, the "tyrant" or "false monarch" of the ancient legends and myths. The idea of independence has, however, decayed into a purely external and political meaning with no reference to the inner justification and resonance of the idea. It now often means little more than an ideological affirmation of the sovereignty of egoistic idiosyncrasy. Authentic independence, however, on an individual and communal basis, means, among other things, the invitation to love and serve the common good under freely chosen obedience to a higher law.

PRACTICALITY: HONEST PRAGMATISM OR BLIND MATERIALISM?

One of the most hidden aspects of the ancient wisdom is the demand to verify for oneself all ideas about human life and the nature of the world, to shun blind faith no matter how exalted the pedigree of a teaching or a teacher. From the Buddha's legendary admonition to his pupils to be "lamps unto yourselves," to Socrates' insistence on the need to free oneself from the thrall of opinion, to Jesus' saying, "Know what is in thy sight and what is hidden will be revealed to thee,"[4] there exists a powerful current of spiritual pragmatism in the ancient wisdom. Truth must be *experienced,* and not only believed in as dogma or inferred on logical or conceptual grounds. And through experience, actual inner facts and tangible results become the test of one's inner search. This aspect of the ancient wisdom operates as a weapon against one of our chief weaknesses: the tendency of ordinary imagination to take the place of reality—the tendency to imagine that one loves, serves, knows, understands, when the facts are actually otherwise. At a certain point, in its American incarnation, this general direction of the ancient wisdom became identified with what was at first simply the healthy, mundane pragmatism that gave modern science so much of its external power, and that gave the main currents of American philosophy so much of their refreshing honesty and common sense. However, with the passage of time, the ideal of pragmatism has become a deeply entrenched prejudice against the very possibility of a real world behind the world we perceive through ordinary sense perception and logic. The need and the possibility of inner, nonsensory experience was forgotten, and the demand for spiritual honesty has now degenerated. In the main corridors of science and academic thought, American honesty most often expresses itself as little more than materialistic cynicism.

THE RULE OF LAW: GUARDIAN OR USURPER OF CONSCIENCE?

In *Common Sense* Thomas Paine ringingly articulated America's fundamental attitude toward the law. Attacking the principle of *monarchy* (what we would now call totalitarianism), he declares: "But where is the King of America? I'll tell you, Friend, he reigns above and doth not make havock of mankind like the Brute of Britain." Let the world know, he continues, "that in America THE LAW IS KING."

A profound idea is at issue here. In the ancient teachings the laws of nature and the moral law not only converge, but are one and the same. Ultimate reality and ultimate goodness blend into one. The human community is charged with the task of ordering its life according to the same kind of objective principles by which the cosmos itself is ordered. And these objective principles, which can unite people rather than divide them, must be sought within the conscience of the community.

The Founding Fathers sought to create a structure of government that would protect and preserve the ongoing work of society to orient itself through the dictates of conscience. As Thomas Paine also recognized, there exists a fundamental distinction between the laws of government and the laws of society. Government is protective and essentially punitive; while society is creative and essentially beneficent. The American government was made for the purpose of protecting the American society. The former required negative laws and the ultimate support of physical force; the latter encouraged the intercourse of human souls in search of conscience. Government is the realm of legality; society is the realm of ethics. Law is the guardian of conscience.

How far we have come from this idea! The litigiousness of our culture is a clear sign that the legal is usurping the role of the ethical. Laws and statutes, no matter how carefully devised, can never take the place of individual ethical choice and action. The mechanisms of the law can never take the place of moral feeling. The fact that in our collective and individual life the legal system is being used to solve ethical problems is evidence that America's original idea of the supremacy of the law has been so degraded that the law is in danger of becoming no less a tyrant than the old "Brute of Britain."

THE NOBILITY OR THE SLAVERY OF WORK?

From its very beginnings, America embraced the necessity of hard work not as an evil but as an expression of self-respect and independence. Americans have always understood the obligation to "pay one's way," but in its origin this attitude toward life was inseparably connected to the sense that human beings were on earth to serve some purpose far greater than their own satisfaction or comfort and even greater than what is ordinarily understood as love or charity. To be free and independent was to be worthy of a task placed upon us by God; all our functions and capacities—physical, mental and emotional—were to be engaged. It was understood that our life was not given to us for ourselves alone and that human beings would be granted a certain greatness only to the extent that they sought to be able to serve God and their neighbor. Human beings were born to live and work in the midst of the forces of life, to build and create and bring nature to perfection—but all as a service: that is, as part of a life that progressively frees itself from egoistic desires and illusions.

Reflecting the influence of this idea, Americans have traditionally—as part of the idea of America—spurned idleness and the craving for unearned goods. The self-respect of Americans has traditionally been linked to "payment," not solely from egoism but, on the contrary, as an aspect of humility and as a sign of communal interdependence. The community depends on each individual's efforts, while at the same time each individual's life is mystically supported by a certain grace pouring through the community. Activity without the recognition of grace was practically the definition of the sin of pride. But also: the recognition of the need for grace without a commitment to active work was no less a mark of pride, the egoism that overestimates one's own importance in the scheme of things and that forgets that even God is engaged in a dramatic struggle in the midst of His creation.

That this general understanding of the meaning of work has been translated into the driven-ness and slavery of work characteristic of our present culture is one of the great ironies of our history. Most of our work in the short run or the long run often serves only the tangle of unnecessary desires and unstable standards of self-worth from which the ancient wisdom has always sought to free us precisely through hard work within ourselves and outside ourselves.

FREEDOM OF SPEECH OR EMPTY TALK?

At the deepest roots of the American ideal of free speech lies an understanding of what is necessary for the conscience of the community to be heard. Every individual must be free to express his or her mind and his or her personal sense of what is right and true. The aim is to foster the expression within the community of the voice of justice and divine common sense. The approach to truth is a communal process; no single individual can find it alone or impose it on others. Thus, the ideal of free speech is inextricably linked to freedom of thought, and both freedom of thought and freedom of speech have their ultimate justification when serving the aim of opening to the inner and outer ideal of Truth, the great self within the individual and the higher intelligence and moral power of the community.

But what does free speech mean in our present culture? How much of what we prize as the right to free speech is based on a loneliness that makes us yearn for others to pay more attention to us? How to understand the decay of this ideal into the sanctification of superficial opinion, on the one hand, or commercial communication, on the other? How to understand that we are losing the *knowledge function* of the community, that the hard work of thinking together is being eclipsed by the addiction to information and empty verbal or electronic "conversation" and by our society's attachment to applications of knowledge that bring only egoistic and often illusory gain?

The American Soul

The aim of this book is to look in a new way at the fundamental ideals and values that have shaped the American nation and that now are affecting the entire world. The task is to separate out the political, sociological and economic aspects of "America" that by themselves tend to set us against each other, and to rediscover in the American vision the transcendent ideas that can bring and keep people together, both as individuals and in collectivities, for the purpose of serving the good. It is this goal of bringing people together under the guidance of conscience that lies at the heart of the idea of democracy in its uniquely American form.

But the question that now needs to be asked concerns the interior, human meaning of this fundamental goal of democracy and the inner as well as the outer conditions that are necessary for its realization. Can there be any real and enduring relationship between disparate peoples and nations unless there also takes place within the soul of the individual human being a similar movement of relationship between the disparate parts of oneself? Can there be an American nation unless there also exists within oneself a unified *American soul?* And if there is a failure of the American vision, with all that this implies for the safety and survival of our world, might it not be because we have failed to understand the metaphysical and psychological requirements of the ideals that have shaped our nation? This is what it means to think in a new way about America.

History shows us many examples of teachings and visions that began as unifying forces but eventually set people against each other. Wars of religion are only the most obvious examples. Almost without exception, the great reformers within every spiritual tradition have sought to restore its original vision by re-establishing the internal, psychological meaning of the ideals and symbols that define the teaching. The great mystical existentialists of the Christian tradition, for example, such as the Desert Fathers in the early centuries of our era, or Meister Eckhart and the men and women he influenced in medieval Europe, show how the commandment of love is meant also to be experienced within oneself: as the interior penetration by a forgiving, reconciling energy. The point is that until our individual inner disharmony is healed by this energy there can be no harmony, no enduring love, in relation to one's neighbor. The great visionaries of the Judaic tradition, for their part, show that a man or woman cannot truly trust in the God of the universe, the creator of the material and the moral world, until he or she can begin to trust in the divine self within one's own body and mind. Likewise, the Sufis, the mystics of Islam, the religion of submission to Allah, speak always of the fundamental need for the ego to submit to a godlike power of love and intelligence within oneself.

Similar examples could be found in all the great wisdom traditions of the world, Eastern and Western, including of course the teachings of Africa and the American Indian. And we find the same note sounded by masters and teachers who are not associated with what we usually think of as "religion." Socrates, in Plato's *Republic,* speaks as clearly and forcefully as any mystic of the primary and fundamental need for a human being to understand reality and the moral law by working first for interior, personal harmony of mind, desire and will.[5]

When any great metaphysical or moral teaching becomes interpreted in a purely external way and applied solely to the political, sociological or economic sphere, it can only result in "the same old story," the setting of men and women against each other. When the followers of Christianity or Judaism or Islam lose the internal meaning of their teachings, when it is forgotten that the world is what it is because human beings are what they are, and that nothing essential in human life can be changed for the better without first attending to our inner disharmony, then, inevitably, there arises the dominance of "politics," leading to violence and war in all its many forms.

The purpose of this book is to call for the return of the inner meaning of America to our hearts and minds. Of course, when we speak of the ideals of America we are not speaking of a whole spiritual tradition, such as Christianity or Judaism, nor are we even speaking of a great, systematic philosophy such as that of Plato. The "American philosophy" in this sense is not an intact revealed teaching that one might wish to see restored or adapted as a guide to the inner life. Nothing could be more misleading or, in its way, dangerous than to equate the American ideals with teachings that, on the whole, have come to us from a higher level of mind.

Yet the American philosophy contains fragments, very precious fragments, of ideals and visions that most certainly do have their origin and root meaning in what Aldous Huxley termed "the perennial philosophy," the teaching that lies at the heart of all the authentic spiritual traditions of the world. These fragments, which comprise the basis of the American philosophy, are infinitely precious because they are all that many of us have to show us the direction back toward the real meaning of human life in this desperately troubled modern world. By opening ourselves to the internal meaning of these fragments, we have a chance to start the journey toward wholeness in ourselves and toward the real feeling for our neighbor that is the only sure support and purpose of what could rightly be called democracy. For all we know, this may be our last chance to move toward a worldview that can orient us toward the real world, rather than the illusory world, with all its attendant violence and meaninglessness, in which most of us now live.

And now, let us begin to look in a new way at our world, ourselves, our America.

II.

In the Beginning

TWO

REMEMBERING AMERICA

I was born in Philadelphia and grew up loving America. My immigrant grandparents spoke with tears in their eyes of the goodness of America, and my father held out Abraham Lincoln as little lower than God. But my teachers in school made the story of America suffocatingly boring. Who cared about these silly-looking men in powdered wigs and buckled shoes? Who cared about this gray William Penn whose stone image collected pigeon droppings atop gray City Hall in gray Philadelphia? Who cared about Pilgrims crossing the ocean, eating turkeys and being befriended by curiously uninteresting Indians?

And who even cared about the Declaration of Independence or the "Constitutional Convention," a phrase whose meaning I could not even register at the age of seven or eight? Countless were the field trips to Independence Hall, each exceeding the previous one in raw tedium. The Liberty Bell with its famous crack: a bad joke. And our teachers, strutting in the classroom or leading us on trips: what pathetic figures they were, bumbling and gurgling about Washington and Jefferson and Madison and "freedom" and "tolerance" and "equality." Yet I loved America, and, down deep, I still do, as do almost all of us, no matter what we may condemn as unjust, ugly or evil about this country.

What did I love? Was it more or less than what any child loves about his or her native land? Any normal human being grows up loving life, family, the trees and sky, the house one lives in, the sounds of one's language. Was my love for America any different from the Japanese child's feeling for his or her country, or the feeling of the English child, or the Spanish or the Australian or the Russian? I only know that while loving America I could not tolerate what people told me, officially, about America, nor what I saw that was officially America. If Philadelphia was America, then I had no interest in it. Official America was not what I loved.

THE FLAG

Then there was the flag, the Stars and Stripes. I remember the fervor with which we young children protected the flag. If you allowed the flag to fall, even if it barely brushed the ground, and even if it was only one of those cheap paper penny-flags that abounded on the Fourth of July, even so, the flag touching the ground was a grave sin that one could redeem only by instantly kissing it. But even this act of redemption was never felt as complete, and there was the sense that allowing the flag to touch the ground left a permanent black mark on what religious people might call the soul. Kissing the flag allowed one to go on living without being immediately killed by God, but the black mark remained forever.

At the same time, stories about the origins and significance of the flag only brought bored smirks to our faces. And if, God forbid, one of the older children should start talking about the history or importance of the flag, that was enough to relegate him or her to the outer darkness of weirdness and idiocy. Yet the flag was sacred.

I remember long moments staring at it, wondering to myself how a piece of cloth could have such power. I remember handling it and feeling electricity in the very fabric. Only now do I see where that electricity came from. The fact is that with the flag I was actually drawn to give all my attention to something in and for itself. My mind could not explain the flag, and, as I have said, I sharply rejected almost every piece of lore and history about it. I did not want and could not bear for any thoughts to interfere in my experience of the flag. As a young child, even as a young adolescent, the flag was a rare and precious occasion for the experience of pure attentiveness. We were told the flag was sacred, and this caused us to give all our attention to it. After that, it was really our attention itself that made the flag sacred, far more than the little we knew about its history.

Yet that little was important. We needed to hear something, something strong, about blood and sacrifice and the sky and the stars and nature and struggle—all in a kind of disordered mix, but enough to touch our hearts. After that, however, it was the electricity of our own consciousness that made the flag sacred.

Obviously, children everywhere have such experiences. America was sacred for me in the sense in which I have just defined it—that which glows in the light of a full, open-hearted inner awareness unmixed with thoughts and explanations that do not acknowledge the inner life. From this it is possible to see why the official history of America never corresponded to my childhood love. The fact is that for me, and for many people like me, the ideals and history of America, in the way they were explained to us, ignored and often contradicted the sense of the sacred that we felt as children.

And yet, at the same time, something in the American vision is still alive and real enough to encourage us to go on searching for that sense of deep, free inner human presence. I am now saying that what we call the ethical, the moral, the spiritual, in the American or any other value system, finds its ultimate support and foundation in the experience of pure human presence, and that it is only this experience that makes possible authentic freedom of speech and action, or independence of the mind and heart, or what we might call "self-reliance" (to use Emerson's term), or true respect for my neighbor—democracy. In brief, the ideals of America can point us to a sacred inner state, but we have almost entirely lost this meaning of America. It is necessary to recover it. As a child, when I loved America, I loved freedom, hope, nature. I loved, in my childlike way, the authentic inner possibilities of human existence.

THE HYPNOSIS OF HISTORY

Perhaps someone will object that even for our Founding Fathers, America meant many things, most of which were not very "spiritual" or "inner." For many of the Founders, perhaps, it meant mainly political independence, economic security, property rights. And perhaps it will be said that even many of those who came to America seeking religious freedom may also have been motivated by political factors. Perhaps it will be objected that to speak of American ideals in terms of interior freedom is to project a contemporary spiritual concept onto our past. My response is that all these concerns will find their proper place once we ourselves face the question of the true basis of moral ideals. And if we use language that has a distinctly contemporary flavor, it is because we need to speak of things that we know about. We need to understand what *for us* is the real meaning of the sacred in human life. If we can touch that question authentically, we can begin to unravel and reconstruct the meaning of our past. And we can reasonably grasp what the sacred may have meant to our forefathers. Because, although the present is not the past, although modern times are astonishingly different from earlier times, although the world has changed almost beyond recognition in two hundred years, we are still human beings in exactly the same sense as were the Franklins, Jeffersons, Penns and Lincolns of our common past. I wish not to be seduced by the hypnotic gaze of "history." Certainly we need accurate historical facts and plausible hypotheses; but above all we need a sense of what a human being is and can become. Only with that is it possible to venture into the study of history and intuit what is essential, and through this to initiate a conversation with the past that serves our present need. Without this, *all* we will have is history, as an infinity of information, facts, theory, thoughts, hearsay—material that serves any and all purposes. History without philosophical vision is chaos, a toxic infinity.

THE HOPE OF AMERICA

What did I love when I loved America? This question cannot be separated from the question of life itself. What do I love when I love life? What do we hope for from life? Above all else, America meant hope, the hope that good would conquer evil and that I myself would be on the side of the good. America meant hope that one would be judged by something in one's heart—something that was one's own self, and not by external factors like wealth or class or looks. I remember this feeling of hope and trust in a universe that accepted one's true inner self, one's inner goodwill, one's real wish to serve—all in oneself that hides and is afraid to come out, and is incapable of coming out amid the contradictions and injustices that make up ordinary everyday life.

This is an elusive point, yet it is common to all the great wisdom teachings of the world—the idea that deep in oneself there is goodness or even, though one wouldn't use this word as a child, "divinity." But this inner goodness retreats and hides; the world is too much for it. Can it really be that at the depth of reality it is this inner goodness that counts and nothing else?

THE PLEDGE OF ALLEGIANCE

I am trying to articulate this feeling of hope, as it is sensed by a child, in the correspondence between one's inner depth and the structure of reality. Here is another memory that may throw light on this question.

We used to have a ritual "pledge of allegiance" to the flag. Where I went to school, in Philadelphia, "the cradle of liberty," we performed this ritual every morning. It comes back to me very vividly. I see myself at seven years old, eight years, ten, thirteen. I see spring, winter and fall outside the window and feel it in the air. I sense the children around me—the good friend, the girl I have a crush on, the enemy I fear. I smell the smells of the children, their skin, their hair. I see their bodies—fat and thin, beautiful and absurd.

We have all been told to stand. The energy and optimism of the morning are in my breast, the muffled giggle, the anticipation of learning and expressing myself. "I pledge allegiance . . ." My hand is upon my chest. For a long time, I did not understand what was meant by "place your hand on your heart." What was my "heart"? I did not know. I only knew that standing there in the early morning, with all the smells and sounds and emotions, with the clean sense of morning, free from fear, at the moment I put my hand on my chest, *I came into myself.* A space appeared in my body; I sensed my weight and the force of gravity. All by itself, my head straightened; a gentle process of relaxation began and a current of life flowed in me, a current which I did not experience under any other conditions.

"I pledge allegiance to the flag of the United States of America and to the republic for which it stands, one nation,* indivisible, with liberty and justice for all." The words meant little to me. In the early years I hardly even understood what they meant—"indivisible," "republic." But the state of being *in myself* never failed to evoke a powerful feeling of respect. I did not know then that what I respected was myself! I was told this ritual was for honoring the flag or America. But, as I see now, that was wholly secondary to my feeling for the state of my human presence.

In any case, there came a time—perhaps I was ten or twelve years old—when a change was made in the form of the pledge of allegiance: at the word "flag" we were now to extend our hand from our chest outward toward the

---

* The phrase "under God" was not introduced until 1954.

flag. That change spoiled the whole ritual for me. I vividly remember how that movement of putting my arm out took away from me everything I was feeling. Even from the very beginning, even with a mind as young as mine was, I thought: "this is phony, this is crap." I sensed the whole hypocrisy and stupidity of reverencing a flag, a piece of cloth. I sensed the shallowness and artificiality of everybody's gesture, and I especially felt this shallowness in my own gesture. Somehow, all that was in me as a sense of self was spilled out through that motion of my arm toward an external object, a stupid piece of cloth. And the worst of it was that no one acknowledged this change of meaning, this deterioration of the experience—not my teachers and not my classmates, though, to tell the truth, I barely acknowledged it to myself. It was an extremely strong experience, but my "conscious" mind was hardly able to put words on it.

The Loss of the Holy

But this was also what had happened any number of times when I went to the synagogue. How many times I would stand next to my father or my grandfather, a man of overwhelming physical power with a wild heart that brought him into ferocious confrontations with my grandmother, a man who radiated nothing but freedom and strength to me, but who, holding the holy scriptures in his hand, would stand and bow his mighty head—and I along with him—to intone, in Hebrew, words that evoked a mysterious God who really did exist and really was judge of the universe and of myself. I stood. I bowed my head and looked uncomprehendingly at the Hebrew letters in front of me. And then we sat down and things happened in the old, tedious way again and I didn't know what to do with the sense of the holy that still reverberated in me. In the wordless, sensitive heart of a young boy, I saw that the holy was dissipating and that no one noticed it or cared—on the contrary, they even pretended it was still there.

In my adolescence I consciously turned away from the religion of my grandparents and my childhood. I turned toward science and philosophy, toward nature and the freedom to think and see and move. I remember a sense of who I was that began to develop in me—in my very body, my movements and postures. I did not really know or acknowledge what was influencing me, what was entering into me to form my persona. But I read, I studied; like everyone else I went to movies, I read newspapers; I was awkward with girls and bewildered by sex; I played baseball and football and went to the games; I was shy and blustering at the same time; I played cards; I won and almost never lost; I prowled the museums and bookstores; I continued to exult in the woods and parks of Philadelphia, where my deepest, most intimate moments, mystical in their silence and sense of a sacred presence, took place next to streams and places with names that had great, unformed power for me: Wissahickon, Schuylkill, Tedyuscung, Tulpehocken. (Much later I discovered that many of these places, especially around the Wissahickon Creek, were considered sacred by the native Indians.) I did not think very much of America as such, nor of myself as an American. I was just myself and felt a sense of becoming uniquely me—although, as I see now, right under the surface (a very thin surface), I knew I did not know who or what I was.

YOU ARE VERY AMERICAN

What was my surprise, then, when a greatly respected friend and mentor, a man in his forties, very wise and strong and magical to me at the age I was—seventeen, a bright high school graduate on my way to glory with a scholarship to Harvard—this man, a transplanted Hungarian Jew who had seen and done everything in life and whose word soon became law to me, this man after my first serious meetings with him, looked at me with his intensely sensitive eye and said, "You are very, *very* American!"

I was shocked. And strangely hurt. I asked him what he meant. "Your movements," he said, "have the freedom of the plains." I tried to take this as a compliment, but I knew it wasn't meant that way, not entirely. One of the most striking things about my friend—Béla—was the postures he took:

well formed, elegant, strong; always the sense of a man with a spine. I knew that my own postures and movements were loose, uncentered, careless— and somewhere, even at that relatively young age, I did understand something of what he meant by calling me "American." At the same time, Béla really did love this aspect of America, what he called "the plains," by which he meant the whole of the American West, the infinite stretches of nature, sky, mountains, virgin forests, endless fields and desert. Béla had driven back and forth across America and had seen more of the country than most Americans had. "You're the wind blowing free," he said to me—I who felt anything but free, who sensed myself as anxious and incapable alongside my exceedingly fragile overestimation of myself.

Béla loved America and, although I was disappointed to be called "American" by him, what he loved was the same thing I loved about America. It was freedom—unformed, yes, but open to any kind of possibility. Being unformed, it was highly charged with energy. It was the future. It was not what is given, what is inherited, what is born into a man or woman. It was not *ethnic.* To be American was not to be born anything at all.

To put it another way, to be American was an idea, not an inescapable, organic given. America is a nation formed by philosophical ideals that have been thought through by human beings—it is the only nation in the world that is so constituted. America is not a tribal, ethnic or racial identity. It is a philosophical identity composed of ideas of freedom, liberty, independent thought, independent conscience, self-reliance, hard work, justice.

This is both the weakness and the strength of America. To love America is not to love one's roots—it is to love the flower that has not yet blossomed, the fruit as yet unripened. To love America is to love the future, and perhaps it is this that sets the love of America apart from what men and women of other nations feel about their native land. One is born Greek or German or Japanese. But to be born American does not mean the same thing. One becomes American. One cannot become German or Greek or Japanese in that way, just as one cannot change one's bones or the color of one's skin. But there is *something* in oneself that can be changed. What is it? There is something in oneself that can develop and evolve. What is it?

AMERICA AND REALITY

At the same time, this something that is free and undeveloped in our-selves—it can go down as well as up; it can bring degeneration and unhap-piness; it can twist human life away from its root and meaning, rather than allowing it to grow through the nourishment of root, sun and air. What is that part? Whatever name we give it, it is tied in some way to the mind, to thought and the formation of ideals. No nation that we know of on earth has ever been formed around the centrality of that part of human nature. Cer-tainly, within every culture there have been groups and associations of men and women who have striven to develop their moral and spiritual natures—such undertakings are at the heart of culture. But no nation itself, no people that we know of has constituted itself solely around this part of human na-ture as its center of gravity.

America is a creature of the mind, and its encounter with physical na-ture is still in its beginning stages.

> The land was ours before we were the land's.
> She was our land more than a hundred years
> Before we were her people.

So wrote Robert Frost in his poem "The Gift Outright." Americans im-posed their ideals and mind upon the geography of the American continent. We did not grow organically out of the land, the climate, the food, the shapes and spaces, the air and water, the skies with their particular stars and planets. No, we brought our ideas and ideals and our own varied tribal residues to an alien and nearly virginal natural world. Here, of course, we met the American Indian, who, in large measure, had in fact evolved in the geography of America in that organic sense of human development that was precisely what we lacked. We need to understand that the encounter of Eu-ropean Americans with the geography and native peoples of America forms a decisive element in who we are now and need to become. And this is far from a simple question. To answer it, we will have to free ourselves from a tendency to romanticize the Indian way of life while yet seeing even more clearly the exalted truth of the teachings upon which their society was based. Since the modern world now faces the agonizing question of the encounter between the human mind and the reality of nature, this question of our relationship to the Native American people and way of life becomes an icon of the whole problem of humanity's present life-or-death confrontation with the world of nature.

But in order to begin by understanding our own uniqueness, to understand the feeling that many of us have toward our native land—to see what we love when we love America—it is necessary to attend to this singular fact about our history as a culture: that "the land was ours before we were the land's," that is, that we imposed our minds upon a land which had not really nourished the growth of our minds. We emigrated here and sought to make the *here* into something we had previously conceived of, independently of what this place may have required. From the Puritan or other religious communities' attempts to make America into a "new Jerusalem," to the mercantile and business interests' plundering and exploiting the rich land through the industrialization of the human substance—namely, through slavery and, after slavery, through technology—we have imposed our mind upon organic nature in an especially stark manner.

WHAT DO WE LOVE WHEN WE LOVE AMERICA?

I see now once again the figure of William Penn. Who, really, was this Quaker with the broad-brimmed hat and the somber cravat? Is he more than a statue atop City Hall? More than a painting in which he and some other "Quakers" stand under trees exchanging goods with Indians whom the artist has drawn in that stiff way that the Indians were often portrayed? Who or what are these "Quakers"?

As I was growing up in Philadelphia, somewhere off to the side of my awareness, just barely in view, there hovered this figure of William Penn—

not the Penn of the gray statue; not the Penn standing under the tree with the boring Indians; no, some other man, some other meaning that I knew was there but which *I did not want to understand.* All I knew was that it had something to do with God. And I did not want to understand that, to go into that. I had had enough of God in the synagogue and at the hands of hostile redneck Catholic kids or in what I heard about the Christians who hated the Jews and kept us from the good things that America promised us. This "Penn" was Christian in some other sense I did not understand. Or, which came to the same thing, he was *not* Christian in some sense I did not understand and did not want to understand.

AMERICA AND THE MYSTICAL COMMUNITY

But off to the side of my awareness I could not help but hear something about the beliefs and practices of the "Quakers." Information about them seeped into my skin from the air around me in Philadelphia. And off to the side, very, very far off to the side of my awareness, yet burning with a strangely intense light, was the word, the idea, the image: *the inner life; silence; conscience.*

As I grew up, I remained impervious to the meaning of the signs of Quakerism all around me—Quakerism not only as a specific religious sect, but as reflecting the strong current of communal mysticism that took root in early colonial America, especially in Pennsylvania. That William Penn founded Pennsylvania to be the home of such communities had no meaning for me. How was I to know—who was there to explain to me that so much of what I loved about America had its roots and deeper meanings in the teachings of these mystical communities?

A MYSTICAL NATION?

But what kind of mark on our culture did these mystical communities really leave? Does America itself have a hidden mystical core? There are those who think so, a few scholars and spiritual seekers who call attention not only to these communities, but to many of the Founding Fathers' affiliations with Freemasonry.[6] Scholarly controversies aside, the fact is that many of the ideals that Americans now consider definitive of our nation were introduced and developed by these mystical communities, and the original and deeper meaning of these ideals may be astonishingly different than what we now understand of them. For example, the ideas of human equality and independence in these communities are rooted in the notion that God, or "the inner light," exists within every human being, and that the aim of life revolves around the endeavor and the necessity for every man or woman to make conscious contact with this inner divine force. This interior divinity—in William Penn's language, "the inner Christ"—is the source of true happiness, intelligence and moral capacity, and is meant to be the guide and ultimate authority in the conduct and assessment of our lives and obligations.

Seen from this perspective, no human being can have ultimate authority over another, not because the individual has the right to satisfy the desires of the body or the ego; not because every individual has the right to plot the scheme of his or her own actions with respect to the social, economic or sexual aspects of life; not because every individual has the right to say whatever he wants to say. No, a human being is his own authority only because he has within him the inner Christ, the inner divinity.

MYSTICAL EQUALITY

To be sure, the New England Calvinist/Puritan notion of human equality had a more negative cast, but it still reflected the same philosophical dimensions of the idea. In this more negative version, all men and women are equally sinful: all fall equally short of what God demands. Being principally negative in cast, this version of the idea did not imply individual responsibility of choice and action as clearly as did the more positive concept, save for the demand on the individual to submit to the truths of Christianity and the Bible. Nevertheless, the notion of the self and of human equality in both cases points to a dimension of consciousness and experience far different from, and far deeper than, the aspects of the human self which are emphasized in contemporary political and ethical theory.

The doctrine of the self put forward by mystical communities like the Quakers dictated that every individual seek to consult the inner divinity for guidance in the conduct of life. But what *is* that inner God? When I go back in my memory to the experiences that brought me the greatest joy and hope in my youth, I find myself remembering the ideal of *understanding*— in front of the greatness of nature. I also find myself trying to understand, *for myself* and *on my own,* the demands and claims of religion and all other forms of authority that the culture presented to me. When I began to grasp the idea of "independence," my first and earliest sense of it thus had nothing whatever to do with material things or social success. It had to do with some mysterious sense of an *independent awareness* within myself that was at the same time an awareness *on the side of God.*

MIND ON THE SIDE OF GOD

When I say that I sensed my mind on the side of God, what I am speaking of is nothing as simplistic or external as the notion that the American nation was God's chosen nation—even when I was a child, and even at the height of the Second World War, I was wary of that idea. What I am speaking of had to do with *thought.* In my most intimate self there was thought, the mind, perception, seeing, understanding, pondering, wondering, imagining. There was in myself a feeling of inner vision. No matter what happened to me; no matter what I was told; no matter what I feared or loved or hated; no matter what disappointments came my way, or pain or injustices, there, in myself—it *was* myself—there was the mind, my thought, my *awareness* informed by great ideas. And I had the distinct sense that this awareness, actively informed or accompanied by ideas which I would give my conscious attention to—that this awareness, this mind, this thinking, was on the side of God; that is, it was somehow recognized by the universe as what was important in myself. I had the vague, inarticulate feeling when I was trying to think in this sense that I was doing the only thing that was really in my power and for which I was really morally responsible. One could say, perhaps, that at that early age I was drawn to contemplation rather than action, but to put it that way would be misleading. In my young heart, I also felt the need for action, the need to *do* the right thing. But—at least before I went too far into the socially conditioned world of adolescence—my strongest and deepest connection with the need to act came from the sense that really good or right action could emanate, and perhaps could only emanate, from that inner mind which was myself and was on the side of God! Without trying to make myself seem in any way unusual, I wish to say that at a very early age there was playing out in myself the same drama that played out in the mystic communities of colonial America concerning the dialectical relationship between contemplation and action, ending in the momentum of events that drew the American nation away from contemplation toward a nearly total emphasis on action. In this sense, one is tempted to say that in its absorption into action and doing, America entered a long adolescence at the beginning of the nineteenth century.

The point I wish to make now is that what I loved about America had a strange and intimate connection to the call of my own independent mind, the selfhood, the "divinity" within myself. What was this connection between something so big and external as the image of America and the secret, intimate sense of my own self and mind? I cannot say for sure—as children we heard again and again of freedom, freedom, freedom; all men created equal, equal, equal. These ideas and much else like them were presented as social ideals, religious in their ultimacy and metaphysical in their seriousness, quite as heavily metaphysical as anything I heard in the synagogue. But they were received by the child as ideas to be *thought about*. It was secondary, in a way, that they were ideas about society and duties; what was primary perhaps was that there were ideas that begged to be thought about. To some extent, therefore, whenever I was presented with "America," it was in the form of ideas that invited me to think, to enter my intimate mind, even if only briefly and superficially. America was an *idea!* What other country can say that?

AMERICAN NATURE

In Philadelphia, there existed parks that were actually small, preserved enclaves of wilderness. These were not the manicured, path-marked parks where people came in their Sunday clothes and sat on clean benches. Philadelphia had plenty of those parks; they were part of the metaphysical dungeon of my childhood. In the parks I am speaking about, the wild Wissahickon Creek sang and roared; no paths, no benches, no mental plans; only wild forests, nests of trees and grass, black soil under decades of glistening oak leaves, harboring nightcrawlers and a million kinds of insects; parks where snow and ice covered joyfully treacherous waters; parks where one could get lost, or even spy in the heaven of one's mind an Indian tracker from the world of real nature and God. In these parks, I loved nature, and nature in her impartial way loved me without indulging me. And this nature was America. I knew that. America was nature and my mind was nature because I felt nature and God in the same place in myself where I thought, where I pondered and meditated on everything. Nature called to the feeling part of the mind. And isn't this the source of real science and real religion also? Nature/America was the home of the real part of me, my feeling, loving, awestruck, eager mind that wishes to see and know and from which—if God is good—my action will emanate.

And something like this, all this, in its way, I only later discovered was believed and held by none other than William Penn and the spiritual communities who were the first to settle Pennsylvania.

Here, finally, is William Penn writing of the inner God and connecting it to man's capacity for true reason and thought. In such words, we can begin to see the metaphysical meaning of what a Thomas Jefferson or perhaps even a Benjamin Franklin—both of whom spoke of life independent of the

claims of religion yet who could certainly be described as spiritual men—
meant by the ideal of reason. We can glimpse why they and so many others
who brought America to birth considered *reason* the highest principle in
man, reason which we at our own peril equate with the ordinary functions
of our everyday "thinking" mind.

William Penn:

> That which the People call'd Quakers lay down as a Main Fundamen-
> tal in Religion, is this, That God, through Christ, hath placed a Prin-
> ciple in every Man, to inform him of his Duty, and to enable him to do
> it; and that those that Live up to this Principle, are the People of God,
> and those that Live in Disobedience to it, are not God's People, what-
> ever Name they may bear, or Profession they may make of Religion.[7]

But what does it really mean that the ideal of independent reason refers to
something other than what we usually call thought? When the Founding
Fathers held up reason in the place of religious faith, were they advocating
the kind of intellectual activity that figures so prominently in our present
culture—in science, education and the professions?

I think not. Nor, on the other side, do I think that when William Penn
or the leaders of the mystical communities of early America speak of the "inner light" they are referring to some purely emotional or irrational experience. When a Franklin or a Jefferson praises reason as the ultimate guide to
human life and when a William Penn or a Conrad Beissel (the founder of the
Ephrata community in Pennsylvania) speaks of the inner light or inner
Christ, are they really speaking of totally different things, or is there a relationship, perhaps even a convergence, between these two elements within
the human psyche, which we in modern times seem to regard as completely
separate?

The fact is that the Founding Fathers' ideal of reason has in it quite as
much warmth as light; and the ideal of the inner Christ in the Colonial
mystics has in it quite as much light as warmth. To repeat, the question we
are in front of is the nature of human reason. To take on that question,

we must be prepared for some surprises concerning the actual level of penetration and grasp in our own thought. We shall see, perhaps, that it is not the greatest minds of the Enlightenment who are over-estimating the power of human reason; it is we who wrongly estimate this power by identifying what we generally experience as thought with the power of the mind that they were referring to a scant two hundred or so years ago.

THE IDEA OF THE GOOD

In order to go into this question, it is necessary to recognize that the teachings that lie at the origins of Western culture—Judaism and Hellenic spiritual philosophy—called all human beings to search in themselves for a capacity of the mind in which objective perception and moral will converge into one power. Psychologically and metaphysically, truth and value were seen as two aspects of one whole. In the philosophy of Plato, the highest capacity of the human mind involves the direct knowing of that which is at one and the same time ultimately good and ultimately real, what Plato called the *Idea of the Good.* This capacity of the mind, this level of *reason,* represented, for Plato, a power in the human soul which could properly be called godlike. Plato sharply distinguished this capacity from the logical-deductive operation of the mind and also from the mental functions of combining concepts, generalizing from data and forming workable hypotheses. In a word, Plato differentiated the highest level of reason from everything we would recognize as scientific, mathematical or analytic knowledge. For Plato, "reason" is a direct intuition of objective reality and objective value. And in order to activate this capacity, an individual had to struggle against the seductive forces of the lower forms of thought, which, when allied with what the Founding Fathers called "the passions," seduce us into believing that they are the doors to the real world. To the modernist claim that scientific and scholarly knowledge seeks objectivity by distancing itself from the emotions, Plato would probably have replied that such a separation of knowing from feeling cannot yield anything like true knowledge. Certainly, reason must free itself from the thrall of the passions, but not from the exquisite and essential subtlety of the feeling/valuing component of the mind, a component which is an absolutely necessary part of authentic human reason.

WHEN TRUTH BECOMES LOVE

Many centuries before Plato was formulating this philosophy, long before Athens began its rise to glory, the prophets of Israel brought forth the idea of one all-powerful and all-beneficent God, the transcendent heart and mind of the universe. To know God, to touch rightly this mysterious Unity, one had to obey, hear, listen—*feel,* "love the Lord thy God with all thine heart, and with all thy soul, and with all thy might."[8] And in order to feel, to love, that is, to strive to submit to this transcendent Unity, one had to strive for *understanding.* In the Hebraic vision, an individual does not know first and then, afterward, feel—one cannot know what is true without *at the same time* feeling what is good. The fundamental property of the universe itself is the mysterious convergence of being and value. God brought the world into *being* and saw *immediately* that it was good. This is very far from the modern ideal of reason, with its mode of knowing in the way that a machine "knows"—collecting information, combining and projecting theories and explanations independently of both passion, in its negative sense, *and* feeling, in the sense of an indispensable organ of perception. The Platonic/Hebraic marriage of knowledge and ethics—the ancient name for this marriage is *conscience*—is very far from our modern idea of reason. But how far is it from the ideal of Reason that animated the mind of Franklin or Jefferson when they spoke of nature and nature's God? Their God was truth. They prayed with the mind, though not only with the mind. But they saw that the mind had been left out of the established religions—or, worse, that it had been enslaved by them, by dogma and superstition, just as the individual man or woman had been enslaved by monarchy. When Truth becomes one's God it becomes more than the kind of alienated thinking that has characterized the modern ideal of reason. It becomes love as well.

Never mind that this God of Truth was soon to become the tyrant of the alienated intellect, the tyrant of merely logical, mechanistic thought. Such tyranny may be considered the degeneration of the vision of the Enlightenment. Never mind the degeneration for now. Consider only the fullness of the original vision and the need to bring it back, to redefine our dominant ideal of the authority of reason.

THE GOD OF FRANKLIN

Once again, Philadelphia. Once again, the young boy of ten or twelve, and the young adolescent—myself. But this is not the wild Wissahickon, and I am not leaning against a sun-warmed rock weeping with joy and wonder. I am in a big stone building; yet a comparable quality of feeling is here being awakened in me.

The place is the Franklin Institute, the first in America of what we now call science museums—where the visitor operates exhibits illustrating scientific principles. Whatever I have understood of the sacredness of scientific reason had its origin there—just there under the name and image of Benjamin Franklin.

I vividly remember my first and most formative experience there. It was a school field trip. As usual, the class had started at Independence Hall and the Liberty Bell, but instead of returning to school afterwards, the bus brought us to a monumental, colonnaded building bearing the inscription "In Honor of Benjamin Franklin." The name of Franklin was vaguely depressing to me—as omnipresent a name as that of Penn and equally representing "Philadelphia."

I remember that winter day with its brilliant sun that gave no warmth. Shivering and sullen, I trudged up an endless number of stone steps, carefully negotiating the black ice that covered them. Adding to my bad mood was the hovering presence of Allie Nemiroff, the fattest kid in the universe, who never, ever stopped talking and who, because of our last names, was, it seemed, destined to accompany me throughout my life on earth and possibly beyond.

Allie kept up an endless stream of chatter as he absurdly turned sideways to pass through the turnstile. It was absurd because his midsection was even bigger sideways than it was frontally.

With Allie's babbling pouring into my brain, I found myself standing in the high, echoing entrance hall of the Institute and then moving with the class toward a stairwell, next to which was a strange metal bowl suspended from way on high, many stories up, and constantly moving in slow motion a few inches from the ground. Out of the bowl, sand poured in a slow stream, making ever-changing geometric patterns. "Foucault's Pendulum," Allie babbled into my ear. I couldn't make out what our teacher, Miss Hackett, was saying. "It moves forever," Allie said; "it never stops. The rotation of the earth makes it move forever. You couldn't stop it even if you tried. No one can."

WHO OR WHAT IS BENJAMIN FRANKLIN?

As the class started up the stairs, I took in the statue of Benjamin Franklin in the center of the entrance hall. I hated statues of all kinds, but there was something about this one that attracted me. I wasn't sure, at that moment, what it was supposed to be a statue *of*—I mean, I knew it was Franklin, but from the statue I wasn't sure what Franklin was supposed to stand for. It was a large, realistic representation of the older Franklin sitting in a massive chair, all white stone, probably marble. I half-consciously wondered why so much fuss was made about Franklin. William Penn—well, he founded the city and was "religious," highly moral and all that. Various generals also I understood. Presidents I understood. Patrick Henrys and Paul Reveres I understood: why *not* have statues and other things celebrating these people, even if it was all ultimately tedious. But there was something about Franklin that didn't quite fit in with all these other icons. And I couldn't quite decide—in my feelings—whether it was because in some way Franklin was better or in some way worse than the other heroes. I tentatively decided (or, rather, vaguely felt) that it was the latter: Franklin was, I felt, somehow less noble—and was so in some manner I didn't understand. (When, years later, I heard about his exploits with women, especially in his old age, I was not surprised and even felt in some smarmy, vaguely puritanical way vindicated in my childhood feelings about him.)

THE RED BUTTON

We entered the hall of exhibits on the second floor with Allie babbling about what we were about to see. He had been here before with his father. The class clumped around a rectangular glass box about six feet long and three feet high, resting on a wooden platform and containing two large, shiny metal spheres several feet apart—or so I remember. "This shows the electricity in lightning," Allie babbled as he pushed me from behind with his huge stomach and forced me physically into the backs of several thin girls. Irritated, they stepped aside as Allie continued, unconsciously, to push me forward. Even as Miss Hackett was saying something about the exhibit, Allie kept snorting in my ear: "The power in these metal balls is enough to kill an elephant. But it's kept in check by the diameter of the static force." Although I knew relatively little about electricity, it was obvious to me that Allie knew less than nothing. He wasn't saying anything, he was just *saying,* just as some people chew gum or others fidget. Allie fidgeted with words and hadn't the slightest idea of what gobbledygook he was saying. As I was slowly, inexorably pushed toward the front of the group, I caught fragments of what Miss Hackett was saying. Her words were partly the same as Allie's—electrical force, positive and negative poles—and I recognized that she was speaking about solid scientific facts. But, as always, they bored me. I was suspended in limbo between Allie's fantastical babbling and Miss Hackett's dull, lifeless recitation of fact. Then, suddenly, Allie's stomach pushed me out into the front row, where I saw an enormous and mysterious red button under the glass box. I could not take my eyes off that button.

Miss Hackett called on Mary Gourley, whose mouth was full of metal and who always did the right thing, to go press the button.

Mary trotted properly up to the button, stuck out her clean, pink index finger and pushed. A jagged bolt of brilliant white light streaked between the spheres, accompanied by a loud report that knocked me back on my heels.

The class was moving as Miss Hackett started talking about the next exhibit. I stayed in my spot, staring at the spheres and the red button. "That's lightning," said Allie, pushing me with his body. I did not actively resist; I more or less allowed myself to be pushed to move with the class. But I remember the word "lightning" and its action on me. The *label* drained away my sense of wonder. "Oh, that's *lightning.*" Lightning! Nothing terrified and amazed me and filled me with wonder more than the experience of lightning during a storm. And here, I had been struck in my eyes and heart by the same phenomenon—and there was a button, too, that I could press; I could nearly touch this blazing force. But—oh: that's *lightning.* Fine, and we move on to the next exhibit.

The Secret of Franklin

I was only a young boy. None of this was explicit in my consciousness, really. Except just then I recalled the image of Franklin that had been drilled into us a thousand times, his experimenting with the lightning in the sky. And how pragmatically useful it all was, how much he understood about harnessing its power for the benefit of man. This was the Franklin Institute, after all, where the main purpose was to show how the discoveries of science can help the industrial and technological march of mankind. It was Franklin who pioneered all that. But I felt, in my boyish way, that I had touched a secret about Franklin, and that I had touched *his* own secret. That was all I felt, nothing more. Franklin's love of nature and his love of mixing

his mind, his thought, his perception with the great laws of the universe—
whether or not it had any use at all—that was Franklin's secret. Or a great
part of it.

I am now blending what I felt as a boy with what I have come to know
now about Franklin's life and work. But the seed of this sense of Franklin began there, in the Franklin Institute, when I was passively moving from
exhibit to exhibit. Franklin has puzzled and intrigued scholars with his mixture of spirituality, canniness, worldliness, patriotism, egoism and adventur-
ousness. But the man played and worked with lightning! What does that
mean? The man *did* things. He went into the world of nature and into the
world of affairs and into the world of ideas and into the world of war and
peace and into boudoirs and courts and forests and oceans—and did look and
experiment with little or no safety net of preconceived ideas. He worked with
lightning. What does that mean? Oh, it's lightning. Next exhibit.

A DANGEROUS MIND

The love that is part of the mind, and the mind that is in the heart: let us
note one important aspect of this convergence, whether we are speaking
about a religious mystic or an active seeker of philosophical wisdom such as
Franklin. This convergence is often experienced and lived as something *dangerous.* History, especially schoolbook history, has cast a pall of niceness over
the great spiritual figures of early America. People like Penn or Jonathan
Edwards or Roger Williams, whatever the facts of their sometimes jagged
biographies may be, come to us through the soft haze of accepted historical
success (be it only in their fame). We do not feel the adventure and the risk
in their enterprise—I mean the interior adventure and risk. Perhaps some of
these individuals, from certain points of view—or some whom historical
events have not crowned with "success"—are regarded as fanatical, as religious "zealots" (a word that lets us be comfortable about other people's inner wildness). But it is rare for us—I think I speak for more than only
myself—to appreciate the personal encounter with fear that these early

Americans must have experienced. That, in the midst of this fear, there were some who remained calm and sensitive, who did not always react solely out of concern for their own nearest interests, who actually sought to reason and think well about the situation of their nation and its endeavor, who even were sometimes able to think and *act* out of nonegoistic motives: this is not often appreciated as we read our history.

A god who is held only in psychological or physical safety—what sort of god is that? A comfortable Christian or Jew or Buddhist may be far less of a spiritual man or woman than a Benjamin Franklin searching in his mind for an understanding of right action when his world is under siege and his life is threatened and he is steering the future hopes of his country in a foreign land while afflicted with the combined devils of physical pain and illness and universal fame and adulation. The man worked with lightning.

The sound of that bolt of electricity repeated in my head as I moved with the class and as Allie Nemiroff continued to dump his word-sounds into my ear. When the class turned a corner, I slowed my pace and drifted toward the rear of the group. Finally, I stopped. Allie did not notice at all and simply went on waddling and gabbling with the others. I spied some kind of exit door and, without even wondering where it led, pushed it open and went through.

ANOTHER ROOM

I was suddenly in another exhibition hall, a huge cavernous space in the center of which, dwarfing everything else, was an immense black Baldwin locomotive. It was like seeing an elephant or a bear for the first time not in a zoo, but in reality. Without a protective fence or a moat, even a large bird, even a cow looks formidable, and this was an elephant, a tiger, a 350-ton locomotive as big as a house.

The sense of its power was overwhelming. It attracted me; it did not frighten me. Yet I felt it was in some way as alive as any animal. I walked over to it. There were other people next to it, including a few children. I saw that the children were climbing into the cab. I was going to do that, but first I just stood close to the wheels, about six inches from them. I remember those wheels—black and shiny steel, taller than I was, taller than a full-grown man. I peered through the wheels into the mechanism under the locomotive—the gears, the giant bars and rods. I understood that *man* had built this. That meant—not God, not an animal, not nature, but *man.* And was I not also *man?* It was for me a whole new coloration to the sense of wonder that I touched in the Wissahickon or on a clear, starry night sitting on the front steps of my house looking up at the sky. I felt awe, but it was awe in front of the mind of man. The mind of man, which was also—was it not?—the mind of nature. And it was *my* mind—was it not?

TECHNOLOGY AND THE SACRED

There was something I, as man, was supposed to *do*—that is what this locomotive evoked in me—some risk to be taken, some brave action that was needed. And it involved an intensely active relationship to nature, the same nature I had until now seen and felt with such deep, but static, feeling. The fusion of mind and feeling involved, all by itself, the possibility and demand of *action,* an involvement of the moving and thinking and feeling human *body,* my body.

Never mind the degeneration of this impulse from which our whole culture suffers—never mind that this impulse to work with the forces of external nature, to shape nature, to build, to fix, this impulse that brings technology into the world—never mind how it has decayed into exploitation and manipulation and the threat to the life of the earth. Think only of the original deep roots of this impulse, the roots in the human spirit.

It is deeply spiritual to seek anything, anything at all, from a source in oneself that has no name, that is a formless observing and feeling, that wishes only to understand and serve with body, mind and heart. Think of a man such as Franklin not as a wise old sage—which is how some people picture him; or merely as an inventive bourgeois capitalist; or as a noble patriot—no, don't think of Franklin in these terms. Think of him as a great and honorable and extremely fragile child set on his own, with no guidance but his own eyes and mind, not able to believe stories that have led others nowhere; think of him as trying anything and everything, with nature, with his fellow man, with God even—only for the sake of understanding reality and participating in the forces of creation. To see in Franklin an icon such as this is, I believe, to approach the sacred root of America's involvement with technology—and here, by technology, is meant not only complex physical machines, but social machines constructed of great wheels and levers to enable the human community to advance. The Constitution of the United States is in its way a great machine just as in the more familiar sense is the immense black locomotive that I marveled at in the Franklin Institute.

INSIDE THE MACHINE

On a narrow iron ladder, I climbed ten feet into the air and clambered into the cab of the locomotive. Suddenly I had entered another world, small and intense, a cave-like space dense with power, a fantasy of knobs, handles, levers and gauges in glistening black iron and gleaming brass. Like all the machines of the pre-computer era, the instruments in the cab of the Baldwin seemed to be a materialization of universal principles, a physical meeting-point between great invisible laws and the human hand.

Today's machines are different. What meets us in today's technology is primarily the logical function of the mind encoded in a circuitry invisible to the eye and ungraspable by the hand. In today's machines, based as they are upon the computer, our own exteriorized logical mind stands between ourselves and material instruments *that require the engagement of the body and the will.* This needs to be emphasized. Today's machines require little or no *will*, little or no physical/self-mastery to operate. The body is very nearly unnecessary.

Inside the engineer's cab there was a little boy of about seven sitting on the knee of a lean old man, doubtless his grandfather. The grandfather had snowy hair and smooth pink skin and was wearing a white shirt with the sleeves rolled up. A fine plaid sports coat was hanging from one of the levers. The pleasant smell of the old man's cologne filled the cab and, over-all, I had the feeling he was from a very different social class than myself— maybe he was a very rich man; it felt that way. The boy was also well dressed—with a little plaid sports coat of his own, creased pants and shiny shoes. Intimidated, I stood near the ladder and watched as the grandfather showed the boy how the locomotive worked. I was dying to sit in the engineer's chair and work the levers myself. The boy's thin arm reached toward a brass lever and his little fingers grasped it. "Oho!" said the grandfather, "that's going to speed us up!" and with his own large, bony hand, he helped the boy turn the lever all the way toward full throttle position.

To my astonishment, the locomotive actually started moving! I didn't know that the museum had set it up to move very slowly a few feet forward and backward when the throttle was turned. The little boy smiled in wonder at his grandfather, but it took me a very long second or two to realize that the damn thing was not in some nightmarish way suddenly going to accelerate through the walls of the room. I actually moved toward the ladder to save myself, and as I did, the old man, apparently aware of my reaction, looked at me with an extraordinary smile—relaxed, compassionate, strong. I could see his wrinkled face and blue eyes and thin, long blade of a nose, as though under an engineer's cap, and would not have been surprised to learn that in his life he had actually driven a machine like this one.

As I realized what was actually happening, I experienced a double sense of wonder at the boldness of man: not only to build such an immense machine capable of channeling huge forces of fire and steam, capable of putting together tons of iron and steel, building thousands of miles of rails, digging coal from the depths of the earth to burn in the cabin of the metal megalith and power it back and forth over the reach of an entire continent; not only to be able to do all that, but then to toss it into a museum for children as though this huge, dense, heavy, complex, metallic machine were a toy for little fingers to play with. Having come from the demonstration of lightning into the cab of this giant powerhouse of a machine, I took in the impression of this strong old man with his relaxed alert eyes and his big, bony, powerful hand and I wondered to myself: am I the boy or the man?

THE GREATNESS OF FRANKLIN

This experience in the institute named for Benjamin Franklin comes to me very sharply when I now think of what we know of Franklin's life and of his own relationship to the forces of nature and human society. Why should he not be for us an icon of man's courageous mind? And of America's ability to invent solutions for material problems? If the American "religion" had saints, surely Franklin would be the patron saint of man's power to intervene in the world of nature and society. Because we see now that man has intervened wrongly and foolishly, do we then turn away from this uniquely human and deeply American capacity to repair and even improve on the way things are in the external world of nature and man?

We need to re-mythologize our heroes. Of course they were only human beings like the rest of us, and of course their motives and behavior were often anything but noble. But they had great gifts and, due to fate or chance or perhaps providence, great currents of human and social energy passed through them. And because they were in a specific place and time where these currents met and acted, their capacities and individualities became, at least to some extent and for some period of time, larger than life; the actions and ideas that passed through and from them created not only the American nation but—to a very large extent—the whole modern world itself. And that means you and me and almost every one of us.

In a recent conversation with a German businessman, who was also a professor of economics, a colleague of mine asked about Europe's emerging role in the modern world—a united Europe rivaling the power of the United States. "Yes," he replied, "but the United States is still by far the most important nation in the world. *All* the forces of the earth are pouring through the United States. All the forces of the earth are concentrated there. Europe's economic power, or Japan's economic and political ferment, or all that is happening in Russia or Eastern Europe, or China's immensity, or Africa or the Middle East—it is all coming together and pouring through the government and people of America and the American land. It is up to America how all these forces will meet and act on each other and resound back into the world, the earth. Population, environment, morality, technology, medicine and old age, the preservation and destruction of tradition; new knowledge, new values—all, everything, is coming together in America in one or another of its effects or phases. What happens in America is what will determine the development and action of all these forces."

What ideal figure or ideal of human action can we find that can meet the challenge of this perception of the world? To study, even superficially, the life of Franklin is to encounter a man who engaged in every movement of the world of his time, who steered through every current and wash of history and nature, a man within whom or next to whom the future—which is our present—was continually coming into existence. Franklin was an important scientist in a golden age of science when great minds were creating modern science out of the unknown; Franklin was a dynamic and innovative businessman in the era when modern capitalism was just beginning to take form and the whole idea of modern business was just being born; he was a master of the creation of associations, social, governmental, and academic. Our plan of postal service, insurance, roadways and governmental planning all owe their birth greatly to Franklin's uniquely active and socially ingenious mind; Franklin was a master diplomat and negotiator who, in his later years, helped in his way *as much as Washington* to win the Revolutionary War—through his exceedingly bold and wise and *lucky* actions in Paris, drawing in French military and financial support for his newborn country.

THE ART FORM OF AMERICA IS GOVERNMENT

As for the birth of what is surely the greatest creation of the American nation, the Constitution, we know only that Franklin was there, in the hot summer of 1787, watching and waiting and speaking, arguing and listening—a man of revered status who, at the same time, failed to win his own points, but who rose above the defeat of his own cherished and highly intelligent views about the structure of government—in particular, the question of representation in Congress proportionate to population. The great art form of America is government and especially the Constitution. Other nations and cultures have produced cathedrals, epics, poems, music, systems of philosophy that far surpass what America has brought forth. But let those who ask what of transcending stature our nation has created turn their eyes to our form and structure of government. That is the American art, a work of human hands and minds that can stand, in a certain way, alongside many of the greatest achievements in the history of the world.

And in this art form, it seems to me, America is pointing to the most essential art form of the future—the art of human association, the art of working together as individuals in groups and communities. This is the essential art form of coming humanity. Without it, nothing else can help us. It is through the group, the community, that moral power and a higher level of intelligence can be sought, if only we can discover the way of constructing association with others in communities, groups and combinations of men and women.

What, then, did Franklin bring to the Constitutional Convention in the early mornings of that asphyxiatingly hot summer of 1787? Consider Franklin's concluding words to the assembled representatives. Read them for what they can represent about the inner demand upon individuals who seek to work with each other in order to touch the intelligence needed for serving a greater aim. Read them for what they can represent about the practical meaning of reason as a spiritualizing force within ourselves and how it can only arise in us through the struggle to listen to our neighbor. Consider the paradox: reason in its spiritual, metaphysical sense is at the same time the most individualistic and most communalistic of human capacities. Reason is the light from within myself *and* reason enters us only as we open to our neighbor. Of course, it cannot be stressed too often that here we are not speaking of the kind of reason that is commonly meant by the word in our present cultural environment, a calculating automatism that can easily isolate and divide us from each other and from nature. What we are speaking of is reason as the calm flame within, which every great metaphysical and spiritual teaching throughout history has sought to activate within us.

Consider first Franklin's motion for prayers at the Convention. It is the Philadelphia State House at the end of June. The delegates have been meeting for a full month, a month of deep distrust—wrangling, quarreling, outrage, bitterness, self-serving politics, fear and recriminations. The war against Britain is history. The colonies are free and independent, but the structure of their relationship is too weak to bind them together with anything but the ties of immediate expediency. Therefore, even the fact that the delegates have come together at all to reexamine their relationship is something of a miracle.

A month, then, has passed. Franklin, who does not speak much, rises on his gout-ridden legs. "Mr. President," he says,

> The small progress we have made after four or five weeks' close attendance and continual reasonings with each other, our different sentiments on almost every question . . . is, methinks, a melancholy proof of the imperfection of the human understanding.

Franklin is about to interpret this situation in a unique manner—not as a sign of human contentiousness only, or of greed or egoism only, but as an indication that the delegation must surely *feel* its lack of wisdom, must surely *feel* its need for a higher source of reason and understanding. Whether any individual delegate does actually feel this is another matter. But Franklin's words serve to point them toward such a perception of their own need. He goes on:

> We indeed seem to *feel* our own want of political wisdom, since we have been running all about in search of it. We have gone back to ancient history for models of government, and examined the different

forms of these republics, which, having originally formed with the seeds of their own dissolution, now no longer exist; and we have viewed modern states all around Europe, but find none of their constitutions suitable to our circumstances.

Having succinctly stated the situation they are all in, Franklin puts the question: why have we all not turned for help to that which is higher than ourselves?

> In this situation of this assembly, groping, as it were, in the dark to find political truth, and scarce able to distinguish it when presented to us, how has it happened, Sir, that we have not hitherto once thought of humbly applying to the Father of Lights to illuminate our understanding? In the beginning of the contest with Britain, when we were sensible of danger, we had daily prayers in this room for the divine protection. Our prayers, Sir, were heard, and they were graciously answered. All of us, who were engaged in the struggle, must have observed frequent instances of a superintending Providence in our favor. To that kind Providence we owe this happy opportunity of consulting in peace on the means of establishing our future national felicity. And have we now forgotten that powerful Friend? Or do we imagine we no longer need its assistance?

I picture Franklin pausing at this moment to see if his words are having an action on the delegates, reminding them of what a man is willing to let go of when the need for a greater force in oneself is felt and understood. But I do not picture Franklin believing that his words are actually going to turn the tide and bring harmony to the delegation. He is too worldly-wise to expect that. And yet, or so I see him, he himself knows that the nation is confronting the same level of danger that it faced in 1776. Perhaps he sees it in himself—that he is too ready to give up listening, too ready to let things go by power plays and egoism, the all-too-familiar forces of wishful thinking and paranoia. Perhaps he is not only addressing the delegates, but himself as he continues:

> I have lived, Sir, a long time, and the longer I live, the more convinc-
> ing proofs I see of this truth, *that* GOD *governs in the affairs of men.*
> And if a sparrow cannot fall to the ground without his notice, is it
> probable that an empire can rise without his aid? We have been as-
> sured, Sir, in the sacred writings, that "except the Lord build the
> house, they labor in vain that build it." I firmly believe this; and I also
> believe that without his concurring aid, we shall succeed in this
> political building no better than the builders of Babel; we shall be di-
> vided by our little, partial, local interests, our projects will be con-
> founded, and we ourselves shall become a reproach and a bye-word
> down to future ages. And, what is worse, mankind may hereafter,
> from this unfortunate instance, despair of establishing government
> by human wisdom, and leave it to chance, war and conquest.[9]

"Chance, war and conquest": to the founders of America—to Franklin, Jefferson, Washington, Adams—these were the only factors that history showed
as the origins of nations. America was to be the first nation created intentionally by thought and moral choice.

Franklin ended his speech with a motion to hold prayers every morning
that the delegation was in session. The motion was almost unanimously
defeated.

Of course, we must not be naive about Franklin's intent in making this
motion. He was no tin saint, no preacher-man. As Catherine Drinker
Bowen has observed in her account of this moment in the Constitutional
Convention,

> Benjamin Franklin was possessed of so much wisdom and political
> acumen that there is no telling which quality was uppermost, impel-
> ling this speech . . . [The] scene had urgency, danger, drama. A Georgia
> delegate, William Few, described that morning of June twenty-eighth

as "an awful and critical moment. If the Convention had then ad-
journed, the dissolution of the union of the states seemed inevitable."
Yet whether the Doctor had spoken from policy or from faith, his
suggestion had been salutary, calling an assembly of doubting minds
to a realization that destiny herself sat as guest and witness in the
room. Franklin had made solemn reminder that a republic of thirteen
states—venture novel and daring—could not be achieved without
mutual sacrifice and a summoning up of men's best, most difficult
and most creative efforts.[10]

The days, weeks and months passed by. The heat increased, the wrangling
and quarreling went on, the danger of dissolution increased. How often it
must have seemed that the colonies would break apart—that fear and mis-
trust and individual opinion would prevail, or that the final resolution
would be a weak and ineffectual document that, in the absence of obvious
external danger, would only hold the colonies together until the next crisis
or the one after that blew them apart. How clear it probably would have
seemed to an outside observer that no real depth of unity would ever be
achieved by these men who in general sought not a deep and greater good
for the whole, but only a greater good for their own interests. And when,
such an observer might have wondered, when ever in the history of human
affairs has a collection of individuals, without clear and present external
danger, formed a union that served anything but selfish purposes? And
when ever in the history of human affairs has a selfishly motivated union
ever endured past the ordinary crises that visit all groups and communities
and nations? Was this group of men seeking to form a purely economic
union? Then a force greater than economic forces might soon destroy it.
Was it to be a military union? Then forces greater than military factors
alone would soon destroy it. Was it to be merely legal, merely political,
merely expedient? Then forces of all kinds would soon destroy it. What
sort of forces are these that break apart legal, economic, military bonds?
The answer to this question begins within the psyche of all men and
women: they are the forces that we loosely label psychological or ethnic or

tribal—forces of fear, false imagination, subjective philosophy, fanatical religion.

And yet a union was formed, a union beyond economic, military, legal, religious or political bonds, a union that has lasted amid forces that in the past two centuries have broken down every other government in the world. The Constitution of the United States has allowed the coherence of a people and a nation within whose geographical and psychological borders all the immense forces of human life on earth have played and clashed with an intensity beyond any imagining.

What force lies at the origin of the Constitution of the United States, beyond what may be labeled economic, political, legal, military or religious influences in any of their obvious meanings? What enabled the Constitution as we know it to come into existence?

Is not the answer to this question to be found in the nearly superhuman struggle of individuals to listen to each other? If we are to discern a spiritual resonance in the founding of America, will it not be seen mainly in the effort of individuals to open their minds to each other when almost everything in them is pulling them into isolation? I do not say that all or even many of these delegates of the Constitutional Convention undertook soul-searching efforts, or that they listened to each other for the purpose of spiritual freedom. This group was not a collection of spiritual aspirants. Nevertheless, we can take the "miracle" of the formation of the Constitution as a great external sign of a process that can take place when individuals come together to seek understanding and right action. If government is the art form of America, if the Constitution is the masterpiece of this art, then there must lie within the process of its formation lessons that we shall need to learn as the modern era spills into the new millennium. *The art of the future is the group.* The intelligence and benevolence we need can only come from the group, from associations of men and women seeking to struggle against the impulses of illusion, egoism and fear.

A WONDROUS ENGINE

And now here is Franklin at the end of the Convention, on the very last day, September 17, 1787. The sweltering heat, finally, has broken; a hint of autumn is in the air. In front of the delegates a document has been placed that reflects the summer's entire fabric of dispute and argument, thought and passion, secret meetings, manipulations, interior sacrifices of personal agenda, long pulses of outrage and fear, resentment and hope—a document reflecting all the questions and issues voted upon and discussed: the proposed Constitution of the United States of America which, as the basis of free government, would be described years later by John Adams as "a complicated piece of machinery, the nice and exact adjustment of whose springs, wheels, and weights, is not yet well comprehended by the artists of the age, and still less by the people."[11]

A wondrous engine, like the immense locomotive standing in the great hall of the Franklin Institute. Franklin rises, holding the papers on which his speech is written. He hands them to James Wilson, the narrow-shouldered, bespectacled delegate from Pennsylvania. Wilson reads aloud:

> Mr. President,
>
> I confess that I do not entirely approve of this Constitution at present; but, Sir, I am not sure I shall never approve it; for having lived long, I have experienced many instances of being obliged, by better information or fuller consideration, to change my opinions even on important subjects, which I once thought right, but found to be otherwise. It is therefore that, the older I grow, the more apt I am to doubt my own judgment of others.

Is this "politics" on Franklin's part? Or is he squarely acknowledging that he must sacrifice attachment to his own "wisdom" in order to allow the action of the *group intelligence?* Let us remember that on many major issues

Franklin's views have been overridden: he had, for example, strongly advocated proportionate representation in the Congress based on state population and had argued against the equal representation rule of the Senate; and he was strongly against salaries for the president and the congressmen, having spoken passionately about the corruption that salaried leadership would bring. At the same time, he is, after Washington, the most respected man in all of America. Yet, at the Convention, he has personally "won" very little. The speech continues:

> Most men, indeed, as well as most sects in religion, think themselves in possession of all truth, and that wherever others differ from them, it is so far error. Steele, a Protestant, in a dedication, tells the Pope, that the only difference between our two churches in their opinions of the certainty of their doctrine, is the Romish Church is *infallible*, and the Church of England is *never in the wrong*. But although many private persons think almost as highly of their own infallibility as that of their sect, few express it so naturally as a certain French Lady, who, in a little dispute with her sister, said, "But I meet with nobody but myself that is always in the right." *"Je ne trouve que moi qui aie toujours raison."*

> In these sentiments, Sir, I agree to this Constitution, with all its faults—if they are such; because I think a general government necessary for us, and there is no *form* of government but what may be a blessing to the people, if well administered; and I believe, farther, that this is likely to be well administered for a course of years, and can only end in despotism, as other forms have done before it, when the people shall become so corrupted as to need despotic government, being incapable of any other.

THE METAPHYSICS OF DEMOCRACY

Again, the question insists itself: is this only pragmatic politics on Franklin's part, or is he fully acknowledging that the group has received a wisdom that surpasses the intelligence of any one individual? Here we touch on what may be called the "metaphysics of democracy"—the idea that authentically human vision and energy come through the association of equals seeking to serve a greater aim and intentionally struggling with the attachment to their own opinions.

Certainly, in the history of the world's spiritual traditions, one often finds reference to the guiding wisdom that is said to appear through the co-operative work of a community of spiritual seekers. Of course, it would be misleading to compare the association of delegates at the Constitutional Convention to a community of spiritual disciples. For one thing, the authentic spiritual community has received a certain definite knowledge and energy from its teacher, and the inner intention of the individuals is to free themselves from the thrall of worldly selfhood in order to be touched and directed by a higher force. The mythic figure of the Divine King and the historic and semi-historic figures of the Divine Lawgiver—Moses, Mohammed, Manu, Asoka—communicate the idea that the organization of human life in the world requires a transworldly intelligence. In the disappearance of the founding teacher, in the conditions intentionally prepared by such a teacher that obtain after his or her death, the source of this transworldly intelligence and energy, at least temporarily, falls upon the group which has most intensely received the teacher's guidance, generally a small group of advanced pupils. Obviously, this is not the "delegation at the Constitutional Convention."

Then why bring in this reference? Because the fact is that something truly remarkable did take place at this meeting of ordinary men in the summer of 1787. And the fact is that something this extraordinary lies at the very foundation of our nation and even, to a significant extent, at the roots of modernity itself. Something redolent of the miraculous is at work here, some collective human action is at work here that can serve as a *symbol* of the power of authentic community. We need to re-mythologize our past, to rediscover the heroes and the values that call to us from the processes of human reality in our past and in our own lives. Set aside all we heard as children about these Founding Fathers—these men were not especially noble and pure; but set aside also, or at least take a distance from, all the information that much revisionist scholarship tells us about the prejudice, self-interest and greed of many of them. Between, or rather above, these two opposite poles—the sentimental and the cynical views of our history—there hovers the element of symbolic reality, of an actual process that took place in actual history which yet at the same time has about it the fragrance of a process that could lead all men and women toward the moral power and intelligence we are searching for. This kind of process took place during that blistering Philadelphia summer—the process of a group of ordinary human beings *listening* to each other, not as people usually listen, but as people *can* listen: from a source deeper in themselves which opens them not only to the thoughts and views of their neighbor, but to something wiser and finer in themselves and, perhaps, in the universe itself. The Constitutional Convention is our specifically American symbol of the *art and power of the community.* It is the community which can bring what no individual can bring, what every individual desires and what, today, we all despair of finding: moral vision and moral power. And, in my view, it is Franklin and, as we will see, Jefferson who can serve as our heroes, embodiments, of faith in the community. Here, again, is Franklin—the concluding notes of his speech on the final day of the Convention.

"I doubt," says Franklin,

whether any other convention we can obtain, may be able to make a better constitution; for, when you assemble a number of men, to have the advantage of their joint wisdom, you inevitably assemble with those men all their prejudices, their passions, their errors of opinion, their local interests, and their selfish views. From such an assembly can a perfect production be expected? It therefore astonishes me, Sir, to find this system approaching so near to perfection as it does; and I think it will astonish our enemies, who are waiting with confidence to hear, that our councils are confounded like those of the builders of Babel, and that our States are on the point of separation, only to meet hereafter for the purpose of cutting one another's throats. Thus, I consent, Sir, to this Constitution, because I expect no better, and because I am not sure it is not the best.[12]

With this, after an appeal for a vote of unanimity, the speech of Franklin ends.

AN ORDINARY MAN

Back at the Franklin Institute, the old man and his grandson have left and I'm alone in the cab of the Baldwin, feeling the heaviness of the locomotive, the heaviness of iron and steel and—although of course not in these words—the astonishing passivity of metal and matter. I marveled that man could make such a machine as this out of hard, cold, unmoving matter. And for what? That question was already on the horizon of my mind—for *what* was such a machine created? To answer what needs or purposes of humanity? While marveling at this meeting of human thought and cold metal—while being spellbound by man's, my, power to put "handles and levers" on the body of dead nature itself, with my eyes bulging and my heart pounding amid the gauges and the thick, black tons of iron, with tears in my eyes, still the thought was already forming itself: For what? For commerce? For things? To carry automobiles? Furniture? Coal to heat houses so that people could do stupid, meaningless things in them? So that people could eat and sleep and go to the bathroom and yell at each other and get bored and tired and excited at nothing and disappointed and self-satisfied and kill and subjugate and . . .

Even at this young age the paradox of human life on earth had already become my nearly constant companion.

And was this not the paradox of Benjamin Franklin? This wise philosopher, sensitive to God without falling prey to religious dogma and naiveté. The revered sage who yet made shrewd business deals, handled lightning, tilted with foreign kings and ministers, pioneered new science and technologies, forged all kinds of associations for business and civic protection, all the while cutting a figure with women and savoring the delights and refinements of the flesh and the persona. Wise, canny, clever, dangerous, brilliant, ingenious, spiritual, artistic, charismatic, famous and silent Benjamin Franklin. Our King Solomon? Our Merlin? Our American symbol of the man alive in two worlds—the world of the spirit and the world of matter. Does one really trust Franklin? It is foolish to take him as saintly, and it is equally foolish to take him as worldly. *We do not know Franklin* because we do not know this meeting place between the worlds that Franklin can represent for us. He is our symbol of the search in ordinary life. And if he went too far into the life of the world, if even he underestimated the seductive power of money, fame, power and knowledge; if Franklin made only tiny steps in the direction of inwardness (and who are we to say how far he went?)—even so, he can become our symbol of the search in the midst of life. If even Franklin failed by falling into the outer world, it is because America itself fell like that so early in its life.

To repeat: we do not quite trust Franklin because we do not understand the intrinsic contradiction of the spiritual search in the midst of the forces of life—sex, power and money. We trust the "official" religious saint, perhaps, who achieves sanctity through retreating from worldly life—the hermit in the desert, the monk in his monastery. And we understand, and therefore in a certain sense we trust, the man or woman engaged only in the outer life with no spiritual motivation at all. But we do not grasp the co-existence of these two directions in any individual or in ourselves. We admire, but do not know, the man who lives in two worlds. In the legends, he is the trickster: no one really trusts him, not even God. He is the magician—what does he really want, what does he really serve? He is Solomon, the ancient King who symbolizes both worldly power and service to God at one and the same time. And this figure, this symbol of the divine King, was already almost entirely degenerated in seventeenth- and eighteenth-century Europe. Monarchy had entirely lost its aura of the sacred. The actual monarch was, in England and for the early Americans, hardly more, and often much less, than an ordinary man—often, in fact, a despot, an oppressor of the body and the spirit. Yet the ancient meaning of the ancient symbol had to return, but now in another outward form—no longer a king who receives his power and wisdom from God, but a kingly ordinary man who receives his power and wisdom from a god within. If Protestantism brought to Christendom the revolutionary doctrine of the priesthood of believers, then America brought to the world the revolutionary doctrine of the kingship of ordinary man. But, as the symbol of Franklin informs us, it is no simple thing to be an "ordinary man"—a human being acting in the world of matter under the inward rule of the search for the spirit.

Very well, if one wishes, one can read Franklin's letters and study the vast body of historical material and come to a more or less scholarly estimate of Franklin's actual personal qualities. But remember, history is an endless maze; he who enters the labyrinth of historical fact and speculation without a guiding thread may never find his way out again. By all means, let us study the historical Franklin, the historical Jefferson, the historical Lincoln. But if we wish to rediscover the values that can guide our present life, we must also remember that history itself, by itself, can never give them to us. It will—like the universe itself—only answer the questions we ask it. And if we ask history—the history of America—for guiding images that can help our present need for meaning, then our American history will begin to give us our old images and heroes in vibrant new colors such as, for example, Benjamin Franklin, the American symbol of the spiritual search in the midst of ordinary life, and our Constitution as the material symbol of how a community can receive the wisdom that is denied to any one individual.

"There he is, Miss Hackett!"

I stared down into the flushed face of Mary Gourley, who always did the right thing. The braces on her teeth gleamed as she stretched out her bare, bony arm and pointed a narrow finger at me.

Miss Hackett rolled up to the locomotive like a field truck, the rest of the class trotting hurriedly behind her. With everyone looking at me, I felt like I was a hundred feet in the air. I saw Allie Nemiroff's face, round as a pie, his mouth still moving.

Not only did I seem a hundred feet in the air, I felt strong, stronger than I had ever felt before. I clutched the black iron frame of the cabin.

"Come down here this minute!" said Miss Hackett.

"Why?" I said. I was amazed at myself. No one had ever responded like that to an order from Miss Hackett.

She, however, did not choose to explain herself. To my astonishment, and that of the class, she grabbed the bars of the iron ladder and, heels and all, started climbing up to get me. There is this vivid memory in my mind of the brief moment when Miss Hackett and I were together in the cabin. I remember her strangely gentle, magnolia-like cologne, her livid face and her dark, angry eyes. I remember the moment standing with her—she was actually shorter than I was, but she was built like a tank. She didn't say anything more; she just looked at me with those powerful, dark eyes. But there was no question about it—she actually smiled tenderly at me.

I happily climbed down the ladder and from that moment on, not only did her explanations no longer bore me, either there or back at school, but even the fatuous blather of Allie Nemiroff no longer annoyed me. However, the righteousness of Mary Gourley continued to torment me.

But now, George Washington.

THREE

THE MYTH AND
THE CHARACTER OF
GEORGE WASHINGTON

A New Kind of Symbol

It is impossible to understand the miracle of the Constitutional Convention or, for that matter, anything at all about the meaning and origins of the United States, without re-assimilating the figure of George Washington. More, perhaps, than any other single factor, it was the presence of Washington in the Philadelphia State House that prevented the parties and factions from shattering into dissolution. And while it is clear from the historical records that Franklin lent not only his presence but his gifts as a thinker and negotiator to the Convention, it is also clear that Washington's immense influence had to do not so much with what he said or did, but simply with his presence. As Garry Wills has so effectively shown,[13] at the Convention and throughout his career, Washington's power and stature—unequaled by any other American of his time, and equaled later only perhaps by Lincoln—derived primarily not from what he did, but *from what he did not do*. A nation

and a culture like our own, which thrive on ever-accelerating outward motion and "doing"—this nation began with a man whose action was in its
way a renunciation of action. The "note" sounded by Washington is that of
letting-go. This is not to claim that Washington's actions were equivalent to
the mysterious gesture of non-action that characterizes the power of spiritual masters. Compared to such spiritual action, Washington's deeds are
surely as much a part of the world of "illusion" and "the flesh" as any other.
But within that "world of the flesh," Plato's "world of coming into being
and passing away," the world and the everyday life we all inhabit, Washington can serve as an entirely new kind of symbol. Within this, our, world
of restless and increasingly meaningless action, Washington's actions have
the perfume, however faint, of non-action, of a different kind of movement
that is possible within the life of every man and woman. To see this, to allow Washington to be re-mythologized in this way, takes very little re-
positioning of the information and legends and historical assessments about
him that we already have.

Consider, for example, his resignation in 1783 as commander-in-chief
of the American forces, a step which historian Gordon S. Wood calls "the
greatest act of his life."

> Following the signing of the peace treaty and British recognition of
> American independence, Washington stunned the world when he
> surrendered his sword to the Congress on December 23, 1783, and
> retired to his farm at Mount Vernon. . . . This self-conscious and un-
> conditional withdrawal from power and politics was a great moral ac-
> tion, full of significance for an enlightened and republicanized world,
> and the results were monumental.

Wood continues:

> His retirement had a profound effect everywhere in the Western
> world. It was extraordinary, it was unprecedented in modern times—
> a victorious general surrendering his arms and returning to his farm.

Cromwell, William of Orange, Marlborough—all had sought political rewards commensurate with their military achievements. Though it was widely thought that Washington could have become king or dictator, he wanted nothing of the kind. He was sincere in his desire for all the soldiers "to return to our Private Stations in the bosom of a free, peaceful and happy Country," and everyone recognized his sincerity. It filled them with awe. Washington's retirement, said the painter John Trumbull writing from London in 1784, "excites the astonishment and admiration of this part of the world. Tis a Conduct so novel, so inconceivable to People, who, far from giving up powers they possess, are willing to convulse the empire to acquire more." King George III supposedly predicted that if Washington retired from public life and returned to his farm, "he will be the greatest man in the world."[14]

Who was this man? *What* was he? Ralph Waldo Emerson, with his usual clairvoyant precision, summarizes the riddle of Washington:

> The head of Washington [probably the Houdon bust] hangs in my dining room for a few days past, & I cannot keep my eyes off of it. It has a certain Appalachian strength, as if it were truly the first-fruits of America, & expressed the country. The heavy leaden eyes turn on you, as the eyes of an ox in a pasture. And the mouth has a gravity and depth of quiet, *as if this man had absorbed all the serenity of America, & left none for his restless, rickety, hysterical countrymen.*[15]

As for modern historians and biographers, each in his or her own way bows before something that seems both inscrutable and strangely commanding of respect in the facts and legends about Washington. Noemie Emery, for example, introduces her 1976 biography by speaking of the inassimilable image that Washington presents to Americans. "He is known," she writes, "but what as? Very little, usually, and that little indeterminate and dim."

> Time has done little to reduce the image of the big man on the white horse, insufferably righteous, or the man who had such trouble with

his teeth. Neither is much use to the scholar, seeking intellectual connections to history, or to the lay reader, seeking emotional connections to his life.

Or, we might add, to the American man or woman seeking ideals and images of authentic meaning lying at the origin of our modern world. Emery notes that "Washington's canonization has made orphans of us all. . . . It sets a dead echo at the center of American history, delegitimizing the first facts of our creation and nature." Referring to Emerson's observation cited above, she writes further of the strength and the enigma of Washington:

> This strength has been a burden on America, and America has taken its revenge. No great man in history has a name so lifeless or a monument so featureless and blank. Jefferson and Lincoln, adoptive saints of the democracy, dominate their own memorials; Andrew Jackson's very horse breathes fire; Washington's tribute alone reveals no warming touch of flesh.

And then, in a passionate survey of Washington's whole life, Emery continues:

> He began a great world war when he was twenty-two years old, was branded an "assassin" in the courts of Europe, and chided for barbarity by Voltaire. In the war that followed [the French and Indian War, 1755–63], his pride, insolence and insubordination were famous— and infamous—among British and colonial commanders in the skirmishes against the French. Eaten by a fierce ambition, he pursued fame relentlessly, missed it, and discovered later, when it came unbidden, that he had somehow lost the taste. He proposed to one woman while in love with another, married the first in a mood of almost bitter resignation, and found later that this, too, could change. Cool, aloof, and distant, he was known for the cold qualities of what Jefferson called his perfect justice, yet Jefferson, and others, sensed

the hidden violence; portraitist Gilbert Stuart observed the hidden lineaments of all the strongest passions and said that if he had lived among the Indians, he would have been the most fierce of all the savage chiefs. The results of those banked fires were apparent then and still endure: the army saved, the union soldered, the ambitions, flames and talents of Hamilton, Jefferson, John Adams—the most contentious lot to co-exist in any house of government—overmastered and subdued.

Hundreds of pages later, the biography concludes:

His passions, gigantic and troubling, were the bedrock of his genius, controlled to provide discipline, loosened to unleash the welding power that sustained and settled the nation he helped to form. On these passions, now chained and now explosive, rested the United States.[16]

A FALLIBLE HUMAN BEING; A GREAT AND GOOD MAN

Obviously, with Washington we are dealing with an individual and a symbol that America has not yet been able to assimilate. As Noemie Emery tellingly observes, the Washington Monument itself has an abstract invisibility about it—as though at the root of the American nation is an incomprehensible and yet overwhelmingly powerful force. "No American is more completely misunderstood than George Washington," writes James Thomas Flexner, arguably Washington's greatest modern biographer. "My continuing effort," he writes, "has been to disentangle the Washington who actually lives from all the symbolic Washingtons, to rescue the man and his deeds from the layers and layers of obscuring legend that have accreted around his memory during some two hundred years. . . . I tried to forget everything I had ever heard about George Washington. . . . I determined to start with a blank canvas."

What was the result? Flexner continues:

> I found a fallible human being made of flesh and blood and spirit—not a statue of marble and wood. And inevitably—for that was the *fact*—I found a great and good man. In all history few men who possessed unassailable power have used that power so gently and self-effacingly for what their best instincts told them was the welfare of their neighbors and all mankind.

Referring to the modern debunking tendency to pull down American idols, Flexner writes further what amounts to an unwitting confession that the life and character of Washington intrinsically compel symbolic understanding. *The facts themselves*—as do all important truths—speak great *meanings* if we have the ears to hear them:

> Most of the brickbats now being thrown at Washington are figments of the modern imagination. In being ourselves untrue to the highest teaching of the American tradition, we of this generation have tended to denigrate that tradition, to seek out all that was unworthy, to emphasize whatever justifies national distrust. In so doing, we have discarded an invaluable heritage. We are blinding our eyes to stars that lead to the very ideals many of us most admire: the sanctity of the individual, the equality of all men before the law, government responsive to the people. . . . To find again the American ideals we have lost, we may not return to our national beginnings with the blinded eyes of idolatry or chauvinism. Let us examine deeply every flaw, every area, where George Washington and his fellow Founding Fathers were untrue to what they professed. Let us examine Washington not as the spotless figure delineated by infantile fantasies or by self-seeking wavers of the flag. Let us determine without prejudice exactly what happened, exactly how men behaved. If we do this, we shall, so I am profoundly convinced, find, in the dark valley where we often stand, inspiration.[17]

What Flexner speaks of—the meanings that arise when one allows in the facts—describes what I myself experienced as I became more familiar with the life of this man who until now had never been more to me than a childhood cliché, or even a joke. A certain hope and faith appear when, without forcing, we allow great ideas to meet facts about history or nature that until now have floated unattended or have been self-servingly perceived in the flood of information that submerges our culture and keeps from us the experience of meaning, which we need as we need air to breathe.

The life of Washington, then.

A MAN OF ASTONISHING STRENGTH

Flexner begins by dispelling the common belief that Washington was by birth and training a rich, conservative, British-oriented aristocrat. Not so: "No other President of the United States before Andrew Jackson was as much shaped by the wilderness as Washington, and he had less formal education than did Jackson, than Lincoln even." The details about his early years, including his conduct in the French and Indian War, altogether speak of the man's *physicality.* What does it really mean that he was born and grew up in the wilderness? Previous generations of Americans have tended to take facts like this as evidence of a great man's ability to overcome the limitations of his upbringing and, by his own efforts, to enter fully and masterfully into the cultured, civilized world. But can we not take it in quite another way—that Washington, like Jackson and Lincoln and many other great Americans, grew up more in direct relationship to nature—and not only to external nature, but to the forces of nature within oneself, the physical body with its specific energy and intelligence. We need to look more closely at this aspect of Washington's life to see what it can tell us about his character.

It is important to realize that the moral and philosophical ideals of the Enlightenment, with its emphasis on the power of reason, were held by men and women who were profoundly engaged and absorbed by the life of the body. Life in colonial America, even in the most refined of city environments, was far, far more physically challenging in every detail than we can imagine today. Speaking to one's neighbor, traveling from one place to another (not to mention crossing the wild ocean on a month-long, perilous voyage), procuring food, making the tools and furnishings needed, building one's house, dealing with matters of cleanliness and hygiene, dealing with light and darkness, cold and heat, dealing (in the cities, and mostly they were hardly what we would call cities) with vermin and offal—all this made demands upon the physical body of a kind that is completely alien to most of us in the modern world. And as for life outside the city (and this accounted for more than 90 percent of the population of America), the need for physical strength and resourcefulness far exceeded the demands we experience in the everyday life of the Western world. And even in that world, it seems that Washington stood out as a man of astonishing strength, stamina and physical courage. Flexner speaks of his "amazing body," describing his actions serving under the British general Edward Braddock near Fort Duquesne in 1755. Violently stricken with dysentery, the young Washington kept his calm as the British soldiers suddenly began retreating in panic and falling around him. Braddock himself was mortally wounded. Hysteria and death were everywhere.

> Braddock indignantly denied Washington's request that he be allowed to lead the provincial troops into the woods and "engage the enemy in their own way."
>
> The officers on their horses were perfect targets. One after another they went down. Washington's horse was shot from under him. He leapt on another. Bullets tore his coat. Braddock toppled over. Washington's second horse crumpled; his hat was shot off. However, as he later wrote, "the miraculous care of Providence . . . protected me beyond all human expectation." He was now "the only person then left to distribute the (wounded) general's orders." This he was hardly able to do because his sickness was rising upon him. The dead

and dying lay in piles. The survivors, no officers being left to stop them, were at long last saving themselves by running away. Having loaded Braddock into "a small covered cart," Washington led into retreat those men who could move and had remained to be led.

The wounded Braddock ordered Washington to ride back forty miles through the night to summon reinforcements. Washington's amazing body summoned up the necessary strength, although he recalled that illness, fatigue and anxiety had left him "in a manner wholly unfit for the execution of the duty. . . . The shocking scenes which presented themselves in this night march are not to be described. The dead, the dying, the groans, lamentations, and cries along the road of the wounded for help . . . were enough to pierce a heart of adamant, the gloom and horror of which was not a little increased by the imperious darkness occasioned by the close shade of the thick woods." At times, he had to crawl on hands and knees to find the road. Washington reached his objective, but the reinforcements he had been ordered to call forward were too terrified to march.[18]

From ancient times to the present, of course, combat in war has called up countless extraordinary actions and human capacities. What is interesting in such descriptions of Washington, however, is how they continually recur in relation to all periods of his life. Washington's leadership during the Revolutionary War, for example, is characterized not so much by brilliant maneuvers, but by an incredible capacity to persist in the face of uncertainties, agonizing betrayals,* frustrations and prolonged desperate physical demands that would have stopped almost any other man. And not only to persist, but to persist with an air of profound calm and, as is continually remarked by his contemporaries, a grace and majesty of the body. During the winter of

---

*The most famous, of course, being the treason of his trusted companion Benedict Arnold. The incapacity and the frequent unwillingness of the Congress to properly support the campaign was an ongoing, deeply dispiriting trial for Washington and his troops.

1777–78 at Valley Forge, for example, the ragged troops suffered cold and hunger as well as neglect by Congress. Washington was being accused of inactivity for failure to attack Howe's forces in Philadelphia. Although such accusations, writes Dr. Algigence Waldo, a surgeon of the Connecticut line,

> brought "blame on His Excellency [as Washington was often called] . . . and disgrace on the Continental troops . . ." Washington, "by opposing little more than an equal number of young troops to old veterans, has kept the ground in general, cooped them [the British] up in the city, prevented their making any considerable inroads upon him, killed and wounded a very considerable number of them in different skirmishes, and made many proselytes to the shrine of Liberty by these little successes, and by the prudence, calmness, sedateness and wisdom with which he facilitates all his operations.[19]

The winter of 1779–80 at Morristown, New Jersey, was, as historian Barbara W. Tuchman describes it, even more severe than the year at Valley Forge.

> Rations were reduced for already hungry men who had been shivering in the snows to one-eighth of normal quantities. Two leaders of a protest by Connecticut regiments demanding full rations and back pay were hanged to quell an uprising. In January of 1781, Pennsylvania regiments mutinied and, with troops of New Jersey, deserted to the number of half their strength before the outbreak was suppressed. At the frontiers, Indians out of the woods guided by Loyalists were burning farms and homes and massacring civilians. Even to keep an army in the field was problematical, because soldiers of the militia had to be furloughed to go home to harvest their crops, and if leave were refused, they would desert. Fighting a war in such circumstances, said General von Steuben, the army's Prussian drillmaster, "Caesar and Hannibal would have lost their reputations."[20]

The period of 1779–80, according to Tuchman, which followed the great disappointment of France's initial military failures on behalf of the colonists, the loss of Charleston, the two bitter winters unsupported by Congress and the public—as well as the betrayal of Benedict Arnold—was "the worst year of the war when the Revolution sank to its lowest point." Washington suffered "discouragement close to despair."[21]

Perhaps all wars are like this; perhaps every organized, prolonged effort of men to kill each other falls under the laws of chaos and despair and blind, stupid chance masquerading as the designs of providence; and perhaps the demands of leadership in war always are such as ultimately call forth the best or the worst in any man. However that may be, it is hard to believe that any American would not be astonished and awed by learning of the demands placed upon Washington during the Revolutionary War and by the qualities of spirit that, by *all* accounts, he exhibited in leading a ragtag army against the greatest military force in the world, facing the incredible impotence and meanness of his own countrymen in Congress and among the colonies, facing the fear and explosive resentment of his bewildered troops and staff—while yet earning the deepest love from all who served near him; buffeted by the forces of an international catfight between France and England within which the emerging American nation lay exposed like a featherless bird. It is impossible not to be stopped when one sees, at every point throughout the war, accounts like the following description of Washington's bearing—here during a visit in 1778 to a newly established hospital near West Point.

WASHINGTON'S PRESENCE

> The appearance of our Commander in Chief is that of the perfect gentleman and the accomplished warrior. He is remarkably tall, full six feet, erect and well proportioned. The strength and proportion of his joints and muscles appear to be commensurate with the preeminent

powers of his mind. The serenity of his countenance, and majestic gracefulness of his deportment, impart a strong impression of that dignity and grandeur, which are his peculiar characteristics, and no one can stand in his presence without feeling the ascendancy of his mind, and associating with his countenance the idea of wisdom, philanthropy, magnanimity and patriotism. There is a fine symmetry in the features of his face indicative of a benign and dignified spirit. . . . He wears his hair in a becoming cue, and from his forehead it is turned back and powdered in a manner which adds to the military air of his appearance. He displays a native gravity, but devoid of all appearance of ostentation. His uniform dress is a blue coat, with two brilliant epaulettes, buff colored under clothes and a three-cornered hat with a black cockade. He is constantly equipped with an elegant small sword, boots and spurs.

Smith quotes this description in full "because it gives a vivid if familiar picture of Washington and serves to remind us how much his mere appearance among his scattered brigades meant in preserving morale and how much he *embodied,* quite literally, the Continental Army."[22]

Encountering Washington among his staff at his headquarters some days later, the same observer writes: "He is feared even when silent and beloved even while we are unconscious of the motive . . . a placid smile is frequently observed on his lips, but a loud laugh, it is said, seldom if ever escapes him."[23]

I am calling attention to something which has not, as far as I can see, been emphasized in all the descriptions of Washington's character and qualities—something having to do with the relationship between moral power and how we are placed within our bodies. We are accustomed to think of moral qualities in terms only of observable behavior and inner intentions. But if we call to mind our own experiences in this realm, we may see that moments of hard-earned ethical action—moments approaching the exercise of altruistic will, for example—always involve an unusually vital relationship between mind and body. True impartiality in life, the quality of calm that carries the current of intense moral sentiment and intelligence, is invariably accompanied by a mysterious lightness of the body, bringing with it a capacity to act that is paradoxically inseparable from the power to wait and *refrain from action.* If Washington is to be re-mythologized in the light of the ancient legend of Cincinnatus,* as the hero of *exalted non-action,* we are obliged to consider very seriously Washington's (and the archetypal, original American's) *physicality,* that is, the relation to the body that characterizes a more fully developed man or woman. When Thomas Jefferson said of Washington that he seated himself better upon a horse than anyone of his time,[24] we are not to smile at that nor relegate it to the trivial. On the contrary, it may serve as a vivid image of the relationship between genuine physical presence and moral authority. As such, it can help us ponder the meaning of the word "character," considered as a quality of the whole human being rather than as the exaggerated development of one part of an individual at the expense of the other parts.

Having underscored this point about Washington's physical presence (and we shall encounter something comparable with Lincoln), we may now consider more familiar examples of what the world has called his "greatness."

The Paradox of Greatness

At the same time, it would be a mistake to pass too quickly over certain aspects of Washington's life prior to 1775, when he assumed the command of the Continental Army. Following Flexner's account, we come to ques-

---

*See Garry Wills, *Cincinnatus: George Washington and the Enlightenment,* which brilliantly develops Parson Weems's comparison of Washington to the fabled Roman general who is called from his small farm to lead the army against a sudden invasion and who, after saving the empire, turns away from glory and returns to his quiet private life.

tions about Washington that our discussion has prepared us to face in a new way. For example, why was it that, as Flexner expresses it, "when [Washington] was hardly beyond his teens, many of his associates were already convinced that his destiny was importantly linked with the destiny of America"? In the context of this question, Flexner refers to Washington's well-documented amazing capacity to place himself in the most dangerous combat conditions, with men falling all about him, without once suffering injury. "That his perfidious Indian guide [this episode occurred during the early encounters between the British and the French] should, even at point-blank range, have missed Washington in the wilderness seems reasonable, but it is strange that during the Braddock massacre, when every other mounted officer was struck, he remained uninjured. And then there was the time he rode between the two firing columns, striking up the guns with his sword. In subsequent years, during the Revolution, Washington was again and again to take the most foolhardy risks, but the bullets, although they tore his clothes and killed his horses, never touched his body."[25]

There are countless examples along these lines, not all of them involving Washington's boldness or "foolhardiness." Providence, or chance, spared him dramatically during the retreat at the battle of Brandywine. Here Patrick Ferguson, the commanding officer of the Loyalist forces, a proud Scottish aristocrat and crack marksman (who invented the breech-loading rifle) had Washington square in his sights and could easily have killed him. In Ferguson's own words, "It was not pleasant to fire at the back of an unoffending individual who was acquitting himself very coolly of his duty, so I let him alone."[26]

Of course, many famous and infamous leaders—such as Napoleon and even Hitler—seem to have led charmed lives, at least for a period of time, and, concerning this aspect of Washington's life, Flexner comments:

> Washington's seeming invulnerability to gunfire, more suited to mythology than factual history, was observed—he commented on it wonderingly himself—but it was only the most exotic aspect of that

charisma which brought him so early the confidence and respect of his fellowmen.

"Too early," says the biographer,

for he was entrusted with responsibilities beyond his ability to handle. Not only did his inexperience make him sometimes militarily inept, but he never understood the wider implications of the situations in which he was involved . . . in action he could be rash, brash, impolitic, over self-confident. He made dreadful mistakes.

And yet, when he resigned, as still a very young man:

It seems amazing to find an *officer corps of frontier fighters* saying farewell to a commander not yet twenty-six as follows: "In our earliest infancy, you took us under your tuition, trained us in the practice of that discipline which alone can constitute good troops. . . . Your steady adherence to impartial justice, your quick discernment and invariable regard to merit—wisely intended to inculcate those genuine sentiments of true honor and passion for glory, from which the greatest military achievements have been derived—first heightened our natural emulation, and our desire to excel."[27]

We have before us, then, the following image (and this remains true throughout the whole of Washington's life): a man of extraordinary physical harmony and energy, a man in whom great and furious passion co-existed with qualities of impartiality, judgment, justice and an emotional balance that almost invariably evoked unagitated love and reverence in those who served him; we have a man of great ambition whose actions, at the same time, stand apart from the actions of all other men of his time for their restraint and self-sacrifice. We have a man universally admired in his time as perhaps the greatest man in the world continually showing traits of fallibility, weakness and travail; a man who represents, in a word, that most astonishing of combinations: the extremes of the all-too-human alongside the extremes of highly developed powers of will, courage, impartial love and the capacity for right action.

It is this co-existence of profoundly opposing moral qualities that must take first importance for us if we wish to find new mythic power in the life and character of Washington.

Again, this is not to say that the man Washington was a saint. It *is* to say that chief among Washington's exceptional qualities were factors that reflect onto our own human plane the qualities and ideals of the inner search that is possible and necessary for our era and our civilization. Figures such as Washington, Lincoln, Jefferson and Franklin are deep archetypes in our shared American psyche—they are there, still radiating energy and power. We need to attend to these "demi-gods" within our common psyche and, by looking at them in the light of our present need, allow them to conduct awakening associations rather than serve merely as cues for agitated "doing" or cynical withdrawal.

The simultaneous existence in Washington of extraordinary selflessness and intense ambition, dispassion and passion, "non-action" and boldness, heart-rending gentleness and terrifying ferocity invites us not only to ponder the paradoxical qualities of human nature as such, the existence within every human being of traits and "personalities" totally at odds with each other, but also to consider another feature of his nature, equally well documented by his biographers: namely, his striving and his capacity *to see his faults as they really were and to work on freeing himself from them.*

Washington's striving for self-improvement showed itself early in his life when, in his teens, he laboriously copied out for himself a French book of moral axioms dating back to the sixteenth century. He kept adding to this book throughout his life as a support for his ideals of self-mastery, balanced judgment and action, courage and civility. In this, he shared the spirit of his age, which saw numerous self-improvement societies in the colonies, especially in Philadelphia, often inspired by the work of Benjamin Franklin.

These rules, which Washington held in such high regard, ranged from a few genteel rules of social etiquette to profound principles of conscience demanding the cultivation of compassion, self-respect and inner collectedness. A few examples:

> "When you speak of God or his attributes, let it be seriously, in
> reverence and honor."
> "Be not hasty to believe flying reports to the disparagement of
> anyone."
> "Speak no evil of the absent . . ."
> "Labor to keep alive in your breast that little spark of celestial
> fire called conscience."[28]

THE AMERICAN IDEAL OF SELF-IMPROVEMENT

The ideal of self-examination and self-improvement, of working intentionally and methodically on one's faults, has always been—in one form or another—characteristic of the American psyche, the most well-known and well-articulated example of it as an interior ideal being the account given by Benjamin Franklin in his *Autobiography*. A look at Franklin's narrative— partly tongue-in-cheek though it may be—will help us to re-position the figure of Washington as a symbol not of quaintly conceived fantastical perfection, but of the possibilities in every man and woman to find a self-discipline that liberates our capacity to serve the common good.

THE MORALITY OF SELF-IMPROVEMENT

It should be noted that it is when the ideal of self-improvement is torn away from the ultimate context of service to others, when it is pursued primarily for one's own individual benefit, that it can become the also typically American, but hardly admirable, obsession with personal material gain, success, prestige—including the modern self-involved goal of personal psychological gain, that is, the obsession with "happiness."

Once again, then: Benjamin Franklin. Prefacing the account of his youthful experiment in self-improvement, he writes that his upbringing and education in religion had inculcated in him a great respect for the principles of all authentic religious teachings, even though certain aspects of his own and other religions struck him as unintelligible or of doubtful truth. His main difficulty with established religion, however, had to do with its incapacity to help individuals be of service to each other and its tendency to set people against each other, rather than to support the formation of community. Again and again, with Franklin, with Washington, with Jefferson and Lincoln, with all the American "demi-gods," it is the same thing: they are all *gods of the community, gods of moral care.* That is what they strove for; that is what the immense forces of the times allowed them to reach for by drawing all their talents into astonishing manifestations and political creations—documents, laws, bills of rights, the creation of a "new world." The times and the forces made them larger than life, overshadowing how they sometimes actually lived in their all-too-human lives, how they failed, individually, to *be* the gods they have become and need to become again as symbols of our own moral aspirations. "I respected [all the religions]," writes Franklin, "tho' with different degrees of respect, as I found them more or less mix'd with other articles, which, without any tendency to inspire, promote, or confirm morality, *served principally to divide us, and make us unfriendly to one another.*"[29]

TRUE RELIGION AND THE GENERAL GOOD

The essence of what Franklin and, it is clear, what Washington and Jefferson as well conceived of as "true religion" is found in this same part of the *Autobiography.* Here, in Franklin's words, are the elements of the foundational early American religious creed:

"That there is one God who made all things.

"That he governs the World by his Providence.

"That he ought to be worshipped by Adoration, Prayer and Thanks-
giving.

"But that the most acceptable Service of God is doing Good to Man.

"That the Soul is immortal.

"And that God will certainly reward Virtue and punish Vice either
here or hereafter."[30]

Again and again, the center of gravity of all philosophy, religion and public
action is service to humanity—under the "look" of God. This center of
gravity must remain in our mind when we consider the struggle for individual self-improvement which lies so deeply at the root of American energy. And we must also keep this context clearly in mind when we consider
the motivation, in Washington and in many other of the Founding Fathers,
which may seem to us now as superficial and vain—namely, their preoccu-
pation with what they referred to as "fame." This word meant something
very different, and much more honorable, than what we mean by it today—
it implied becoming *worthy* to be known and respected by others.

To complete the setting of Franklin's early experiment in self-
improvement, we may cite his observations about the motive force of
history—namely, that all the bloodshed and violence of human history are
rooted in mankind's incapacity to will the general good.

Notice, here, Franklin's condemnation of what in the infant nation
came to be called "the spirit of party," understood already by the young
Franklin as a form of collective selfishness. Washington struggled greatly,
but in vain, against the growth of this spirit of party during his own presidency. Although the structure of the United States' government allows for
and even encourages the clash of differences among individuals and groups,
and although the United States Constitution realistically previsions the
forces of special interests and self-centeredness in the conduct of govern-

ment, the unspoken undercurrent of early American idealism holds out the goal of the striving to work on one's own moral defects—through self-struggle and education—in order to approach the capacity to will what is good for the whole of humanity. Carried too far without the concomitant inner struggle for individual self-improvement, therefore, the spirit of party by itself, although it need not bring down the physical structure of the government, inevitably destroys the moral foundations of the community.

The following, then, is from Franklin's "Observations on My Reading History in Library, May 9, 1731":

> That the great Affairs of the World, the Wars, Revolutions, &c. are carried on and effected by Parties.
>
> That the View of these Parties is their present general Interest, or what they take to be such.
>
> That the different Views of these different Parties, occasion all Confusion.
>
> That while a Party is carrying on a general Design, each Man has his particular private Interest in View.
>
> That as soon as a Party has gain'd its general Point, each Member becomes Intent upon his particular Interest, which thwarting others, breaks that Party into Divisions, and occasions more Confusion.
>
> That few in Public Affairs act from a meer View of the Good of their Country, whatever they may pretend; and tho' their Actings bring real Good to their Country, yet Men primarily consider'd that their own and their Country's Interest was united, and did not act from a Principle of Benevolence.
>
> That fewer still in public Affairs act with a View to the Good of Mankind.[31]

If we would understand the ideals which Washington sought to serve, we must see that the impulse to serve the general good, the struggle to be free from the principle of personal gain, presented itself under the aim of serving the country, the new America. That such an impulse later becomes distorted into the often profane impulse of crass "patriotism" (masking material or psychological self-interest) should not blind us to what love of country meant for Washington, Franklin and Jefferson. It meant service to God through love of mankind. Similarly, that the ideal of self-improvement became in the nineteenth and twentieth centuries an instrument for the obsession with "success" and material gain should also not blind us to what it meant for the founding Americans—namely, the struggle for what we now might call inner change, or perhaps even "inner transformation." In an earlier era, such a goal was referred to, generally, under the once very live and valid word, "character."

Toward Moral Perfection

"It was about this time," writes Franklin, "that I conceived the bold and arduous Project of arriving at moral Perfection. I wish'd to live without committing any Fault at any time; I would conquer all that either Natural Inclination, Custom or Company might lead me into."

What follows is nothing less than a report of the younger Franklin's methodical program of self-study and inner self-development. We need to look at this account with clear eyes. To the modern reader it may sound either naive, shallow, puritanical or satirical. D. H. Lawrence, for example, in his *Studies in Classic American Literature,* saw in it all that was stultifying, self-repressed and materialistic in the American character. But it is none of these things. It represents, rather, an old and rather wise man's artful use of the literary form of autobiography for the purpose of introducing his skeptical, pragmatic, yet spiritually hungry American readers to the reality of the inner world, and to the necessity, known from the most ancient of times, of an active struggle with oneself, a struggle which alone can lead to a life of authentic self-worth and the capacity to serve. It is, I think, the description, however preliminary, of a practical, experimental spirituality—

stripped of all sectarian, religious associations and language. That Franklin casts this material in a form that is often light and self-ironic only shows that he is keenly aware of the subjectivity of his readers—and their allergy to pious moralizing.

> As I knew, or thought I knew, what was right and wrong, I did not see why I might not *always* do the one and avoid the other. But I soon found I had undertaken a Task of more Difficulty than I had imagined. While my *Attention was taken up* in guarding against one Fault, I was often surpriz'd by another. Habit took the Advantage of Inattention. Inclination was sometimes too strong for Reason. I concluded at length, that the mere speculative Conviction that it was our Interest to be compleatly virtuous, was not sufficient to prevent our Slipping, and that the contrary Habits must be broken and good ones acquired and established, before we can have any Dependance on a steady uniform Rectitude of Conduct. For this purpose I therefore contrived the following Method. . . . I included under Thirteen Names of Virtues all that at that time occurr'd to me as necessary or desirable, and annex'd to each a short Precept, which fully express'd the Extent I gave to its Meaning.

> These Names of Virtues with their Precepts were:
> 1. TEMPERANCE: Eat not to Dulness. Drink not to Elevation.
> 2. SILENCE: Speak not but what may benefit others or yourself. Avoid trifling Conversation.
> 3. ORDER: Let all your Things have their Places. Let each Part of your Business have its Time.
> 4. RESOLUTION: Resolve to perform what you ought. Perform without fail what you resolve.
> 5. FRUGALITY: Make no Expence but to do good to others or yourself: i.e. Waste nothing.
> 6. INDUSTRY: Lose no Time. Be always employ'd in something useful. Cut off all unnecessary Actions.

7. SINCERITY: Use no hurtful Deceit. Think innocently and justly; and, if you speak, speak accordingly.

8. JUSTICE: Wrong none, by doing Injuries or omitting the Benefits that are your Duty.

9. MODERATION: Avoid Extreams. Forbear resenting Injuries so much as you think they deserve.

10. CLEANLINESS: Tolerate no Uncleanness in Body, Cloaths or Habitation.

11. TRANQUILLITY: Be not disturbed at Trifles, or at Accidents common or unavoidable.

12. CHASTITY: Rarely use Venery but for Health or Offspring; Never to Dulness, Weakness, or the Injury of your own or another's Peace or Reputation.

13. HUMILITY: Imitate Jesus and Socrates.[32]

Again, we must try to separate our perception of Franklin's "experiment" from what this sort of program became in the nineteenth and twentieth centuries. What Franklin is giving here, and what was of such an influence in the life of so many of our Founding Fathers, is a reflection, in Enlightenment, "scientific" language, of the sort of program of self-struggle that has always formed the basis of the search for inner freedom and moral power. It is an echo on the modernist plane of a very ancient, interior discipline. Therefore, we are quite wrong to imagine that when men like Washington or Jefferson or, later, Lincoln strove for self-improvement they were trying merely to make themselves over with a naive understanding of how human nature can or cannot change and for what purposes it can change. If we would appreciate anew our heroes, and especially Washington, we must see what is really involved in such programs of self-development considered as echoes, however faint, of great and ancient traditions of inner search.

WILL

And what is involved, first and foremost, in these programs of self-improvement is the exercise and development of a capacity which has almost entirely disappeared from our contemporary ethical discourse, the capacity designated by the word *will*.

Concerning this word and what it means, and its fading relevance in our era, I can report that I have often asked groups of students, young and old, to list what they consider the virtues of a morally or psychologically developed man or woman. Not once has the word *will*, or its equivalent, been brought forth. Compassion—yes; wisdom—certainly; kindness, love, intelligence, sensitivity, fairness, insight, harmony, tranquility, joyousness, selflessness, honesty, spirituality (the vaguest of these terms)—but not once will, self-mastery, the capacity to keep a promise made to oneself or to another, the capacity to work toward a goal one has carefully and thoughtfully established for oneself, the sensitivity not so much to others, but to one's own deepest obligations, along with the resolve to carry them out.

When, therefore, Washington is spoken of as a man of exemplary self-discipline and perseverance, these qualities cannot be separated from his capacity and his struggle—so widely observed in him—to accept criticism, to study his own mistakes and to work over time to correct them. Together, these qualities comprise an essential element of the ancient and eternal virtue of will.

OR ARE WE ONLY VICTIMS?

To re-introduce will into the ethical and psychological discourse of our time is to re-introduce the possibility of assuming an active stance toward our inner and outer difficulties. Such a stance is opposed to the generally prevailing view that we are, on the whole, victims—psychologically, economically, biologically, sociologically, historically—even cosmically.

The victim mentality has become pervasive in our present era for several reasons. In the first place, there is the development of modern psychology, which, primarily through psychoanalysis, has persuasively attempted to identify factors in childhood and in the social environment that decisively shape the patterns of human behavior, thought and feeling. According to this view, our inner lives, and much of our outer lives, are made up of effects of causes, some very distant and indirect, that have acted on us originally from outside ourselves and continue to influence us through their action within ourselves in regions of our minds of which we are unaware (the unconscious and the subconscious). This doctrine of psychic determinism presents itself simply as a logical extension of the view that in the universe every event has a cause. Since the human psyche is also part of the universe, events within the psyche must also have causes that have determined them to be what they are. This general view completely contradicts the whole idea of human freedom, upon which the social order—law, education, morality—is based. For many decades this psychic determinism has been the prevailing view in psychology, but without really influencing people's feeling for themselves in their daily lives. Even though the science of psychology told them that all their inner emotions and thoughts were effects of unseen causes, and not—as it may have seemed—aspects of their free will, people have been quite content to live their lives and sense themselves as freely choosing men and women. The influence of the theory of psychic determinism has been buffered off from the general conduct of life, a conduct based on assumptions that have flatly contradicted that theory. Theoretically, one could accept that there was no such thing as free will, but in fact one actually lived as though one could choose and will.

It has been the same situation with regard to theories of social, historical and economic determinism, such as Marxism, which taught that forces operating through the masses of humanity decisively determined an individual's material, social and psychological condition. Such theories had great impact, especially in Eastern Europe, Russia and Asia, but in the United States they remained largely speculative and marginal. America, after all, was born in the fire of a revolutionary rejection of social determinism, even though with its acceptance of slavery it actually substituted one class system for another, a class system now defined in racial and economic terms. The Civil War was the result of this self-contradiction—the contradiction of a society founded equally on the doctrine of equality and the reality of racial slavery. This self-contradiction is not yet resolved or healed in the hearts and minds of Americans.

But we need to ask: what do questions of social justice or psychological causality mean without a vision of the structure of human nature, of what it means to be human? Is man fundamentally a *passive* being—existing solely at the mercy of psychological, social or historical influences? Or, on the contrary, does he have something *active* within himself that distinguishes him from all the other creatures of the earth?

INNER FREEDOM

In this question lies the whole issue of human freedom, and a renewed meaning of America and the American revolution.

Without a doubt, every hero of the American pantheon is a representative of the idea of freedom. Are we limited to conceiving that freedom only in external, political terms? Or are we not obliged to return as well to the inner meaning of freedom as a relationship between parts of oneself? What, after all, could be the ultimate value of outer freedom, of liberty in the external sense of the term, if inwardly we are and must remain enslaved and tyrannized? For, let us emphasize again, the deepest spiritual source of the early colonists' rejection of political and religious tyranny was that such tyranny prevented them from searching for *inner* freedom.

It is quite wrong to think of the origins of America only in economic or political terms without acknowledging the fundamental place of the inner search in the minds and hearts of the early colonists. It is true that over the years the religious motivation of the colonists has been sentimentalized—to the point of absurdity and unreality. Scholarship and common sense have done much to correct this sentimentalized picture by pointing out the economic, political and military factors involved in the movements of peoples from England and Europe to America and the westward expansion of the United States. But all this scholarship leads to an equally false and, in its way, equally absurd picture of the forces behind the origins of America when the power of authentic spiritual need and practice is not recognized.

Among those who came first to the Northeast from England, Germany and Holland were very many who brought with them plans for a life of interiority, even to the point of various forms of monastic communitarianism. And of this substantial number, almost all brought as well texts which served to guide the inner work of self-perfection under the teaching of what we must in a definite sense term "mysticism" or "esoteric spirituality"— usually of a Christian stamp, but often with or alongside the admixture of Kabbalistic or Hellenic (Hermetic) esoteric spiritual psychologies. The communal experiment at Ephrata, Pennsylvania, discussed in Chapter Nine, is an outstanding example of what we are speaking of, but it was in its way equally true of New England religiosity and many other spiritual communities. In all these cases, in varying forms and degrees, an interior work of self-perfecting through obedience to the inner authority of God was sought, based on a vision of the structure of the human self that places physical and psycho-social desire under the potential authority of the will. The work of self-perfecting was understood exclusively as an inner struggle to free oneself from the overmastering influence of bodily desire and addictive passions, such as greed, envy, sexual craving (lust), discouragement (sloth) and so forth. All these weaknesses, taken together, came under the principal heading of the sin of *pride*—or what we might nowadays call "ego." In this context, sin referred to an internal state, not necessarily to external behavior, although, to be sure—and this is of utmost importance—evil external behavior, "crime" in the full sense of the word, was the inevitable result of inner disorder.

Correspondingly, virtue was also understood as an internal state and virtuous outer action the inevitable result of inner order. The spiritual practices of the early colonists, the German Pietists as well as the English Quakers and many Puritans, involved a program of self-perfection or "self-improvement" in the sense of an active struggle to allow a higher, stronger, but far more subtle force than pride or the ego to enter into the realm of one's personal, psychological experience. Benjamin Franklin was fully aware of these programs of inner struggle. He personally printed the texts and tracts of some of the most serious of these groups in Pennsylvania. The young Franklin's program of self-improvement, *as portrayed by the older Franklin* in the *Autobiography,* cannot be understood without recognizing its affinity with these spiritual disciplines, which resonate to the ancient, practical systems of spiritual psychology. It is a great mistake to look at Franklin's program, as did D. H. Lawrence, only in the light of the bourgeois or self-aggrandizing and naively materialistic "self-help" fads of nineteenth- and early-twentieth-century America. If we would remythologize the roots of our culture in order to rediscover the soul of America, we need to see such ideals as those expressed in Franklin's autobiography in the light of their connection to the deeper currents of mankind's spiritual search.

The ideal of self-improvement—an ideal that resonates to the great wisdom traditions of human history—lies at the heart of early American individualism, and it is one of the things we most admire in the life of a man like Washington. In recent times, perhaps, that kind of admiration has lessened because of the degeneration of our common understanding of what self-improvement really once meant. But this degeneration of the ideal should not blind us to how Washington may have regarded it. We need to accept the possibility that Washington and, to one degree or another, all who pursued this ideal struggled in the light, however faint, of a very great and honorable human possibility—and struggled with extraordinary energy and courage.

The Most Influential Man in Our History

THE DOWNFLOWING STREAM

With these considerations in mind, we can now look more directly at the actions of the mature Washington, remembering that he is our nation's chief symbol of will and self-mastery. The hints we have found about the deeper interior meaning of these virtues in the writing of Franklin, and in the intellectual atmosphere of early American spirituality, will enable us to regard Washington's actions not solely as external political measures, as many historians and political observers have regarded them, but as gestures that can relate the beginning of the United States—which means the beginning of the culture in which we now live—to the ancient and downflowing stream of knowledge of how to work toward self-perfection.

I am not so foolish as to say that this way of regarding Washington's actions should replace the interpretations and explanations of them that historians have offered. But we must be aware of interpretations that, implicitly or explicitly, subsume the actions of individual men and women under the rubric of motivations that are depressingly and, actually, unrealistically non-transcendent: motives of personal power, cunning, greed, fear, ineffectual moralism, sentimentality, cowardice, resentment, revenge. To look at the actions of great men and women from this perspective may serve as a necessary corrective to sentimentalism and false idealism. But to look at such actions solely or mainly in this way is to deny the real motivations that actually operate in much human action—nobler motivations that, however they play themselves out in the rough and tumble of historical accident, are as much a part of human nature as the fears and cravings with which modern psychology and our own honesty have made us so familiar. It is also to deny the action of what may be called the downflowing stream of spiritual ideals and methods which, for their part, originate in the wisdom teachings of the past. It is to deny the existence of great knowledge and authentic disciplines of self-perfecting. It is to deny that spiritually developed human beings, through various means—including religious teachings, philosophies, art, manners and customs—fashioned ideals and forms that were specifically designed to enter into the stream of human life and thought and have an action on future generations. Many of the ideals which touched our Franklins, Washingtons and Jeffersons came from such origins, flowing down to them from the powerful sources of spiritual knowledge and personal systems of moral self-discipline that have formed the true foundation of every great culture worthy of the name.

Let us return, then, to where we began with Washington: the most influential actions of the most influential man in American history are movements of stepping back and the surrender of personal power. The most decisive actions of America's great symbol of will are actions of letting go.

THE GREAT RENUNCIATION

In his *Circular to the States,* dated June 8, 1783, Washington resigns his position as commander-in-chief of the victorious revolutionary army. It is the eve of the formal creation of the United States of America, conceived by its creators as the most immense, idealistic communal experiment in the known history of the world. The actual words of the Founding Fathers show how they considered the importance for the world of the American experiment. To them, and to none more than to Washington, the birth of America represents the first attempt of its kind in human history to bring moral and spiritual values into the day-to-day life of mankind, and to them the very future of the world depends upon this effort. And Washington knows it is he, more than anyone else, who represents the meaning of America to the people. Yet at just this most crucial moment in the process of the nation's birth, *he steps back!*

"The Citizens of America," he writes,

> placed in the most enviable condition, as the sole Lords and Proprietors of a vast Tract of Continent, comprehending all the various soils

and climates of the World, and abounding with all the necessaries and conveniences of life, are now . . . acknowledged to be possessed of absolute freedom and Independency; They are, from this period, to be considered as the Actors on a most conspicuous Theatre, which seems to be peculiarly designed by Providence for the display of human greatness and felicity.[33]

Seeds of Darkness

Neither Washington nor any other of the founders, nor of course we ourselves, can comprehend, really, the huge, open possibility for human life represented by the American world—with its seemingly infinite space, natural resources, soil, air, water, life upon life, much of it untold and even as yet unseen. It can only be ideas and ideals that enable a morally normal man or woman to regard him- or herself, his or her nation or people as beings privileged to hold the ownership and trust of such a world. Washington believed in God; it can only be because his ideals were felt to come from God that he felt enabled to equate America with the Americans lately arrived from the Old World. No one, not Washington, not even Franklin nor Adams nor Hamilton, not even Jefferson, could have imagined truly what America was as a geographical, biospheric reality—not to mention as a land that would draw to itself all the peoples and forces of the earth. Their very vision made them blind, and how could it be otherwise? What they saw was great, and we must try to honor it and them for seeing it; but, as is the law of human life, what they failed to see was equally great. They were not of the stature of a Moses, Jesus or Buddha; we must both re-mythologize what was great in them, and also confront what they failed to see.

Thus, Washington could not, really, see the whole of America, and—sincere as his moral struggle, his battle of the will, was—he did not and perhaps could not see the nature of the American Indian. The full reality of the American Indian spiritual tradition was surely invisible to many of our greatest forebears, just as was the human essence of the black slaves. But if we would morally judge our forefathers rightly, we must also rightly appreciate what was both right and wrong in them. The lesson we can take is not that we ourselves are morally superior to them; the lesson is surely that evil conceals itself in the heart of good and that we ourselves, in this very moment, are at least as asleep as we are awake, just as they on their far more influential level were both awake and asleep. Always and everywhere, the forces of the cosmos play themselves out. Always and everywhere good is resisted by evil. Our question is: how to understand that law and how to live so that a harmonizing, reconciling force can act to bring together the good and evil into a new and great creation, both within ourselves and in the world we live in. For this, we need first of all great ideas and ideals that will enable us to become aware of both the good *and* the evil in life. If we would re-mythologize our heroes, let us see in them ideals and standards that bring people and forces into relationship, rather than set people and forces apart from each other. Washington, then, is the hero of will and self-struggle; but it is a will and self-struggle that does not affirm the ego nor destroy its opposite. It is a will and self-struggle that *steps back*—that yields, mysteriously, not like a storm, but like a prayer.

THE RESULTS OF STEPPING BACK

We now follow Washington further in his *Circular to the States,* trying to receive the mythic significance of his act of letting go, remembering that he is voluntarily surrendering a degree of personal, political power that would never again be possible for any individual in America to possess.

"Here," Washington says, in this newly gained world of America, its citizens

> are not only surrounded with every thing which can contribute to the completion of private and domestic enjoyment, but Heaven has crowned all its other blessings, by giving a fairer opportunity for political happiness, than any other Nation has ever been favored with. Nothing can illustrate these observations more forcibly, than a recol-

lection of the happy conjuncture of times and circumstances, under which our Republic assumed its rank among the Nations.[34]

Washington seeks to allow these forces (of "Heaven"), these divinely favoring forces, to act—without the tyrannical imposition of any individual personage. Like all the Founding Fathers, he knows that "monarchy"—the imposition of what we might term the "ego"—cuts the individual and society off from the favoring forces that want and seek what is good for mankind. Washington perceives and trusts that these favoring forces will now operate through the people and by means of social and physical conditions and a structure of government that reflects on earth the nature of the supernal, or spiritual, laws.

> The foundation of our Empire was not laid in the gloomy age of Ignorance and Superstition, but in an Epocha when the rights of mankind were better understood and more clearly defined, than at any former period, the researches of the human mind, after social happiness, have been carried to a great extent, the Treasures of knowledge, acquired by the labours of Philosophers, Sages and Legislatures, through a long succession of years, are laid open for our use, and their collected wisdom may be happily applied in the Establishment of our forms of Government: the free cultivation of Letters, the unbounded extension of Commerce, the progressive refinement of Manners, the growing liberality of sentiment, and above all, the pure and benign light of Revelation, have had a meliorating influence on mankind and increased the blessings of Society. At this auspicious period, the United States came into existence as a Nation, and if their Citizens should not be completely free and happy, the fault will be entirely their own.[35]

Thus, Washington steps back in order to *allow* what is good to act, in order to allow that which is greater than human pride to act in the life of mankind. Surely, no healthier redefinition of the idea of *will* can be imagined: *the voluntary surrender of accumulated personal power for the common good.* Unless Washington steps back, the forces that have created America cannot act. *The people of America will not be able to learn from each other* and will not, each in his or her individual capacity, become carriers of the current of providential power that is eternally poised to pour down upon the life of humanity on earth.

If this sounds like a fanciful overestimation of the value and place of a small group of human beings, the Americans; if this seems metaphysically and spiritually provincial, ignoring the thousands of years of human history and countless great civilizations and cultures of the entire world—east, west, north and south—then so be it. But it is childish, naive or provincial only to the extent that it is taken literally as applied to this or that material grouping to the exclusion of all others. It is anything but childish or naive if it is taken mythically as a new form of the enactment of a drama that is timeless and ever new, a drama of the human struggle to receive the dispensation of Heaven.

THE MEANING OF GEORGE WASHINGTON

Washington steps back to allow the action of the Higher. Regard his stern, yet—in Emerson's words—mysteriously quiet and harmonious face in this way. Regard the mysterious monument—a blank white towering obelisk that suggests no individual subjective quirks or personality features—in this way. Regard Washington as the echo—perhaps the last echo in American history, an echo that sounds, paradoxically, at the very beginning of American history—of self-abnegation, self-effacement. Regard him in this way and study the results of such an act. Study it in its reflection in the inner life of man. Receive it and let it instruct us as a paradigm of the main interior movement of true virtue. That is—*seek the mythic Washington.* Pay less attention to the "historic" man that some have invented on the basis of a demeaned and diminished understanding of the real springs of human nature and on the basis of a diminished understanding of what human beings are on earth to serve. Return to the mythic Washington—which means: return to the real meaning of human life on earth. Do we imagine that America means only money and greed and ugliness, hypocrisy and war and death? That is like saying humanity itself means only these things, and that is to deny—like a hurt and blinded child—the whole question of what humanity and the earth and creation itself are part of.

THE KING OF AMERICA

Washington, then, stepping back, resigning his immense power and potential impregnable "monarchy"—he could have become *king of America.* And he knew it.

> Such is our situation, and such are our prospects; but notwithstanding the cup of blessing is thus reached out to us, notwithstanding happiness is ours, if we have a disposition to seize the occasion and make it our own; yet it appears to me there is an option still left to the United States of America, that it is in their choice, and depends upon their conduct, whether they will be respectable and prosperous, or contemptible and miserable as a Nation; This is the time of their political probation, this is the moment when the eyes of the whole World are turned upon them, *this is the moment to establish or ruin their national Character forever.*[36]

Washington now goes on, referring to the question of the form the confederation of states will take and the question of international entanglements, and referring to questions of a peace establishment and the money owed the army—but ultimately referring to far more universal issues that touch on questions of justice pure and simple, of attention to one's neighbor, of the willingness to sacrifice immediate gain for the common good—issues that we take as merely political at our peril, issues that can echo within the heart of every individual in search of the real source of moral power within. This is the moment of decision of the American nation, the American character—it would surely be foolish to think of this moment as referring only to a particular period in time. It was an essential and decisive moment in the history of America, that is true. But that moment, in its essence, is always in front of us as long as our fortunate political structure allows us the burden and the privilege of making decisions. This moment is an eternally recurring inner moment as well. Not only individuals, but moments of history need to be mythologized—seen, that is, in their profound relevance to what is essential to us, always and everywhere, and now and here in this most critical moment in our history—*now*, always *now*. In this light, regard the next thing Washington says—the man who gave all and received all in leading the nation to its astonishing victory in the war of revolution:

> For . . . it is yet to be decided, whether the Revolution must ulti-
> mately be considered as a blessing or a curse: a blessing or a curse, not
> to the present age alone, for with our fate will the destiny of unborn
> Millions be involved.[37]

THE LAST RENUNCIATION

We are now ready, I think, to take the next step in our re-positioning of the figure of Washington. Let us boldly lift out the interior echoes of what is conventionally regarded as mainly political in the speech that Washington delivered when, for the last time in his life, he stepped back and surrendered his power. We turn to his farewell address as he steps down from the presidency in 1796 at the end of his second term. Three years later, he will die.

He did not have to step down from the presidency. He could easily have won a third term. Even after the battles and turmoils of his second term in office, there is no question that he could have kept the presidency for as long as he wished. Historians cite numerous personal reasons for his decision to leave the presidency, and no doubt all of these factors had their place. No doubt Washington was weary and genuinely longed for a peaceful life at his beloved Mount Vernon. No doubt he was beginning to detect the signs of his own failing mental powers. And no doubt there were other compelling causes—political as well as personal. But from our point of view, the most telling reason was that he stepped down in order to preserve the essence of the American republic—that the leader is freely chosen by and answerable to the people. Had Washington died in office, the whole nature of the office of the president would surely have been different. It could have, and probably would have, been regarded more as a lifelong position of individual power, comparable in many ways to a monarchy.* Washington's withdrawal allowed an election to take place under his living gaze, under the mark of his awareness and approval. His stepping down signified that it is the people and the Constitution that are the only source of authority in the new nation.

THE AMERICAN PRESIDENT

It is important to note that in many essential respects the office of the president of the United States is what it is precisely because of the nature of Washington's character. The historically unique combination of great power and great limitation that distinguishes the American presidency is almost entirely a mirror reflection of the character of Washington. Even with the universal fear of monarchy in the new nation, the Congress and the people were willing to give powers to him that they would have withheld from any other man. In this sense, all the presidencies in American history have been footnotes to that of Washington.

The American presidency is an astonishing blending of power and weakness. The American president has, in his way, even more than a king

---

*Washington probably also feared that if he died in office, the vice president would succeed him as a crown prince succeeds in a monarchy.

the aura of immense power and authority—in part because of the present physical and economic power of America, but not only for that reason. At the same time, the president can really *do* very little by himself. He is the conductor of only one of the three primary forces in the structure of the government. It is only necessary to ask ourselves what inner reality, even what metaphysical principle, is suggested or echoed by this unique combination of individual personhood, immense hierarchical power and equally deep, though often less vividly noted, powerlessness? To what extent does the structure of the American presidency reflect the character of an individual man, Washington, who himself combined phenomenal physical, military and political power with the repeated act of stepping back, stepping down, surrendering?

Echoes from the East

Having gone this far in our "re-mythologizing" soundings, it is hard to resist citing at least one or two passages from across the world. The book is the *Tao Te Ching,* the source is ancient China, and the text is the world's most famous and influential blending of spiritual wisdom and political intelligence:

> If the sage would guide the people, he must serve with humility.
> If he would lead them, he must follow behind.
> In this way when the sage rules, the people will not feel oppressed:
> When he stands before them, they will not be harmed.
> The whole world will support him and will not tire of him.
> Because he does not compete,
> He does not meet competition.[38]

And

> Better stop short than fill to the brim.
> Oversharpen the blade, and the edge will soon blunt.

Amass a store of gold and jade, and no one can protect it.

Claim wealth and titles, and disaster will follow.

Retire when the work is done.

This is the way of heaven.[39]

THE FAREWELL

And now, the Farewell Address of 1796. I intentionally set aside the question of the influence of Alexander Hamilton on the composition of this famous speech. It seems that Washington allowed the opposing ideas of both Hamilton and Madison into this text—just as he struggled to allow the opposing geniuses of Hamilton and Jefferson to operate in his cabinet, under his reconciling eye, during the first term of his presidency.

Washington begins:

> Friends and Fellow-citizens: The period for a new election of a citizen, to administer the executive government of the United States, being not far distant—and the time actually arrived when your thoughts must be employed in designating the person who is to be clothed with that important trust—it appears to me proper, especially as it may conduce to a more distinct expression of the public voice, that I should now apprise you of the resolution I have formed, to decline being considered among the number of those out of whom a choice is to be made.[40]

With a fine mixture of candor, modesty and fatherliness, Washington sums up his estimation of the state of the union and his own efforts during the past eight years to help the new nation set its course. He observes that he has done as much as his limited powers will allow him, and he now sees that the retirement he has long desired is not inconsistent with the welfare of "my beloved country."

But even here, at the very beginning of this speech, where Washington is oratorically expressing his gratitude for the confidence the people have placed in him throughout his military and political career, he brings—perhaps too smoothly to be noticed—telling psychological and philosophical observations of a kind that will sound more and more strongly throughout the speech. Looking at this text now, it is clear that it is far more than what we nowadays label "political." It is, in fact, a speech showing the spiritual dimensions of the question of human government and society, and showing the spiritual meaning of America, conceived not so much as a specific, concrete historical reality, but as an idea and ideal for the whole of mankind.

"Here, perhaps, I ought to stop," says Washington,

> But a solicitude for your welfare, which cannot end but with my life, and the apprehension of danger, natural to that solicitude, urge me . . . to offer to your solemn contemplation . . . some sentiments, which are the result of much reflection, of no inconsiderable observation, and which appear to me all important to the permanency of your felicity as a people. These will be offered to you with the more freedom, as you can only see in them the disinterested warnings of a parting friend, who can possibly have no personal motive to bias his counsel.[41]

"You Are Americans"

And now Washington goes to the heart of his message which, more than two hundred years later, has the power to act with equal force on our understanding of both the inner and the outer meaning of the structure of our social order. The most essential directives of Washington's address are just those that now beg us to "re-mythologize" them, to see in them directives regarding our inner lives as "Americans," that is, as men and women seeking, above all, freedom. Just as over two thousand years ago Plato—of course in a far more systematic and conscious way—brought forth in his most important work, *The Republic,* the idea that the outer form of government must reflect the inner structure and purpose of human nature, so Washington's words here evoke in their way—with less philosophical completeness, but with all the more contemporary vitality and urgency—the interior meaning of the American ideal.

"You are Americans," says Washington;

> you love freedom. Interwoven as is the love of liberty with every ligament of your hearts, no recommendation of mine is necessary to fortify or confirm the attachment.[42]

What kind of liberty? we ask. Is it solely external liberty, or is it also internal liberty that Americans strive for—the liberty of mind and spiritual striving? Isn't the whole purpose of political liberty to support the internal rebirth of the psyche—through learning, through love, through the struggle to serve what is higher than ourselves and to help each other?

In the same way, we may consider the interior meaning of the idea of *unity:*

> The unity of government, which constitutes you one people, is also now dear to you. It is justly so; for it is a main pillar in the edifice of your real independence; the support of your tranquillity at home, your peace abroad; of your safety; of your prosperity; of that very liberty which you so highly prize.[43]

Compare here the culminating vision of Plato's *Republic:* both politically and psychologically, for both the outer and the inner "republic," *unity* is the basis and the source of every other virtue and every other advantage that is proper to a human being and to a moral social order. Through the figure of Socrates, Plato tells us that unity—that is, the internal harmony of the three major forces within the self and within the government—is the virtue from which springs all that is good in human life. And the corruption of unity, disharmony, is the weakness from which arises all that is evil in human life, again in both the psychological and political realms. Here are Socrates' words:

> But in reality justice was such as we were describing, being concerned however, not with the outward man, but with the inward, which is the true self and the true concern of man; for the just man does not permit the several elements within him to interfere with one another, or any of them to do the work of others—he sets in order his own inner life, and is his own master and his own law, in unison with himself; and when he has bound together the three principles within him, which may be compared to the higher, lower and middle notes of the scale, and the intermediate intervals—when he has bound all these together, and is no longer many, but has become one entirely temperate and perfectly adjusted nature, then he proceeds to act, if he has to act, whether in a matter of property, or in the treatment of the body, or in some other affair of politics or private business; always thinking and calling that which preserves and co-operates with this harmonious condition, just and good actions, and the knowledge which presides over it, wisdom, and that which at any time impairs this condition, he will call unjust action, and the opinion which presides over it, ignorance.[44]

Washington goes on:

> . . . it is of *infinite moment,* that you should properly estimate the *immense* value of your *national union,* to your collective and individual happiness; that you should cherish a cordial, habitual and immoveable attachment to it; accustoming yourselves to think and speak of it as of the palladium of your political safety and prosperity; watching for its preservation with jealous anxiety; discountenancing whatever may suggest even a suspicion that it can in any event be abandoned; and indignantly frowning upon the first dawning of any attempt to

alienate any portion of our country from the rest, or to enfeeble the sacred ties which now link together the various parts.[45]

THE UNITY OF AMERICA

Is Washington speaking only of external unity? I think not. Is he then, like Plato, speaking explicitly of internal, psychological unity? Surely not. Yet the manner in which he and the founders of America speak of national unity resonates with metaphysical and spiritual principles. It is impossible to think of the national unity that Washington, Franklin, Jefferson and, after them, Lincoln, speak of as being solely a matter of physical and material advantage and security. Somehow, for Washington, the unity of America is intimately related to the unity and integrity of mankind itself; and, by implication, it must be—and it can be—taken as referring to the need for unity within ourselves and within any intentional community that is established for the moral good, and not only for the material advantage, of its members. Call this a naive belief in the morality of a nation; call it suspect nationalism or patriotism—perhaps that is what it so easily becomes in our hands. But however this ideal of the national unity may have degenerated, at its root—and in our own minds—it can be seen as reflecting the eternal and unchanging laws of moral order within the human self. Human freedom is inseparable from the development of a presiding intelligence and will under which all the forces of nature confront each other in dynamic, moving harmony. And moreover, as the figure of Washington suggests, this overarching, presiding will is not a violent or rigid imposition and intervention; it is an intensely active and watchful stepping back and allowing. Under the eye of allowing and caring and sacrifice of the ego, a force enters into the life of an individual and a nation that enables them to live meaningfully for themselves and effectively serve the source of their existence. Such is the ancient and eternal idea of human nature and human community as mirrors of each other.

FOREIGN ENTANGLEMENTS

In this light, we can now follow Washington's further admonitions, seeing them now not only as prophetic political warnings, but as a lightly enciphered system of spiritual psychology that can exemplify the possibility of internalizing all that we instinctively value about the foundations of the American political system.

For example, the whole question of "foreign alliances"[46] which Washington warned against—and, in so doing, created a dominant force in American foreign policy even up to our present day—this whole issue can begin to resonate in a manner reminiscent of similar warnings voiced by the prophet Isaiah.[47] Washington even uses the religious word "apostate" (apostasy: the abandonment of religious vows) to describe the danger of wrong connections with foreign powers, wrong dependence upon external forces. But, of course, where Isaiah commands Israel to depend upon God, rather than other nations, Washington urges Americans to depend upon their own unity and law. Yet no reading of the prophetic message in the Old Testament can rest content with conceiving God as only an external being; on the contrary, the prophetic voice trembles with the vision of the God above speaking and acting from within the unified self. Read Washington's words, then—certainly in much less intentional yet much more contemporary metaphysical imagery—as referring to the need for both the nation and the individual self to turn within for strength, not to the egoistic impulses of one or another self-serving part of human nature, but to the inner self that represents the fountainhead of inner unity. Isaiah—in great and deep mystical tones—calls it God. Washington calls it the *Union*.

> While then every part of our country thus feels an immediate and particular interest in union, all the parts combined cannot fail to find, in the united mass of means and efforts, greater strength, greater resource, proportionately greater security from external danger, a less frequent interruption of their peace by foreign nations.[48]

Hardheaded realism about the economic and military strength of a united nation? Certainly. But also: read here an outward expression of laws governing the inner world as well—and the power of internal unity within the self with respect to the distractions and illusions that draw human beings into agitation, psychopathy, violence, sentimental fantasy and will-lessness, cruelty born of alienation from the feeling part of the self and all that follows from this.

> . . . And, what is of inestimable value, they must derive from union
> an exemption from those broils and wars between themselves . . .

Read: Inner conflict; inner war—represented by and resulting in literal civil war.

> . . . which so frequently afflict neighboring countries, not tied to-
> gether by the same government; which their own rivalships alone
> would be sufficient to produce, but which opposite foreign alliances,
> attachments, and intrigues, would stimulate and embitter. Hence,
> likewise, these will avoid the necessity of those overgrown military
> establishments, which under any form of government are inauspi-
> cious to liberty . . .

Read also: The inner tyranny of forced interior compliance, where body and feeling languish under the sway of the ego's illusions, fears and cravings.

> . . . and which are to be regarded as particularly hostile to republican
> liberty. In this sense it is, that your union ought to be considered as a
> main prop of your liberty, and that the love of the one ought to endear
> you to the preservation of the other.[49]

THE FORGE OF EXPERIENCE[50]

In a most important aside, Washington now addresses the question of the practical possibility of such a union and, in so doing, brings in a great idea of the Enlightenment, an idea that is crucial to every individual's search for liberty and inner moral development. Is there a doubt, whether a common government can embrace so large a sphere? "Let experience solve it," he says. "To listen to mere speculation in such a case were criminal." We are familiar with the revolution in the sciences brought about by the emphasis on experiment and experience that was brought into Western thought during the Renaissance and the Enlightenment. We are less familiar with the notion that this emphasis on experiment and personal experience—this vision of the need to be free from mere speculation, mere intellectualism or dogmatic, blind belief—was at least as central in the sphere of moral life as well. Washington, Jefferson, Franklin—all of the American symbolic "gods" are telling us in our lives and in our science, in our actions and in our knowledge: *to try things for ourselves,* to learn for ourselves, to work together in the forge of experience and thereby to sense and feel with body, mind and heart what we are and what we need.

All our heroes are telling us: work practically, experimentally, in the realm of the *new*—not, as it has all too often become, in the realm of the merely novel, the merely invented and "original," but in the breathtaking air of the *"unmarked path"* laid down from mankind's ancient past that guides the individual, not as an imposition from outside, but through the voice of one's own unique conscience. Thus, at the heart of, say, the Quaker vision or the mystic Protestantism of a Jakob Böhme or a Conrad Beissel, there lies the real spiritual root of the Enlightenment. It is there where even an Isaac Newton, freely questioning all the science of his time, finds for himself and through experiment, those laws of nature that have been since time immemorial encoded in the enciphered, esoteric teachings of the alchemists, among others. It is the same in the moral and legislative sphere for men like Franklin, Washington and Jefferson. The sphere of human social order is no less a sphere of spiritual experiment than is the sphere of the material world opened up by the new sciences of physics and chemistry. That this world of free experiment in nature and society came into the degraded captivity of materialism and exploitative technology and tyrannical or mob political rule is not the fault of the fathers of the Enlightenment.

"'Tis well worth a fair and full experiment," says Washington. And then he proceeds to the heart of his message.

REASON, LIBERTY, AND LOVE

We can read what follows, in the conventionally established way, as an eloquent, Hamiltonian expression of the Federalist vision of a strong central government. Certainly it is that. But having brought in the far more inclusive perspective of ideas that refer not solely to external political matters, but to the very structure of human nature and the cosmic world, we can listen to Washington's warnings about the "spirit of party" as referring as well to the inner life of the individual.

Washington introduces the whole issue of party and special interest by referring to the different geographical regions of the country and their particular needs. He cites the controversial Jay's Treaty of 1794 with Britain and Pinckney's Treaty of 1795 with Spain, both of which provoked intense and largely unjustified partisan fears and temptations to foreign alliance. He then proceeds to examine the question of party and special interest in a language that is richly meaningful at the three levels of human life: psychologically, politically and metaphysically.

> To the efficacy and permanency of your union a government for the whole is indispensable. No alliances, however strict, between the parts, can be an adequate substitute. They must inevitably experience the infractions and interruptions which all alliances in all times have experienced. Sensible of this momentous truth, you have improved upon your first essay, by the adoption of a constitution of government

better calculated than your former, for an intimate union, and for the efficacious management of your common concerns. This government, the offspring of your own choice, uninfluenced and unawed, adopted upon full investigation and mature deliberation, completely free in its principles, in the distribution of its powers, uniting security with energy, and containing within itself a provision for its own amendment, has a just claim to your confidence and your support. Respect for its authority, compliance with its laws, acquiescence in its measures, are duties enjoined by the fundamental maxims of true liberty. The basis of our political systems is the right of the people to make and alter their constitutions of government. But the constitution which at any time exists, till changed by an explicit and authentic act of the whole people, is sacredly obligatory on all. The very idea of the power and the right of the people to establish government, presupposes the duty of every individual to obey the established government.[51]

It is not only possible, it is necessary, to see in this speech of Washington the *inner* resonance of the American idea of liberty. Freed of all sectarian, religious language and dogma; freed of cant and suggestion; freed of literary or poetic sleight of hand; freed of any sort of demagoguery, Washington's words open us to the interior meaning of liberty as obedience to what is highest within ourselves and within our community. Washington and the Founding Fathers called this "reason." To repeat, this capacity which they called "reason" has little to do with what we usually refer to by that name. It is not something that can be programmed into a computer; nor is it a collection of information and data; nor is it the power to develop ingenious hypotheses for the purpose of short-term prediction and material advantage— all these are capacities of the mind which in their way are shared by the animals and many of which can even be performed better by machines. By "reason," the Founding Fathers are speaking of a power within man that is capable actively of apprehending the essential truth and form of universal reality and morality. It is a capacity that acts independently of individual subjective emotion or instinctual attraction. By being thus independent of emotional or subjective preference, this "reason" is able to be the conduit not only of knowledge but of love, love that is not shackled to the personal and preferential.

The founders of America and the thinkers of the Enlightenment must be understood as searching and thinking in the train of the Judeo-Christian and Hellenic teachings that spoke of the *active intellect* as the most sacred element within human nature—what Plato called *nous,* the governing, presiding force within the inner republic of man. Certainly, one could look at Eastern teachings about the consciousness that is higher than ordinary thought and emotion, and such examinations of the great Eastern spiritual psychologies can help us gain a new perspective on our own Western ideas. But it is not necessary to rely on the Eastern material only—we have this teaching in our own culture; and the Founding Fathers, sometimes knowingly, and sometimes only by unconscious inheritance, were deeply influenced and attracted to this teaching about an independent power of the mind, a presiding power which can legislate to the whole only through the willing consent of the parts of ourselves to be governed by the attention of reason. Read in Washington's phrase "uniting security with energy" a pithy summary of the developed individual as well as the developed state.

Washington continues:

> All obstructions to the execution of the laws, all combinations and associations, under whatever plausible character, with a real design to direct, control, counteract, or awe the regular deliberation and action of the constituted authorities, are destructive of this fundamental principle, and of fatal tendency. They serve to organize faction; to give it an artificial and extraordinary force.

Note Washington's language here. He is warning of the danger that faction, "the spirit of party," can easily acquire an artificial and extraordinary force. A part can take on, or move toward taking on, the power and force that are proper to the whole. The part can try to perform the function of the whole.

This is practically a definition not only of injustice (in Plato's sense) and so-cial disorder, but of neurosis and even physical pathology. Such obstructions to the fundamental principle of the rule of the whole, Washington contin-ues, serve

> to put in the place of the delegated will of the nation, the will of a
> party, often a small, but artful and enterprising minority of the com-
> munity; and, according to the alternate triumphs of different parties,
> to make the public administration the mirror of the ill-concerted and
> incongruous projects of faction, rather than the organ of consistent
> and wholesome plans, digested by common counsels, and modified
> by mutual interests.[52]

THE STATE AND THE SELF

Surely now it is possible, after all that we have considered about the found-ing of America, to interpret the words of Washington not only as a diagno-sis of that which threatens national unity, but as a diagnosis of the dangers threatening the inner life of the individual citizen as well. It is hard to resist seeing the state of the nation as a mirror of our own inner condition. And it is only one step from this comparison to the idea that society always and everywhere is what it is solely because individual human beings are what they are. This is an ancient teaching which is at the same time revolution-ary in that it goes against the prevailing assumptions that we can better our-selves and our lives solely through the machinery of government. It is revolutionary in that it seems to go against the whole idea of America as a world in which government creates happiness.

But, of course, this is not the idea of the Founding Fathers. The philo-sophical origin of the American nation lies in the hope of creating a social order in which the individual is free to search for the inner change that de-velops men and women into authentic, inwardly free individuals. At the origins of America there is never to be found the idea that morality can be legislated; or if it appears, it is soon overwhelmed by the ideal—far more realistic and at the same time far more spiritual—that society needs to create and government protect a material, psychological and metaphysical space within which the individual can search for his or her own conscience. This is the philosophical root of many of the most creative impulses of the American society. It is astonishing and revolutionary only to those who are unfamiliar with the inner spiritual sciences that underlie the teachings of the Judeo-Christian and Hellenic spiritual traditions: the idea, namely, that the world is what it is because man is what he is, that we cannot help the world unless we also help ourselves—not in the sense of self-gratification, but of helping ourselves discover to what greatness we really belong.

The originators of America were not mystics; not monks, not contemplatives. But neither were the most dynamic of them mere materialists, exploiters or cunning businessmen. America was the creation of a collection of men in whom traces of ancient interior spiritual truths were honored alongside the need to organize an immense new world of phenomenal potential wealth and power. This simultaneity of the spiritual and the material was of quite new coloration and energy. This simultaneity was America.

THE SPIRIT OF PARTY AND THE ENEMY WITHIN

When Washington speaks of "the spirit of party" and the danger of "parties," his words, therefore, are also applicable to the parts within ourselves.

> I have already intimated to you the danger of the parties in the state, with particular reference to the founding of them on geographical discriminations. Let me now take a more comprehensive view, and warn you in the most solemn manner against the baneful effects of the spirit of party generally. *This spirit, unfortunately, is inseparable from our nature, having its root in the strongest passions of the human mind.*[53]

Washington is thus speaking, and here quite explicitly and intentionally, of that which lies at the root of human weakness and conflict.

> It exists under different shapes in all governments, more or less sti-
> fled, controlled or repressed. But in those of the popular form, it is
> seen in its greatest rankness; and is truly their worst enemy.

> The alternate dominion of one faction over another by the spirit of re-
> venge natural to party dissension, which in different ages and coun-
> tries, has perpetrated the most horrid enormities, is itself frightful
> despotism. . . .

> But this leads at length to a formal and permanent despotism.[54]

The external despotism of the "monarch" parallels the internal despotism within the individual under the sway of Plato's "inner tyrant," the obsessed ego of the *Republic*.[55]

Here, Washington no doubt has in mind the manner in which Rome passed from a representative republic to the rule of an emperor:

> The disorders and miseries which result, gradually incline the minds
> of men to seek security and repose in the absolute power of an indi-
> vidual. And, sooner or later, the chief of some prevailing faction, more
> able or more fortunate than his competitors, turns this disposition to
> the purposes of his own elevation, on the ruins of public liberty.[56]

Compare Plato:

> Then if man is like the state . . . there must be the same arrangement
> in him; his soul must be laden full of slavery and ungenerousness, and
> those parts of the soul which were most decent are enslaved, but the
> small part most mad and abominable is master.

"That must be so," he said.

"Well, will you say such a soul is free or slave?"

"Slave, surely."[57]

Washington goes on; and what he says is as true of the self as it is of the state:

> Without looking forward to an extremity of this kind (which, never-theless, ought not to be entirely out of sight,) the common and con-tinual mischiefs of the spirit of party are sufficient to make it the interest and duty of a wise people to discourage and restrain it. It serves always to distract the public councils, and enfeeble the public administration. It agitates the community with ill founded jealousies and false alarms; kindles the animosity of one part against another; fo-ments occasionally riot and insurrection; and opens the door to foreign influence and corruption, which find a facilitated access to the govern-ment itself through the channel of party passions. Thus the policy and will of one country are subjected to the policy and will of another.[58]

Read: for both the nation and the individual, internal dissension and dishar-mony open the door to the overmastering influence of external forces.

On a strictly historical note, the American two-party system was a re-markable accommodation which prevented the kind of political fractioning that has characterized many other democracies of the world. At the outset, the American "nation" was at one level no more than a loose assemblage of thirteen states, each with its own sense of itself and its interests. The mira-cle of the Constitution was that it actually brought to all the elements a common law and rule under which each could be free to pursue its own good while at the same time accepting the prime imperative of the general good. And, of course, even after the adoption of the Constitution, there re-mained throughout the country a tangle of conflicting interests and atti-tudes. The historian William Nisbet Chambers observes:

Here were small-freehold farmers and great planters owning platoons of slaves; domestic merchants, shipowners looking to the trade of the ocean seas, and shipbuilders on the coastal streams; struggling manufacturers seeking home markets, and importers and exporters; and artisans or "mechanics." Here also were varieties of ethnic shoots and religious flowerings; divisions between sober "Anglomen" who adhered to English ways as the measure of stability, or sanguine "Gallomen" who saw the French Revolution as the millennium for the rights of man; and cleavage between men who wanted an "aristocratic," consolidated republic, and others who looked towards a "democratic" regime and state rights. In short, the nation was the scene of an indigenous, deeply rooted, conflicting pluralism. In the early American states, the multiform interests, sentiments, and opinions of this pluralism had produced a highly uncertain faction politics of hybrid combinations and perishable alliances. Furthermore, each state had its own taproots of power and its own government offices to fill, and thus its different leaders "ambitiously contending," as Madison put it, for preferment.

"The surprising thing," says Chambers, "was not that America's political founders took so long to evolve parties, but that they managed to bring any order into the nation's politics at all."[59]

Historically speaking, there is no question that the two-party system, as we know of it, brought a great measure of order and unity to the young and growing nation. But what Washington, and others after him, including Lincoln, feared was not the party system as such, but "the spirit of party." By this term he meant the attitude that one's own faction or *part* was more important than the whole; or, what came to the same thing, that one's own party's interests were the same as the interests of the whole. The "spirit of party" meant the commitment to fight for one's own interests and to overcome, or even destroy, rather than learn from the opposition. This view, of course, is intimately related to the adversarial structure of our legal system.

Here we can let Flexner articulate Washington's attitude toward the spirit of party:

> He deplored the adversary theory which sees government as a tug of war between the holders of opposite views, one side eventually vanquishing the other. Washington saw the national capital as a place where men came together not to tussle but to reconcile disagreements. This attitude grew out of his entire experience and also from the nature of his own genius. . . . Washington's own greatest mental gift was to be able to bore down through partial arguments to the fundamental principles on which everyone could agree.[60]

BLESSED ARE THE PEACEMAKERS

In Biblical language, those with this gift are called "the peacemakers," understanding the word "peace" as the Greek *eirēne,* the reconciliation of mutually opposing forces under the presiding vision of the good of the whole.

Such a capacity, within the individual and *by* an individual in the role of leader, allows and even requires that the parts of the social body or parts of oneself strongly confront each other—but *not* as enemies to be destroyed. Washington's great gift of allowing opposition to exist within his administration or under his command, and to bring to this opposition the non-intervening look that is the reconciling force—this gift must be an essential element in our re-mythologizing of the man. It can help us regenerate our image of the democratic process and correct our fantasies that a marketplace of egoistic impulses somehow miraculously produces intelligence and harmony, both in the self and in the society. Washingtonian democracy is not the freedom to try to destroy each other physically or philosophically or morally, but the freedom to bring one's own best thought together with one's best effort to listen and attend to the other. The aim is not to reach the pale and crooked version of mutual accommodation that we call "compromise," which is often either ineffectual or ethically corrupt, but to discover a more comprehensive intelligence that allows each part and each partial truth to take its proper and necessary place in the life of the whole.

To further such a process is the work of the mythic Washington who lies embedded in the whole structure of the Constitution and in the flowing, dynamic wholeness that is represented in the ancient idea of the separation of powers. The same Washington who steps back from material power and thereby conducts moral power is the Washington who allows life-giving confrontation among the parts of the self and the community. Democracy is not chaos, not anarchy, not the passive permission of the parts to do what they want, as they want. Washingtonian—or, if one wishes, *mythic* democracy—is the circulation of higher intelligence and will through the parts as the parts both separate from and confront each other. To have unity, it is necessary to have right separation so that the parts are free to relate to each other as aspects of the whole. Such is the ideal represented at the level of government by the principle of the separation of powers. For such unity, one must struggle to become free from the false separations, the divisions and conflicts that breed violence, a false separation that is represented by what we are referring to as the spirit of party.

THE ROLE OF RELIGION

At this point in the Farewell Address, Washington inserts an especially important and interesting comment about the role of religion in the political and economic life of the nation. Here he speaks almost explicitly about the difference between an individual seeking intensively for self-cultivation of the spirit—such an individual may not need the forms and symbols of the church—and the general process of life in the nation as a whole. The life of the nation as a whole must proceed within the fabric of religious or religiously moral ideals. There can be no democracy and no social survival where the social order is based only on the self-interest of the parts or the individual. There can be no authentic human life rooted in the motive of personal gain—as in the theories of Thomas Hobbes—where the "social contract" is formed in order to ensure the so-called "happiness" of fundamentally self-seeking individuals and fundamentally self-seeking parts of the whole. At the same time, no religion or religious faith can be *imposed on* or *demanded of* people. This is the mystery of the American nation, the paradox that has nourished much that is alive in America for over two hundred years: there *must* be religion (or its intense inner equivalent!) and there *must* be no imposition—physical, economic or psychological—to compel individuals to open their lives to the sacred.

There *must* be a sense of God, and there *must* be the freedom to accept or reject God.

"Of all the dispositions and habits which lead to political prosperity," Washington says, religion and morality are indispensable supports.

> In vain would that man claim the tribute of patriotism, who should labor to subvert these great pillars of human happiness, these firmest props of the duties of men and citizens.—The mere politician, equally with the pious man, ought to respect and to cherish them.—A volume could not trace all their connections with private and public felicity. Let it be simply asked, where is the security for property, for reputation, for life, if the sense of religious obligations desert the oaths, which are the instruments of investigations in courts of justice? And let us with caution indulge the supposition, that morality can be maintained without religion. *What ever may be conceded to the influence of refined education on minds of peculiar structure, reason and experience both forbid us to expect that national morality can prevail in exclusion of religious principle.*[61]

The last line deserves emphasis in order to make clear that Washington and those who shared his perspective did not think of religious symbols and practices as ends in themselves, but as instruments leading toward an inner condition of man, an inner condition which certain individuals might strive for with great intensity under forms not explicitly bound to conventional religious language or rituals.* For certain individuals, therefore, religious symbols and practices may have served mainly as a framework for an inner quest leading to a freedom of spirit transcending all sectarian beliefs. But for the nation as a whole, including the vast majority of those who did not feel called to the inner search, religious belief and practice were necessary in order to maintain a standard of virtue by which, to whatever degree, the lives of all men and women can serve a greater good. Washington's insistence on the need for religion was not a cynical measure to keep the masses opiated, as Marx might have interpreted it. Washington is not cynical, but deeply practical in recognizing in religion the power it can have to help prevent the principle of personal gain from dominating the individual psyche and the life of society, especially a society in which personal liberty prevails.

For Washington and for many of the Founding Fathers—I believe this holds true for Jefferson as well—the idea of freedom of religion opens up in ways that are not what is usually thought. Freedom of religion means not only the liberty to practice whatever religion one chooses. It also means that genuine freedom must, freely and naturally, lead toward and be based upon the religious dimension. *A religion that is not freely chosen is not religion; and a freedom that is not in the deepest sense religious is not freedom.* The present age has tended to emphasize the first half of this proposition and has neglected the second half.

ATTACHMENTS, ENTANGLEMENTS AND INNER SLAVERY

Washington draws his speech to a close by emphasizing and explaining the reason for his view of America's relation to the nations; and it is not difficult to read both an inner and outer meanings in his words. What is true of the nation is true of the self. The meanings of independence, liberty and strength for the nation are strictly analogous to what these terms mean for the individual and within the individual. And what slavish dependence is for the

---

*See, for example, the brief discussion of Stoicism in chapter 1.

nation as a whole in its relation to foreign powers, slavish dependence is for and within the human self in its relation to its own passions and to influences coming from outside.

> Observe good faith and justice towards all nations; cultivate peace and harmony with all. Religion and morality enjoin this conduct; and can it be that good policy does not equally enjoin it? It will be worthy of a free, enlightened, and at no distant period a great nation, to give to mankind the magnanimous and too novel example of a people always guided by an exalted justice and benevolence. Who can doubt that in the course of time and things, the fruits of such a plan would richly repay any temporary advantages which might be lost by a steady adherence to it? Can it be that Providence has not connected the permanent felicity of a nation with its virtue? The experiment, at least, is recommended by every sentiment which ennobles human nature. Alas! is it rendered impossible by its vices?[62]

The chief thing, Washington continues, is to resist what we might nowadays call "attachments" or what another era called the "passions" with respect to the influences of the external world.

> In the execution of such a plan, nothing is more essential than that permanent, inveterate antipathies against particular nations, and passionate attachments for others, should be excluded; and that in place of them just and amicable feelings towards all should be cultivated. *The nation which indulges towards another an habitual hatred or an habitual fondness, is in some degree a slave.* It is a slave to its animosity or to its affection, either of which is sufficient to lead it astray from its duty and its interest.[63]

Having said these words which, with remarkable clarity, echo the ancient teachings about the fallen self—inner slavery is the condition of being devoured by one's own emotions, attractions and repulsions—Washington then proceeds with what can be read as a further diagnosis of inner slavery in both the individual and the nation. With just a very few changes, what follows could have come from the mouth of a Plato or a Jakob Böhme speaking about the inner state of fallen man:

> [Such a nation] is a slave to its animosity or affection, either of which is sufficient to lead it astray from its duty and its interest. Antipathy in one nation against another disposes each more readily to offer insult and injury; to lay hold of slight causes of umbrage; and to be haughty and intractable, when accidental or trifling occasions of dispute occur. Hence frequent collisions, obstinate, envenomed, and bloody contests. The nation, prompted by ill-will and resentment, sometimes impels to war the government, contrary to the best calculations of policy. The government sometimes participates in the national propensity; and adopts, through passions, what reason would reject. At other times, it makes the animosity of the nation subservient to projects of hostility, instigated by pride, ambition, and other sinister and pernicious motives. The peace often, sometimes perhaps the liberty, of nations has been the victim.[64]

What is true—in the nation and in the self—of anger and fear is equally true of absorption into reactions of preferment and attraction:

> So, likewise, a passionate attachment of one nation for another produces a variety of evils. Sympathy for the favorite nation, facilitating the illusion of an imaginary common interest, in cases where no real common interest exists, and infusing into one the enmities of the other, betrays the former into a participation in the quarrels and wars of the latter, without adequate inducement or justification. . . .
>
> The great rule of conduct for us, in regard to foreign nations is, in extending our commercial relations, to have with them as little political connection as possible. So far as we have already formed en-

gagements, let them be fulfilled with perfect good faith. Here let us stop.

Europe has a set of primary interests, which to us have none or a very remote relation. Hence she must be engaged in frequent controversies, the causes of which are essentially foreign to our concerns. Hence, therefore, it must be unwise in us to implicate ourselves, by artificial ties, in the ordinary vicissitudes of her politics, or the ordinary combinations and collision of her friendships or enmities.[65]

REAL INDEPENDENCE

Of course, the world has vastly changed since Washington spoke these words. The United States is inextricably connected not only to Europe and its destiny but to every single region of the earth and every nation and people, and it must act accordingly. But the changing world does not at all affect Washington's admonitions and insight: he is speaking about independence, not isolation. With the nation, as with the self, it is a matter of *how* one is engaged with the world, not so much with the objects of these engagements. It is a matter of attitude, discernment and, above all, freedom from unbalanced emotion. The idea of independence suffers a great distortion when it is treated as isolation. To be independent—in a human sense—is to have one's own mind and conscience, to be capable of consulting one's own understanding and one's own unique feeling without imitation of others and without anxiety about what one imagines will be their opinions and reactions. Speaking in religious language, an individual is said to be independent when he is answerable only to God. Speaking the language of Deism and the Enlightenment, an individual is independent when he is answerable only to—in Franklin's words—the "Father of Lights," the God of Reason (*Logos*) under whose sway all the "lights" (the worlds upon worlds of the inner and outer universe) move in their courses. An individual is independent when, in the terminology of the great philosopher of the Enlightenment, Immanuel Kant, he is answerable only to the "moral law within."

When an individual is open to that inner capacity of conscience, impartial feeling and reason, he or she is then capable of love toward one's neighbor. But it is love that is not subjective and egoistic. It is a love and a hate based on deep, essential perceptions, not on lovesick emotions or egoistic reactions. In this regard, an iconoclastic philosopher like Friedrich Nietzsche, in his powerful and profound denunciation of the pallor of modern reason and its rule, even a Nietzsche has failed to see into the depths and the real roots of the Enlightenment turn toward the god of Reason. We may join Nietzsche in overthrowing the tyranny of mental knowing and feeling, but what we are rejecting is only what has been made of the vision of the Enlightenment. It does not reflect the ideas that called to a Newton in science, or a Kant in philosophy, or a Washington, Franklin and Jefferson in politics and government.

> Our detached and distant situation invites and enables us to pursue a different course. If we remain one people, under an efficient government, the period is not far off, when we may defy material injury from external annoyance; when we may take such an attitude as will cause the neutrality, we may at any time resolve upon, to be scrupulously respected; when belligerent nations, under the impossibility of making acquisitions upon us, will not lightly hazard the giving us provocations; when we may choose peace or war, as our interest, guided by *justice,* shall counsel.
>
> Why forego the advantages of so peculiar a situation? Why quit our own, to stand upon foreign ground? Why, by interweaving our destiny with that of Europe, entangle our peace and prosperity in the toils of European ambition, rivalship, interest, humour or caprice? . . .
>
> Harmony, and a liberal intercourse with all nations, are recommended by policy, humanity and interest. But even our commercial policy should hold an equal and impartial hand; neither seeking nor granting exclusive favors or preferences; consulting the natural course

of things; diffusing and diversifying by gentle means the streams of commerce, but forcing nothing . . . constantly keeping in view, that it is folly in one nation to look for disinterested favors from another; that it must pay with a portion of its independence, for whatever it may accept under that character. . . . There can be no greater error than to expect or calculate upon real favours from nation to nation. It is an illusion which experience must cure, which a just pride ought to discard.[66]

Drawing to his concluding words, Washington then says:

In offering to you, my countrymen, these counsels of an old and affectionate friend, I dare not hope they will make the strong and lasting impression I could wish; that they will control the usual current of passions, or prevent our nation from running the course which has hitherto marked the destiny of nations! But, if I may even flatter myself, that they may be productive of some occasional good; that they may now and then recur to moderate the fury of party spirit; to warn against the mischiefs of foreign intrigue; to guard against the impostures of pretended patriotism; this hope will be a full recompense for the solicitude for your welfare, by which they have been dictated.[67]

A NEW MEANING OF VIRTUE

In sum, the mythic Washington now emerges as a symbol of the new meaning of virtue for our time—or rather, of the ancient, hidden meaning of virtue that has existed through all times, and which needs to be heard anew in our culture: the stepping back, the yielding, the withdrawal—from what? Not from life, not from realism, mental acuity, not from precise action—even sharp, severe action when necessary; the stepping back is the intensely and uniquely human act of freeing oneself from *attachment* to the whirlpool of life. In that stepping back, that self-removal from the condition of being devoured by the illusions and violence of life, the true self begins to emerge, grounded, to whatever extent, in the source of its being; and hence able, to whatever small or large degree, to serve as a conduit force of conscious creativity and care for one's neighbor. This is not some alien, Oriental doctrine, not some strange, occult fantasy; this is Christianity; it is Hellenic spirituality; it is at the heart of the vision of Judaism—it is Western, and, if it be heard once again, it is—strange though it may seem to say so—American. And, perhaps even stranger to say, yet overwhelmingly just and right, it is represented by the figure of George Washington.

FOUR

THOMAS JEFFERSON:
DEMOCRACY AS
THE COMMUNAL SELF

W ho was this tall, vibrant, yet abnormally shy man with the flaming red hair—principal creator of the Declaration of Independence, drafter of the Bill of Rights, master of the sciences and arts of his time; architect and builder of the great house Monticello, archaeologist, shrewd political tactician and diplomat; at one and the same time slaveowner and visionary philosopher of freedom and equality; gifted craftsman, scientific gardener and farmer, pioneering inventor, mathematician and, of course—third president of the United States of America? And what aspects of the legends and counter-legends that swirl around this hugely complex and many-faceted man and thinker are needed for the new story of the American soul?

We will set aside for now most of the man, and try to enter in a new way into the inner meaning of his understanding of democracy. None of the Founding Fathers sought more diligently to establish the relationship between the communal and the individual ideals of self-government—the notion, namely, that in the life of the individual as well as the community, direction must ultimately come from within. Just here it is possible to see unexpected new shadings in the social vision of Thomas Jefferson, to reposition his ideal of self-government so that it reflects what is actually a startling teaching about the power of community. We will see that the Jeffersonian social ideal actually presupposes and supports an exceptional inner struggle on the part of the individual. Ideals and standards of communal relationship that have become rank clichés to us may begin to open to entirely new meanings; and the ideal of democracy may begin to seem more like a script for men and women searching for conscious individuality than a pattern that we are supposed to conform to and obey.

We can interpret the vision of Jefferson in light of the ancient ideal of *voluntary life,* which does not mean a life where the individual gets what he or she wants, but rather a life which corresponds to an individual's *will.* For Jefferson, the aim of self-government is not the satisfaction of desires, but the incarnation of our free will. This is an immense difference, and the confusion of these meanings of "freedom" is one of the misunderstandings that is now threatening the existence and meaning of the whole American experiment.

POLITICS AND THE INNER WORLD

Here, then, is Jefferson writing about the inevitability and even the need for friction in communal and political relationships. Can we hear such passages from a somewhat different perspective than is usual? Is not Jefferson, *whether knowingly or not,* inviting the individual to an inner struggle quite as much as to the resolution of an external problem?

In every free and deliberating society, there must, from the nature of man, be opposite parties, and violent dissensions and discords; and one of these, for the most part, must prevail over the others for a shorter or longer time. Perhaps this party division is necessary to induce each to watch and relate to the people the proceedings of the other. But if on a temporary superiority of the one party, the other is to resort to a scission of the Union, no federal government can ever exist.

If to rid ourselves of the present rule of Massachusetts and Connecticut, we break the Union, will the evil stop there? Suppose the New England States alone cut off, will our nature be changed? Are we not men still to the south of that, and with all the passions of men? Immediately, we shall see a Pennsylvania and a Virginia party arise in the residuary confederacy, and the public mind will be distracted with the same party spirit. What a game too will the one party have in their hands, by eternally threatening the other that unless they do so and so, they will join their northern neighbors. . . . Seeing, therefore, that an association of men who will not quarrel with one another is a thing which never yet existed, from the greatest confederacy of nations down to a town meeting or a vestry; seeing that we must have somebody to quarrel with, I had rather keep our New England associates for that purpose, than to see our bickerings transferred to others.[68]

We can if we wish see here only the reflections of a worldly wise politician. But such observations by Jefferson invite us to think in rather deeper terms than that. For one thing, we immediately realize that all governmental systems are based on a view of the human self, a view of human nature. There can be no politics without psychology. And there can be no psychology without metaphysics, without a vision of the real world. Therefore, we need to take such observations of Jefferson's as clues to the vision of man in the universal world upon which the American civilization is based—and as clues to the role that social interaction, in the form of *democracy,* can play in the inner development of individual men and women. Yes, democratic politics has its distinctive, familiar and powerful external, pragmatic side; but it can, perhaps *must,* have its interior spiritual dimension as well.

IN SEARCH OF THE DEMOCRATIC SELF

We continue, now, with Jefferson's own words. As we listen to him, we ask ourselves: what is the nature of the struggle with oneself that is presupposed by these words? And, further, without this struggle, is the ideal of democracy only another fantasy by which human beings mask their ignorance of themselves?

> I tolerate with the utmost latitude the right of others to differ from me in opinion without imputing to them criminality. I know too well the weakness and uncertainty of human reason to wonder at its different results. Both of our political parties, at least the honest part of them, agree conscientiously in the same object—the public good; but they differ essentially in what they deem the means of promoting that good. One side . . . fears most the ignorance of the people; the other, the selfishness of rulers independent of them. Which is right, time and experience will prove. We think that one side of this experiment has been long enough tried, and proved not to promote the good of the many; and that the other has not been fairly and efficiently tried. Our opponents think the reverse. With whichever opinion the body of the nation concurs, that must prevail. *My anxieties on this subject will never carry me beyond the use of fair and honorable means, of truth and reason; nor have they ever lessened my esteem for the moral worth, nor alienated my affections from a single friend, who did not first withdraw himself.*[69]

I suggest that in such a statement, and there are thousands like it of course, what is presupposed is a distinct and extremely difficult inner struggle with the tendency in all of us to identify ourselves with our thoughts and opinions. The ideal of allowing others the right to their own opinions is everywhere respected in theory; but actually to practice it is quite another matter. Outwardly, the rules of our social order, the rules of democracy, protect the rights of others to disagree; but inwardly, in our own emotional nature, it is exceedingly rare and difficult for us to grant others that right—*at the moment they are exercising it.* Inwardly, it is an exceedingly rare and difficult thing to be democratic in the sense of a willingness and capacity to separate oneself from one's thoughts and freely give attention to the other. And if democracy is not understood in this way as a measure of our individual character and inner life, how does it differ essentially from any other social system that is based on hypocrisy?—systems of social ethics that make us lie to ourselves about our actual psychological capacities. When so many Americans hate and perhaps even wish the destruction of those who disagree with them, is it not partly because democracy has not been understood as a measure of our inner state? When the Church tells men and women to love their neighbor, suggesting it is something we actually can do, is not the result often the masking of our actual incapacity to love, the suppression of passions which gather their strength in the darkness of self-deception and then, all too often, explode into violence while still bearing the banners of religious ideals? Similarly, unless we take the ideal of democracy as a lens to see ourselves as we actually are, this ideal will also become the instrument of the very tyranny it was meant to correct—as war and destruction have so often been carried out under the name of Christian love.

Did Jefferson understand democracy in this way? This is a question for historians, but I think that for us the question is: how are *we* to take the ideals of democracy that he carved out for us? I am suggesting that it is necessary to interiorize these ideals. Unless they become ideals and measures of the inner world, they cannot operate in the outer world. Unless they become metaphysical and psychological, they cannot be political. That, I suggest, is the exceptional quality of American political ideals: they can work in the external world only if they are understood in the internal world.

At the same time, it can be of considerable help to look at how the founders of our country expressed themselves on the question of man's capacity to live according to the principles of democracy. We need to understand more exactly how they saw human nature; it will tell us how we ourselves, as their heirs, understand human nature. We seek to interiorize the ideals of democracy; but in order to do this, we must also see what kinds

of assumptions are in our minds about who and what we are. We need to
look at our assumptions about ourselves and our capacities. We are born not
only into a political system, but into the view of ourselves that goes with it.
"We believed," writes Jefferson,

> that man was a rational animal, endowed by nature with rights and
> with an innate sense of justice; and that he could be restrained from
> wrong and protected in right, by moderate powers confided to per-
> sons of his own choice, and held to their duties by dependence on
> their own will.[70]

Immediately, we are in front of the idea of human rights and capacities
given us by nature (and nature's God) itself. And of course, we hear in this
the most famous and important words of the American nation written by
Jefferson in 1776. But it is not often recognized that these opening sentences of the Declaration of Independence are far more than a political statement. They embrace a powerful psychological and metaphysical claim, an
overwhelmingly influential summary of assumptions about the nature of
the human self and our place in the universal world. And these assumptions
have become *our* assumptions about who we are, what we are and the nature
of the real world:

The Declaration of Independence

> When in the course of human events it becomes necessary for one
> people to dissolve the political bonds, which have connected them
> with another, and to assume, among the powers of the earth, the
> separate and equal station, to which the laws of nature and nature's
> God entitle them, a decent respect for the Opinions of mankind re-
> quires that they should declare the causes which impel them to the
> separation.

> We hold these truths to be self-evident, that all men are created
> equal, that they are endowed by their Creator with certain unalien-
> able rights, that among these are Life, Liberty, and the pursuit of
> Happiness.

Again, we are searching for the philosophical assumptions of our form of
democracy. Whenever we see the idea of *rights,* we must realize that something is also being said about the structure and makeup of the self. We are
being told by Jefferson that we human beings have within us, as part of our
intrinsic makeup, the capacity to intuit the good and the power to will the
good. We are capable of guiding our own lives toward an authentic and
purposive end. Such assumptions about the intrinsic capacities of human
nature contradict the basic thrust of the Calvinistic Protestantism that
played such a dominant role in the settling of the New England colonies.
The Jeffersonian view of human nature is diametrically opposed to the
Calvinistic doctrine of man's essential corruption and incapacity, and ac-
cords great powers and capacities to the human soul. Since every right implies a power, to grant man so many rights can only be based on an exalted
vision of human powers. And to say this is to come directly in front of the
question of whether democracy is based on an accurate assessment of our actual capacities. We are confronted with the age-old but eternally challenging question of what man *is* as opposed to what he can *become.* What may
have seemed questions of only external, political relevance—questions that
one can safely think about without reference to deep metaphysical or
psychospiritual issues—now draw us irrevocably into the heart of spiritual
philosophy.

RIGHTS, DUTIES AND POWERS

Here, again, Jefferson. Is this *ourselves* that he is speaking about? Do such
statements really reflect a true picture of ourselves *as we in fact are?*

> We acknowledge that our children are born free; that that freedom is
> a gift of nature, and not of him who begot them. . . . Every man, and
> every body of men on earth, possess the right of self-government.
> They receive it with their being from the hand of nature. Individuals
> exercise it by their single will; collections of men by that of their ma-
> jority; for the law of the majority is the natural law of every society
> of men.[71]

As Jefferson speaks, our effort is to detect his view of human *capacity* and
not to be distracted by the questions of rights and shoulds and ideals—
brilliantly and movingly though he articulates them. We must try to remember that the vision of what man is is inextricably connected with how
we see our rights and duties, and we must try not to let our emotions about
the latter distract us from seeing the former issues, upon which all legiti-
macy of the latter is based.

> Some men are born without the organs of sight, or of hearing, or
> without hands. Yet it would be wrong to say that man is born with-
> out these faculties, and sight, hearing, and hands may with truth en-
> ter into the general definition of man. The want or imperfection of
> the moral sense in some men, like the want or imperfection of the
> sense of sight and hearing in others, is no proof that it is a general
> characteristic of the species. . . . I sincerely, then, believe . . . in the
> general existence of a moral instinct. I think it is the brightest gem
> with which the human character is studded, and the want of it as
> more degrading than the most hideous of the bodily deformities.[72]

There is no ambiguity here—man is born with the capacity to intuit what
is good and what is evil. Where these are lacking, says Jefferson, this defect
may be corrected by *education.* But unequivocally, for Jefferson, man is inherently endowed with conscience as a part of his nature, just as surely as he
is endowed with the capacity to see, hear and touch. He is endowed, as well,
with educability: the capacity to be improved, to grow inwardly toward the

ideal. And this ideal involves his own individual happiness. Man was not created for misery; he was created for joy and beneficent well-being. This is his right; this is his *duty;* and, obviously, this is his *capacity.*

> If we are made in some degree for others, yet, in a greater sense, are we made for ourselves. It were contrary to feeling, and indeed ridiculous to suppose that a man had less rights in himself than in one of his neighbors, or indeed all of them put together. This would be slavery, and not that liberty which the bill of rights has made inviolable, and for the preservation of which our government has been charged. Nothing could so completely divest us of that liberty as the establishment of the opinion, that the State has a perpetual right to the services of all its members. This . . . would be to annihilate the blessings of existence, and to contradict the Giver of life, who gave it for happiness and not for wretchedness.

> And certainly, to such it were better that they had never been born.[73]

How often do we consider the Bill of Rights in this way as a *metaphysical statement* about the nature of man and his relation to God and the universal order? There is so much anguish about rights in our society that we hardly ever seriously ponder the assumptions about ourselves that these rights are based upon. We are so troubled by the striving to get what we need or want, especially in comparison to what others may or may not have, that our thought rarely moves in a metaphysical direction—in the sense of asking ourselves what these rights are telling us about the structure of our being.

The Bill of Rights

We need to look more closely at this vision of human nature that forms the basis of our Bill of Rights. And if we do, we will find it centered, surprisingly perhaps for some of us, around the mind and the will. We will find that our form of government rests on the assumption that we men and women can think independently and in discourse with others, that we can weigh evidence and information, form opinions that are not wholly dictated by passion, and then act in a manner consistent with our views and moral principles, which themselves have been or can be arrived at on the basis of independent thought and the intuitions of conscience. To the extent that these capacities seem to be lacking in us, that lack can, in general, be corrected through education.

This view of human nature may not seem extraordinary to us, but in fact it represents a fairly exalted view of human capacity. And if it does not seem so to us, if it seems "common knowledge," it may be because we have not really put it to the test. What does it really mean to think independently, for example? Surely it means that we exercise a power of mind and attention unswayed by outer conditioning and suggestion, and unswayed by interior fears and desires. It means, ultimately, the power to think from one's own real self, one's own authentic mind and consciousness. When we begin to put the matter in this way, Jefferson's assumptions about human nature begin to resonate with the vision of the qualities of the self that have been offered by all the wisdom traditions of the world, qualities that are only a result of prolonged inner struggle. At the same time, the great spiritual philosophies of the world—as expressed, for example, in the figure of Socrates—all tell us that we, just we flawed human beings, have the capacity to *begin* thinking for ourselves, to begin striving to find our authentic mind. But, in all cases, this capacity of self-authentic thinking is not something we just do how and when it pleases us, just by the by. Independent thought is never mechanical, never automatic. Therefore, if we hear this view of the human self as something prosaic and "obvious," it may well be because the ideas it represents have degenerated in our minds. And here, as elsewhere, one may reasonably suppose that generations of men and women did not suffer and die, nor live through the extremes of sacrifice, triumph and despair, only so that we contemporary men and women could indulge in what we call "independent thought."

THE PURSUIT OF HAPPINESS

So much is perhaps more obvious when it is a matter of consumerism. The pursuit of happiness, as Jefferson and the Founding Fathers understood it, is surely not the pursuit of consumer products. The happiness Jefferson spoke of is a matter of the spirit of man, his moral and intellectual faculties in harmony with nature as it exists both outside of himself in his environment and within himself in the processes of his own body and soul. As with the spiritual philosophies and traditions of all ages, for Jefferson happiness is not to be equated with the mere satisfaction of desires. And if we assume we understand what Jefferson meant by the pursuit of happiness, and in so assuming if we vaguely feel it has to do mainly with material factors, then it is very likely we misunderstand the bases upon which the American nation was formed. Men and women did not die for the right to unbounded consumer goods.

The point is that Jefferson had to fight for this view of human nature. It was not "common knowledge"; it was, in fact, revolutionary. We think of the American struggle as a struggle for rights; it was, and perhaps still is, equally a struggle for a view of the human self. The First Amendment, the first element of Jefferson's and our Bill of Rights, states:

> Congress shall make no law respecting the establishment of religion,
> or prohibiting the free exercise thereof; or abridging the freedom of
> speech, or of the press; or the right of the people peaceably to assem-
> ble, and to petition the Government for a redress of grievances.

This and the following nine elements of the Bill of Rights were not originally included in the Constitution—in fact, Jefferson was serving in France when the Constitution was being drafted. When the draft of the Constitution was shown to him, he immediately urged that the Bill of Rights be added. It was Jefferson, and perhaps only Jefferson, who insisted that the fundamental laws forming the basis of the American government contain this vision of human nature and the rights that follow from it. It was he who insisted that government be based on ethics, spiritual psychology, and a vision of the universal world. If Lincoln is our icon of individual consciousness, as we shall see, Jefferson represents the interconnection of metaphysics, spiritual psychology and practical political organization.

THE STATE AND THE COSMOS

Writing, for example, on the very pragmatic subject of states' rights, Jefferson draws on nothing less than a vision of cosmic order:

> I do not think it for the interest of the general government itself, and still less of the Union at large, that the State governments should be so little respected as they have been. However, I dare say that in time all these as well as their central government, like the planets revolving around their common sun, acting and acted upon according to their respective weights and distances, will produce that beautiful equilibrium on which our Constitution is founded, and which I believe it will exhibit to the world in a degree of perfection, unexampled but in the planetary system itself. The enlightened statesman, therefore, will endeavor to preserve the weight and influence of every part, as too much given to any number of it would destroy the general equilibrium.[74]

Jefferson represents the strictly American vision of man's divine nature. There is a divinity within ourselves—both in our individual being and in our communal life. This is not Hinduism, though it may sound like it. This is not Christian or Jewish mysticism, though it may sound like it. This is a vision of the meaning of America, in the language of America and on the soil of the American nation.

Such is Jefferson's vision of the self. This is not to claim that Jefferson was anything like what we ordinarily think of as a "mystic." Quite the opposite. He was a great representative of the Enlightenment; he stood as a devotee at the altar of rationality, science and common sense. At the same time, it is necessary to see that all great visions of man and man's duties are in essence mystical, in the deeper sense of the word. The Enlightenment itself, as we shall see, rationalism itself, as we shall see, radiate the same mystic vision of man's nature as do the masters of the path in every tradition. This is not to say anything whatever about Jefferson's interior life or level of being; it is only to point out the ideas and vision which energized him and which, passing through his extraordinarily sensitive mind and heart, energized the American soul.

THE DARK SIDE OF HUMAN NATURE

Yet, as Jefferson also realized with equal force, this vision of human nature was utterly false as a description of ourselves as we are. And to say this is to come toward the second great thrust of the Jeffersonian blending of spiritual psychology and practical politics. This second thrust operates in apparently direct opposition to the first.

In *The American Political Tradition,* Richard Hofstadter opens as follows:

> Long ago Horace White observed that the Constitution of the United
> States "is based upon the philosophy of Hobbes and the religion of
> Calvin. It assumes that the natural state of mankind is a state of war,
> and that the carnal mind is at enmity with God." Of course the Con
> stitution was founded more upon experience than any such abstract
> theory; but it was also an event in the intellectual history of Western
> civilization. The men who drew up the Constitution in Philadelphia
> during the summer of 1787 had a vivid Calvinistic sense of human
> evil and damnation and believed with Hobbes that men are selfish
> and contentious. They were men of affairs, merchants, lawyers, planter-
> businessmen, speculators, investors. Having seen human nature on

display in the marketplace, the courtroom, the legislative chamber, and in every secret path and alleyway where wealth and power are courted, they felt they knew it in all its frailty. To them a human being was an atom of self-interest. They did not believe in man, but they did believe in the power of a good political constitution to control him.[75]

Hofstadter goes on:

There was no better expression of the dilemma of a man who has no faith in the people but insists that government be based upon them than that of Jeremy Belknap, a New England clergyman, who wrote to a friend: "Let it stand as a principle that government originates from the people; but let the people be taught . . . that they are not able to govern themselves."[76]

And further:

If the masses were turbulent and unregenerate, and yet if government must be founded upon their suffrage and consent, what could a Constitution-maker do? One thing that the Fathers did not propose to do, because they thought it impossible, was to change the nature of man to conform with a more ideal system. They were inordinately confident that they knew what man always had been and what he always would be. . . . Since man was an unchangeable creature of self-interest, it would not do to leave anything to his capacity for restraint. It was too much to expect that vice could be checked by virtue; the Fathers relied instead upon checking vice with vice. . . . What the Fathers wanted was known as "balanced government." . . . A properly designed state, the Fathers believed, would check interest with interest, class with class, faction with faction, and one branch of government with another in a harmonious system of mutual frustration.[77]

It is just at this point that the second aspect of Jefferson's view of human nature may be understood. He saw quite clearly the weakness of human nature, and although he nowhere puts this aspect of his vision into a concise philosophical summary, his letters everywhere give evidence of a full and sober acquaintance with the dark side of human nature, a side which of course he dealt with continually in his years as a lawyer. We have seen this sober picture of human nature already expressed in the letters we have cited from Jefferson—to the effect that, human nature being what it is, there will always be dissension and that which Washington abhorred, "the spirit of party."

But the most concise expression of Jefferson's view of this aspect of human nature is to be sought not under his own name, but from the pen of his great friend and protégé, James Madison. In *The Federalist Papers,* Madison carefully enunciates the psychological—or, as we might also say, the psycho-spiritual—basis of the American Constitution. Historical evidence clearly shows the congruence of Madison's and Jefferson's views in this and many other essential elements in the formation of the American governmental system.

In the tenth *Federalist* paper, Madison begins by acknowledging the deep significance of what Washington and others had understood by "the spirit of party." It may even be that he has Washington specifically in mind when he writes of the fears of "our most considerate and virtuous citizens" that "the public good is disregarded in the conflicts of rival parties." Acknowledging the justice of this fear, he goes on:

> There are two methods of curing the mischiefs of faction: the one by removing its causes, the other, by controlling its effects.[78]

But, says Madison, it is impossible to remove the causes of faction without either destroying liberty or attempting to inculcate uniformity of opinion throughout the land.

> There are . . . two methods of removing the causes of faction: the one, by destroying the liberty which is essential to its existence; the other, by giving to every citizen the same opinions, the same passions, and the same interests.

> It could never be more truly said than of the first remedy, that it was worse than the disease. Liberty is to faction what air is to fire, an aliment without which it instantly expires. But it could not be less folly to abolish liberty, which is essential to political life, because it nourishes faction, than it would be to wish the annihilation of air, which is essential to animal life, because it imparts to fire its destructive agency.

As for the second expedient, the inculcation of uniformity, it is as impracticable as the first would be unwise.

> As long as the reason of man continues fallible, and he is at liberty to exercise it, different opinions will be formed. As long as the connection subsists between his reason and his self-love, his opinions and his passions will have a reciprocal influence on each other; and the former will be the objects to which the latter will attach themselves.

THE FALLEN SELF

Observations such as this about the weakness of human reason and its dependent relationship to the passions were common among our more philosophical Founding Fathers. Such observations were common, as well, among the great philosophers who shaped the assumptions of the modern world—Hobbes, Locke, Hume, Kant. And, of course, this kind of psychospiritual insight lay at the heart of the Christian, especially Protestant, contemplative practices that formed the fundamental basis of the lives and ideals of the early colonists in New England, Pennsylvania and elsewhere.

We are speaking here of contemplative Christianity, its insights into the fallenness of the human self. This vision and these insights were restated, shorn of religious and creedal language, by the great philosophers of the Enlightenment and powerfully echoed by the American Founding Fathers, especially by men like Jefferson and Madison. The trappings of Church and dogma were to be abandoned; but the question of understanding the inner life of man, the relationship between man's capacity to see truth and his inevitable passion—this was *the* issue, *the* arena of inquiry, *the* basic realm upon which were founded all principles of human society and government. To ignore this realm, to ignore its spiritual significance, to ignore its centrality in the conduct and the meaning of human life, was—for the likes of Jefferson, Adams, Madison, Washington and Franklin—to ignore not only the most fundamental truths about our human nature, but the basis of human life itself.

The Enlightenment philosophers and the Enlightenment builders of society—and this latter comprises the originators of America—were *spiritual* thinkers or they were nothing. They were not necessarily religious. But they *were* spiritual. They might even have been against religion in its conventional forms. They were openly hostile to the tendency of institutional religion to oppress the free mind and to ally itself with despotic governments. But they were spiritual thinkers in that they, and none more than Jefferson, envisioned the aim of human life as the dwelling in a reality beyond the world of personal gain and loss, the world of physical satisfaction and pleasure. For Jefferson and for all the greatest figures of the Enlightenment, *reason was not what we tend to imagine as reason.* Reason was the realm of human freedom, the realm in which, from the interior of the self, a man or woman could open to the need both to function well in the earthly life we are given *and* at the same time to receive life and vision from a realm of reality beyond what the ordinary senses and passions recognized.

Our Founding Fathers were artists and masters of building a social order. That was their milieu, their instrument, their art form. In other lands at the same time there were great thinkers who created new forms of science, literature, art, symbols. But it remained for the Americans to create or re-create the art form of government known as republican democracy. And an essential element in this art form was their recognition of human weakness and failure. All around our Founding Fathers, the Christian religion called it sin. But a Jefferson, or a Madison, having climbed to another promontory, sees some of the same ultimate truths that Christianity saw about fallen man, but is able and obliged to speak of these truths in a new language, a language that is the harbinger of the inner liberation which reason itself promises within our selves, a language devoid of blind faith, but suffused by the sober faith in a conscious mind: the language of science, of passionate rationality.

PROPERTY AND THE TWO NATURES OF MAN

Madison (and, behind him, Jefferson) goes on, continuing the argument against trying to remove the causes of factions in a free society. Having observed that in their present state, human beings cannot free their reason from the influence of the passions, Madison writes now about the manner in which (fallen) human beings manifest themselves in the world of action and matter. The general expression that is used to refer to the milieu and result of human action in the world is "property." We must note that the Enlightenment idea of "property" is a far wider idea than what we now designate by this term. For the Founding Fathers, "property" refers mainly to what takes place and what comes into being when man functions in the world, when human beings interact with nature and matter. Its contemporary meaning, on the other hand, is generally confined to the legal ownership of specific objects such as real estate. For Jefferson, Madison and the creators of the American government, "property" includes what we nowadays mean by it, but also refers to the general results of the functioning of man in the world—it is a very general and unabashedly metaphysical term. Human beings have faculties and functions specific to our nature as human; we must exercise these functions to live on this earth; and as a result of mingling our functional capacities* with what nature presents to us, "property" comes into being. A social order that severely restricts or suppresses this functioning condemns us to a less than human existence. According to Madison, however, the weakness of human nature is such that:

> The diversity in the faculties of men, from which the rights of property originate, is not less an insuperable obstacle to a uniformity of interests. *The protection of these faculties is the first object of government.*

A social order must be created that allows every human being to manifest his given, outward-directed functions.† But:

> From the protection of different and unequal faculties of acquiring property, the possession of different degrees and kinds of property immediately results; and from the influence of these on the sentiments [emotions] and views of the respective proprietors, ensues a division of the society into different interests and parties.

> The latent causes of faction are thus sown in the nature of man . . .

And these causes manifest themselves inevitably in a social order that allows every individual the liberty to be what he is:

> and we see them [these causes] everywhere brought into different degrees of activity, according to the different circumstances of civil society. A zeal for different opinions concerning religion, concerning

---

* In colonial America these functional capacities themselves, when worked on and developed into "skills," were themselves understood as "property." See Wood, *The Radicalism of the American Revolution,* p. 23.

†It is important to note that the main aim of government is confined to supporting the exercise of the outward-directed faculties of human nature. The inward-directed movement, the spiritual movement, is not a matter of governmental regulation. It is a matter of personal search or conscience. This is the basis of "freedom of religion." Yet it was Jefferson's vision that a true republican democracy can powerfully, but indirectly, support this inward movement as well. Not only can it do so, it *must* do so.

government, and many other points, as well of speculation and practice; an attachment to different leaders ambitiously contending for
pre-eminence and power: or to persons of other descriptions whose
fortunes have been interesting to the human passions, have in turn,
divided mankind into parties, inflamed them with mutual animosity,
and rendered them much more disposed to vex and oppress each other
than to cooperate for the common good. So strong is this propensity
of mankind to fall into mutual animosities, that where no substantial
occasion presents itself, the most frivolous and fanciful distinctions
have been sufficient to kindle their unfriendly passions and excite
their most violent conflicts.

And now, referring specifically to property, Madison continues:

But the most common and durable source of factions has been the
various and unequal distribution of property. Those who hold and
those who are without property have ever formed distinct interests in
society. Those who are creditors and those who are debtors, fall under
a like discrimination. A landed interest, a manufacturing interest, a
mercantile interest, a moneyed interest, with many lesser interests,
grow up of necessity in civilized nations, and divide them into different classes, actuated by different sentiments and views. The regulation of these various and interfering interests forms the principal task
of modern legislation, and involves the spirit of party and faction in
the necessary and ordinary operations of government.

Do we, perhaps, now regard such statements as clichés? Is it so obvious to
us that it is our human nature, with its weaknesses and passions, its egoism
and violence, that requires government and laws? Or can we once again *feel*
what is at issue here?—namely, the fact that our social order is based
uniquely on a very specific idea of man's possible greatness and his actual
wretchedness? Such as we are, we will inevitably take for ourselves and oppress our neighbor—therefore we must be restrained. But such as we are

meant to be, we are a spark of the divine—call it God or the Creator—and therefore we must be free. We are two-natured beings. The entire sense of the Jeffersonian ideal lies in this notion. And so we must create a form of social order, a government, that allows the liberty of free, potentially divine human beings, while at the same time checking the bestial, egoistic forces that in fact dominate our fallen nature. Such is the spiritual logic, the metaphysical logic behind the notion of a government with automatic checks and balances.

HUMAN RIGHTS AND THE TWO NATURES

What we call "human rights," and what Jefferson and Madison called "private rights," refers, metaphysically, to the rights of a human being who has the seed of God within him and who must be allowed the conditions to strive for the development of his relationship to what is highest in himself and in creation. An individual must be free not only to buy things and to own things, but free to think and make moral decisions and conduct his or her own life in a way that does justice to the whole of human nature. Outer liberty is necessary so that inner liberty can be sought. There is no higher justification for it than this.

At the same time, human beings are weak, corrupt, selfish, vain, greedy, brutal, timid, suggestible, hypocritical and violent. They do not understand order and history; they—with very few exceptions—do not and are not able to see the whole structure of societal life; they cannot, in sum, govern themselves. They must be restrained. But—all men are more alike than they have hitherto imagined. Kings are more like commoners than has been imagined. All human beings, as the Christian tradition taught in tones whose shock value continued to echo down to the eighteenth century—human beings are equal not only as children of God, but as playthings of the devil. We must all be governed. But no single individual is intrinsically capable of governing all the others. We are all weak. It is not mainly a special individual or a special group of all-too-human individuals who must govern, but it is God who must govern us—and what is God? God is nature or is first and foremost expressed as nature. And what is nature? Nature is law and forces operating infallibly and perfectly. The government of human beings must be under the same kind of laws that govern nature. Only within the sphere of such laws, laws that true reason can—up to a point— apprehend, can individuals find their way to live together in community and under the governance of chosen leaders. Human society must be a mirror of the vast universal society of God's universal creation: a conscious, conscientious mirror of nature and nature's God.

In this context we can now hear Jefferson, again speaking in collaboration with and through the mind of Madison in the tenth *Federalist* paper. Nature itself operates through checks and balances, through mutual antagonisms. It is through understanding this that government can control, not the causes of human conflict and disorder (faction), but the *results* of this fallibility of our nature. "The inference to which we are brought is, that the *causes* of faction cannot be removed, and that relief is only to be sought in the means of controlling its *effects*." If the following account by Madison sounds overly familiar or idealistic, it is partly because we are no longer galvanized by the vision of who and what we are that lies at the heart of the American governmental system. But it need not remain all too familiar, or all too "political"—that is, it need not remain a conceptual instrument for our habitual externally directed thoughts and action. We can—and I think we must—re-mythologize, that is, interiorize, not only the heroes who already occupy a certain place in our common psyche, but also our governmental structure, the law, itself. This we can do by understanding anew the eternal questions of human nature that underlie the creation of law and the American Constitution. It is the paradox of human nature: we are inwardly free and inwardly slaves at one and the same time; we are gods and beasts at the same time; we are great *and* fallen, strong *and* weak at the same time. It is ideas like these which lie far back at the root of texts which seem otherwise purely political and external. Here, then, is Madison speaking of how the effects of human weakness will be controlled in the new government.

He begins by citing the case where the source of faction and conflict consists of less than a majority of the people. In this case,

> [i]f a faction consists of less than a majority, relief is supplied by the republican principle, which enables the majority to defeat its sinister views by regular vote: It may clog the administration, it may convulse the society; but it will be unable to execute and mask its violence under the forms of the Constitution.

But if a faction, a group whose interest is their own personal gain rather than the good of the whole, consists of a majority, the laws of nature, reflected in the form of republican democracy, still operate to neutralize its threat to the whole. In the following passage, we should note especially Madison's choice of the phrase "ruling passion." This term was traditionally used (and we find it strongly emphasized in Plato's *Republic*) to refer to the overwhelming power of personal emotion in the life of the unregenerate individual; it is nearly equivalent to what we sometimes mean today by the terms "obsession" and "addiction."

> When a majority is included in a faction, the form of popular government on the other hand enables it to sacrifice to its ruling passion or interest, both the public good and the rights of other citizens. To secure the public good, and private rights, against the danger of such a faction, and at the same time to preserve the spirit and the form of popular government, is then the great object to which our enquiries are directed. . . . By what means is this object attainable? Evidently by one of two only. Either the existence of the same passion or interest in a majority at the same time, must be prevented; or the majority, having such co-existent passion or interest, must be rendered, by their number and local situation, unable to concert and carry into effect schemes of oppression. *If the impulse and the opportunity be suffered to coincide, we well know that neither moral nor religious motives can be relied*

on as an adequate control. They are not found to be such on the injustice and
violence of individuals, and lose their efficacy in proportion to the number com-
bined together; that is, in proportion as their efficacy becomes needful.

The italicized sentences express, as clearly as can be expressed, the understanding of human fallibility that lies at the heart of the Constitution. The
Constitution, by creating a sufficiently republican form of government—
that is, not a direct democracy, but a representative form of government
which allows for a mediating force through elected delegates who in their
turn vote the direct actions of the government—absorbs and modulates the
inevitable passions of groups and individuals, and through this structure allows the laws of nature to operate within the nation as a whole. Such is the
metaphysics of the American Constitution.

THE COMMUNAL SELF AS A RECONCILING FORCE

But even with these principles forming the basis of the Constitution, Jefferson was troubled. His powerful sense of human imperfection, which existed side by side with his vision of human possibility, demanded more. As
great as man could be, man as he is had to be restrained from his overwhelming tendencies toward oppression, injustice, greed and tyranny. And
there had to be room, free and clear, for human beings to exercise their freedom, to think—and this meant to think *together,* in *community;* to exchange
with each other in the realm of ideas and perception. There had to be space
for human beings to become improved and perfected by the process of free
inquiry and by the natural obligations of living on the earth and carrying
out their natural, human responsibilities.

We come round again to Jefferson's insistence on adding the Bill of
Rights to the Constitution. Why did he feel it was so necessary to add these
amendments having to do with freedom of religion, freedom of speech, the
press, the right to assembly, the right to petition for redress of grievances
and all the rights protecting the individual in matters of law, arrest, privacy

and personal security? In considering this question we come to the third thrust of Jefferson's view of human nature and the role of community—his vision of the meaning of democracy as a medium through which man may pass from his actual weakness to his possible greatness. For Jefferson, the community, the nation, is, or can be, the conduit for the force that elevates humanity through the dual power of education of the mind and the engagement of heart and body in honest work—all undertaken within the milieu of a free exchange of thought and communal inquiry in search of truth. In short, we are in front of the idea of democracy as the communal self.

For many, including many who were the most ardent supporters of the Constitution drafted in 1787, a bill of rights was unnecessary. Alexander Hamilton, for example, argued that the whole Constitution was itself a monumental "bill of rights" that powerfully achieved all that any additional such articles could hope for. Why, then, did Jefferson insist otherwise? Bills of rights, says Hamilton, are not only unnecessary in the proposed Constitution, but would even be dangerous. They would contain various exceptions to powers not granted; and, on this very account, would afford

> a . . . pretext to claim more than were granted. For why declare that things shall not be done which there is no power to do? Why, for instance, should it be said that the liberty of the press shall not be restrained, when no power is given [in the Constitution] by which [such] restrictions may be imposed?[79]

Hamilton's point is quite reasonable. There is nothing in the text of the Constitution that gives government the right to restrain the press. And since it is a fundamental principle of the Constitution that the Congress shall *have* no powers that are not specifically granted to it, then why specify rights that are not endangered in the first place? Amendments such as this might even afford the malicious a pretext for claiming that the original body of the Constitution intended the Congress to have power over the press!

Hamilton makes equally strong logical arguments with respect to all the other elements of the first ten amendments that we know as the Bill of Rights. To Hamilton, these amendments not only add nothing to what is already granted in the main body of the Constitution, they are in various ways dangerously vague and piecemeal. Drawing to a conclusion, he writes:

> The truth is . . . that the Constitution is itself in every rational sense, and to every useful purpose, A BILL OF RIGHTS. The several bills of rights in Great Britain form its Constitution, and conversely the constitution of each State is its bill of rights. And the proposed Constitution, if adopted, will be the bill of rights of the Union.[80]

Again the question: why was Jefferson so insistent on adding a bill of rights? Or rather, how are *we* to interpret his insistence? How can it help us toward a new appreciation of the meaning of democracy and the meaning of the very idea of human rights?

What is at issue here is nothing less than humanity's hope of growing from what we are to what we are meant to be. Under what communal conditions can men and women grow inwardly, morally, spiritually? The point is that the idea of the "rights of man" which emerged so powerfully from the Enlightenment and through the mind of Jefferson, among others, is not simply and solely a negative concept. "Human rights," for Jefferson, does not mean solely the right not to be interfered with by government; this is only part of it—and of course it is this part that commands so much attention in our present world. But the other part is perhaps even more important: "human rights" means the right to pursue one's authentic obligations as a God-created and potentially godlike human being through the latent power of divine reason (or conscience) within oneself.

The founding of America thus reads out as the attempt to create a form of government within which human society can function as a morally and spiritually educative force.

When Hamilton argues that no bill of rights is necessary, it is because he is attending solely to the political, legal and economic aspects of the structure of government. He is saying that the Constitution as drafted in

Philadelphia contains all the safeguards that are necessary to protect individuals from external oppression and tyranny. He is not concerning himself with the educative aspect of a free society. Hamilton is not concerned with the inner life. That, perhaps, was part of Hamilton's strength; it is around this external aspect of government that his genius is concentrated, and it is from this point of view that we may today understand his conflict with Jefferson.

Jefferson's aim is much more complex, much more mixed than Hamilton's. His aim involves a more difficult mixture of outer and inner considerations, considerations dealing with both external liberty and inward moral development. He is insisting on a Bill of Rights not only because he fears external political oppression—in this he is one with Hamilton. Where Jefferson differs from Hamilton is in his view of human possibility. Both Jefferson and Hamilton, like many of the Founding Fathers, clearly saw the dark side of human nature, and both sought a form of government that would keep this aspect under control—both for those ruled and for those in power—through a mechanism of force and counterforce resembling the way nature itself worked. But, unlike Hamilton, Jefferson also passionately believed in the perfectibility of human nature, the capacity of individual human beings to grow inwardly under specific conditions of communal life and individual effort. Specifically, these conditions, for Jefferson, comprise a life that combines (1) development of the mind through free intellectual intercourse and free access to knowledge contained in books and gained through untrammeled scientific experiment; (2) development of the feelings through the struggle to allow one's neighbor the right to his opinion and his place in the social order; and (3) development of the physical, organic substrate of human nature through a life in direct contact with the earth and its rhythms, its demands, its bounty and its severity: namely, through a life rooted in agriculture.

Mind, feeling, body: knowledge, acceptance of one's neighbor, and work in contact with biological nature and the earth. For Jefferson, the structure of government was to allow these three fundamental aspects of human life to develop together in harmony—*within the individual.* Democracy as a political system was to be the skin and bones that supported and protected the pulsing movement of human life toward the goal of individual obedience to reason and conscience, "Nature's God," within oneself.

As for Hamilton, on the other hand, the outer structure was all that really concerned him—and in this concern he was a master thinker and even a prophetic architect not only of America, but of the modern world itself. Hamilton advocated a strong central government, an active, interventionist central government, whereas Jefferson always stood for a more evenly distributed political system. But that is not the point we are concerned with here. The point, here, is not whether the founding of the United States was based on a new kind of social or moral hierarchy or simply on the firm determination to protect the individual's rights within reason to live in any way he wished. The point is that the new government, in Jefferson's eyes, was to be a shell, an armor, a protective structure that would allow and perhaps, in subtle ways, even support the growth of moral power within the individual members of the society. Democracy, for Jefferson, was to be neutral with respect to sectarian religion, but spiritually and morally positive. Hamilton either did not care about this inner world of the spirit, or did not believe that human beings could escape from their moral degradation. Or, perhaps, he simply felt it was not the place of government to concern itself with such matters. For Jefferson, too, freedom of religion also meant freedom *from* religion in the sense of freedom from imposed or suggested beliefs. Only within the frame of this freedom could individuals have the possibility of discovering the moral and spiritual power of reason within themselves.

WHAT IS DEMOCRACY *FOR*?

Jefferson's complexity and ambiguity about the function of democracy—as opposed to Hamilton's lucid, brilliant, external precision—I see not as a flaw so much as a sign of the scale of the ideals he was grappling with. The fact is, no one expressed so profoundly and passionately the ideals of republican democracy. But his idea of democracy was not purely and simply a negative ideal, that is, the advocating of a form of government whose sole principle was protection *against* something. Jeffersonian democracy represents more than freedom *from*. His ideal of democracy also points us—powerfully, but often without words—to a freedom *for* something! For Jefferson, government is an *active neutrality*.

The whole principle of republican democracy can be re-positioned as a method of social organization in which the mind of the whole is allowed to communicate to and through the parts of which it is composed. To put the point abstractly, the whole is that which radiates and expresses itself through the parts, which in turn are structured and obliged to communicate with each other in order to allow the whole to appear and to survive. To a part, the idea of the whole seems impersonal—literally *impartial*. That is exactly what impartiality is: the perspective that is free from the subjectivity of the part. But one strives to become free from the rule of a part in order to come under the rule of the whole, not in order to come under the rule of what is only another part—either of oneself or of society. To put the matter in this way is to grasp succinctly the problem of modern democracy when, through advocating freedom from this or that party interest or sectarian belief structure, or faction, or class interest, or moneyed interest, it then turns us immediately to the influence of some other part—glamour, fame, sexual satisfaction, ego or any of the other thousand and one impulses that operate within ourselves and within society. Hamiltonian precision is superb, but *for* what?—to what end? With interpretations that rigorously argue only for a negative view of the Constitution and the Bill of Rights, we are given what is only a pure instrument, a social technology. In this view, the Constitution and the Bill of Rights are no more and no less than that—a social technology, a machine which, like every great piece of technology, is relatively neutral. The Constitution and the Bill of Rights set up a governmental structure only then, as it were, to dis-establish it, leading us to the challenge and the need to decide for ourselves what we wish for and how we wish to live.

Yes, this is Jeffersonian, too. But Jefferson's vision goes beyond that. If democracy were only that, then it would be a real question of whether it is at all worthwhile to shake off the tyranny of one part in order to exchange it for the tyranny of another part. Did we fight to free ourselves from the sway of a monarch only in order to come under the sway of consumerism or militarism? Similarly, in one's personal life, does one struggle to become free from one craving or fear only in order to come under the sway of another?

VERTICAL DEMOCRACY

In order to re-establish the idea of democracy, there needs to be a sense that the whole is more than the sum of its parts, that the whole exists at a higher level than the parts. This is, if you like, vertical democracy; what we are now suffering from is horizontal democracy, a view of society in which the value of the whole is purely quantitative. However, an error is no less an error when it reflects the view of everyone than when it reflects the view of the few. In order to re-mythologize democracy, there has to be a conviction and an understanding that the mind of the community, the general will, is in some sense higher than the mind of any individual or party.

The point is that the whole, unity, is—metaphysically and psychologically—*mind*. The horizontal whole is merely a container, but the vertical whole—which includes the horizontal—is a governing, all-penetrating *mind*. Such is the interior meaning of the whole, as expressed by the great wisdom teachings of the world when they speak of the great self behind the ego.

Everything that Jefferson represents can be brought under this heading of democracy as the communal self, the self that is higher and deeper and more whole than the social individuality of any one person or party. Seen in this way, the American ideal of democracy begins to vibrate on the same frequency as the ancient, spiritual ideals of community as the vessel for the reception of higher universal forces. Every great teaching in the history of the world—and not only Christianity—has been brought forward with one or another version of this ideal of community. At the same time, it is possible to say that there is no ideal in human history that is more easily distorted. Again and again, history shows us examples of this distortion: totalitarianism in its countless forms, including forms that are specifically American. Recall that only fifty years after the birth of the American nation, its greatest observer, Alexis de Tocqueville, warned of the danger to America of what he termed "the tyranny of the majority."

The ideal of the democratic, communal self is as strong an American ideal as that of individualism. But it is rarely spoken of explicitly in the writings or pronouncements of the Founding Fathers. We have to find it in between the lines of what they said and at the root of how they behaved. There is a God for Jefferson, for Franklin, for Washington, for Lincoln. It is a higher power that acts within the individual and within the nation— nation here understood not only as a sociopolitical entity, but as a community of souls. This God is not the God of any one church or sect or religion. But it is God in a most meaningful sense—that which is ultimately real and beneficent and powerful in the universe and in the course of human life. This God acts within the individual by means of, and supported by, the community.

The renewed interest in the general form of this idea—in certain respects, what is termed "communitarianism" reflects this interest—should not blind us to the danger of treating the notion of the communal self in a purely horizontal fashion. The communal self of Jeffersonian democracy is not simply the "majority" or the "consensus" in the usual meaning of these terms. The communal self is the mind of the whole; it is unquestionably a mystical reality in the authentic sense of the term "mystical"—that is, unknowable by the ego-driven perceptions of individual men and women or by parties and factions representing ego-driven needs and wants.

On the other hand, to speak of the communal self of Jeffersonian democracy in a "vertical" fashion—as a higher, more spiritual reality—is if anything more dangerous In that such characterizations tend toward totalism, totalitarianism, tyranny, the "false king" of the legends of old. This "false king," the usurper king of spiritual allegory, represents the tyranny of the entrenched ego pretending to be the legitimate ruler of the inner "republic," aided in its rule by powerful and violent forces within the human psyche—what Plato spoke of as the "warrior" element within the self. The communal self of democracy must not be so understood that it leads back to the very thing that the American revolution sought to overthrow—the tyranny of monarchy or something like it not only in the economic and political sphere but in the inner world as well, the world of the mind and will of the individual.

Our inquiry has brought us to the culminating question of the American soul: the question of community and nation. What kind of culture, what kind of organization of human relationships does "America" represent? What do we need from each other? What do we owe each other?

What emerges from this inquiry is the notion that America can neither be understood or endure as a purely external, social, political, economic entity. Nor can human life itself so be understood or endure. Nor can America be understood or endure as a religious or purely "spiritual" entity, unconnected to power and action in the world of matter, power, money and physical force. This vision of a religious or mystical America holds no real connection to the obvious facts of life on earth within which each one of us lives and dies.

Two Americas; Two Democracies

We come to the conclusion that there are two Americas. And it is Jefferson who leads us to that conclusion. There are two Americas and two democracies.

There is the democracy of external order and action: the government of men and women living in the material world, the political world, the world of physical force. American democracy, under the light of Hamilton as well as Jefferson—under the light of nearly all the framers of the Constitution—broke free of political tyranny in order to establish a form of government that maximized individual liberty for every individual. Of course, there were and still are classes of people who do not receive the same degree of liberty and opportunity. The government of the nation is such that there continues to be movement, and there will always be movement, toward establishing liberty and equality for the people. This process is jagged and often violent; it is confused and sometimes so imperfect as to approach the evils in reaction to which it was originally born. But this movement still exists and still can exist—the movement toward a greatly beneficent quality of individual liberty. It is a rare quality in any nation or people of historical record.

But even this degree of external democracy could not exist and will not exist without the process of self-development in individual men and women. Individuals within our democracy cannot conduct their government without the development of their essential nature as human beings. Jefferson and many others identified this process of self-development with the education of the mind. But for Jefferson the education of the mind was only part of the necessary process of individual self-development without which external democracy would inevitably fail or turn into what de Tocqueville warned against under the phrase "the tyranny of the majority."

THE DEMOCRACY OF DESIRE AND THE DEMOCRACY OF CONSCIENCE

There exists another democracy that initiates and guides this movement of self-development. The second democracy, this second America, is not the democracy of personal preference; not the democracy of desire, but the democracy of conscience. Jeffersonian democracy symbolizes the possibility of both democracies existing one within the other, one allowing the other to flourish, each in its own way and at its own level. Hamiltonian or pragmatic, political democracy is one-dimensional, however glorious it may be in its own right as compared to nightmarish forms of gross political tyranny. But Jeffersonian democracy's ultimate aim is to protect the interior democracy. External democracy without spiritual democracy will otherwise inevitably destroy itself and the people within it.*

Can men and women come together and work together under the form of spiritual democracy—that is, toward the mutual goal of a progressive interior opening to conscience? This is the great question of our culture, and of our era: how to preserve and support external liberty in order to work together toward interior liberty? How to see external democracy as an echo or symbol of the inner democracy? May we not look at Jefferson from this perspective, taking his views about the education of the mind, the importance of living in relationship to the land, and the commandments to attend to one's neighbor as a call to search for spiritual democracy within political democracy? We shall return to these questions.

---

*This was the message of Plato in the much-misunderstood section of *The Republic* (Book VIII) where he mercilessly criticizes democracy as a form of government. In fact, what he is attacking is only the democracy of desire.

FIVE

INDIVIDUALITY:
A MEDITATION ON
THE FACE OF LINCOLN

T his face was placed before us when we were very young. We were told he was a great man. We were also told wonderful things about Washington and Jefferson and, in my household, Franklin D. Roosevelt. But only with Abraham Lincoln did we actually sense greatness. I was drawn again and again to his face.

We were told about his great deeds—freeing the slaves, holding the nation together. We were given the Gettysburg Address to memorize and study. But it was not what he did or said that astonished me. It was what was in his face.

We were told about his honesty, his humble beginnings, his simplicity—the whole legend of Lincoln. But the legend did not move me. It was his face. But I didn't know why. And of course I was not alone in this; I don't think any of us knew, even as we grew up, what it was about Lincoln—because none of us really understood what it was about man that was, or could be, great. The ideal of individuality, as a concept, as a word, just grazed the surface of it and then slid off into other things—having to do with what a man or woman thinks or says or does; or having to do with his or her courage or honesty or ability to sacrifice. But for many of us, none of that is exactly what drew us to Lincoln. Or perhaps I should say that all of Lincoln's virtues drew their meaning from something that emanated from his face.

Why? In the answer to this question lies the deeper meaning of the ideal of individuality that was such a beacon to the creators of this country. In the answer to this question lies the deeper understanding of selfhood that forms the basis of the idea of America.

INDIVIDUALITY AS PRESENCE

There exists a remarkable series of paintings from the Egypt of the first centuries after Christ. Known as the Fayum portraits, they are mainly close-up frontal representations of young men and women looking straight out from the surface of the painting with large, dark eyes and with faces that have a beauty and a power that are mysteriously simple. Some scholars see these portraits as the forerunners of the tradition of icons that so marks the sacred art of Eastern Christianity. But we need bring no associations about religion to these faces. To look at them is to see normal human beings. In these faces there is no fear, no tension, no ambition, no self-pity, no sentimentality. Yet they are full of feeling and intelligence. In these faces there is little or nothing of egoism; yet they are intensely individual. They are not "saints"; there are no religious trappings at all in these paintings. These are men and women of mundane society. All one can say of them is that they are *present*. And it is utterly compelling. There are no lies in these faces.

PHOTOGRAPHS

I now have before me a book of Lincoln photographs.[81] It is not easy to look at them freshly and honestly, so overcrowded with familiar associations is this face. What helps is that this particular collection also contains numerous photographs of Lincoln's family, friends and associates. I remind myself that I am looking for the root meaning of the ideal of individuality that lies at the heart of the American experiment. I know—I sense—that a key to this ideal is in the face of Lincoln.

Here is a portrait of Stephen Douglas, Lincoln's opponent in the senatorial election of 1858. Every student of American history learns about the dramatic series of debates between the two men revolving around the slavery issue. But no sense is ever given of what kind of man Douglas was—apart, perhaps, from the characterization of him as a gifted orator and a seasoned, clever campaigner—or the physical description of him as the exact opposite of Lincoln: short, broad-shouldered, compactly built, known as "The Little Giant."

My first response to Douglas's face is one of surprise. It is so human, so vulnerable, so . . . *young.* It is the face of a man who wants something, driven, earnest. A man who is *trying.* It is a face, as I feel it, of a persona, a defiant child masquerading as a man. And next to the portrait of Douglas is a full-length photo of him. Again I am surprised, but I am not sure why. I feel the body explains something. It is as though the body is ignorant—if it is possible to speak in this way of a human body. The posture of the body is driven by the huge head . . .

On the opposite page is Lincoln, age 49. He has not yet attained the political success that he craves. Yet the portrait and the full-length photo do not seem to be the picture of a man of ambition. The body of Lincoln and the face of Lincoln are not just different from those of Douglas by obvious factors of height and weight and posture and expression. There is something *entirely* different in Lincoln. He is a man—like Douglas—driven by ambition, by a desire—but for *what?* He has not yet been elected president. He has not yet become the most powerful man in America; he has not yet suffered the agony of the Civil War. He has not yet gotten all that he wanted and more, only to discover that all along he has wanted something else, something that has no name in the world of politics and society and war and triumph and defeat. Why does the body of Lincoln already seem so free and the face already so quiet, even with its intensity?

I bring myself back to my question about the real meaning of individuality and to another book.[82] Here are two photographs of General Grant taken just around the time Lincoln gave him the main responsibility for conducting the war. A face and body much more mobile than what we see in Douglas, but wholly outward-directed, the sense of an animal, alert, ready to leap, ready to strike; yet in the eyes a child who could easily be hurt, easily cry, ready to feel like a very good boy or to sink into self-pity.

I look now at one of the later photos of Lincoln taken probably around the same time as the photo of Grant. It is April 1864. The war by now has gone far, far beyond what anyone expected. Far, far more death and horror and danger to the republic. Only Lincoln seems able to contain all the death and anguish of the war, all the demons that have been unleashed. His posture is contained, his body seems to contain all that passes in his inward-directed face and eyes. And I see that it is Lincoln's *body* that gives his face such force. The face alone, yes, it is strong, perhaps even spiritual; but with the body, the relaxed body (a grown-up's relaxation, not a child's, not an animal's), everything in the face is rendered more objective; the qualities one feels in the face are verified, rendered part of nature, organic.

Looking at Lincoln in this way, one begins to suspect that over the years the ideal of individuality which lies at the root of the idea of America has become infantilized. The corruption of individualism we now so often see in our culture is a species of arrogance that confirms itself by excluding others and begets conflict with others, opposition, and fear.

To be truly oneself, to be uniquely oneself is to be *I*. This is a state of being that has nothing to do, at root, with this or that unusual or unique subjectivity, this or that unique set of psychosocial characteristics, this or that egoistic affirmation of oneself in opposition to or in comparison with the other.

Every human being is unique in the sense that we receive different material in our education and through the environment in which we develop. Deep individualism does not mean glorifying such differences—that is to trivialize the idea. The point is that to be one's self, one's own unique self, independent of social conditioning, is to participate in the force of *I* that forms the essential nature of every human being. When and to the extent that all the psychosocial aspects of ourselves are irradiated by this force, then a human being, an individual, exists.

Could it be that we glimpse this possibility of individuality in Lincoln's face and that somewhere we joyfully accept the prospect of abandoning our immature idea of individualism?

MASKS

Here are photographs of Edwin M. Stanton, Lincoln's secretary of war; William H. Seward, his secretary of state; William Fessenden, secretary of the Treasury. Here are Lincoln's two successive attorneys general. Here is his great friend Joshua Fry Speed. Here is his son, the distinguished Robert Todd Lincoln, in his mature years as minister to England. Here is Lincoln's successor, Vice President Andrew Johnson, and here is his predecessor, James Buchanan, fifteenth president of the United States. Under Buchanan's picture, the book's compiler writes:

> James Buchanan, outgoing President, looking tired and woebegone
> when, after four years of vacillation and compromise, he turned over
> his great office to Lincoln. Buchanan had failed utterly to meet the
> challenge of South Carolina's secession.[83]

And it seems true enough: Buchanan's face and posture seem to indicate a resolve and strength of character that are strangely non-functional; he seems, as a man, a system of habits, even good habits, that stands in front of something immeasurably greater than he is and which it can hardly even see, far less respond to. Personally, I do not see fatigue in his face, but rather a sort of saddened, blinded resolve. I see a mask.

But isn't that what we see in all these photographs darkened by time?

Don't we see men and women whose masks are uncomfortably obvious when compared to the face of Lincoln? Stanton: "I am firm and strong"—a mask. Seward: "I serve and obey and will uphold the good"—a mask. Patriarchically bearded Secretary of the Navy Gideon Welles: "I will brook no compromise"—a mask. General in Chief of the Union Army George B. McClellan: "Honor above all"—a mask.

It is important to remember that photographic portraits in that era required that the subject tiresomely sit and wait without moving for long stretches of time. The camera, therefore, does not capture the impression of the moment as it can do today, the fleeting smile or flash in the eyes; the sudden look that sometimes appears for a moment between familiar postures. No, here the camera records what the man or woman has worn all their lives under every other smile or frown. It is said, for example, that Lincoln's good humor and playfulness never appear in his photographs.

These old photographs can therefore represent for us the individual stripped to some small degree of his or her "individuality," in the contemporary sense of the term—the fleeting impulses, the "charm" that one sustains for short moments and in immediate reaction to some stimulus. Of course, a great photographer can see through all that and, in one instant, give us the essential person behind the passing facades. But in these old photographs, *time* is the photographer. Time always speaks the truth.

And yet, in these photographs, Lincoln appears intensely individual, intensely alive and singular. This face is a face within which we *sense* the possibility and the right of a man to say *I*. We do not sense that, I suggest, when we look at the other photographs.

The True and the False Individualism

Obviously, the founders of our country did not fight and die for the right to be selfish and self-involved, nor did they make holy cause of the childish impulse to have no constraints upon ourselves, to get just what we like or want whenever or however we want it. They did not risk so much just so that a man or woman could live and act independently of obligation to society. To sense the individuality in the face of Abraham Lincoln is to sense how far we have gone from the true ideal of individualism. Can we recover it?

The American historian Page Smith asks: "If there is such a thing as a uniquely American consciousness, from whence was it derived?" The most fundamental force in the shaping of the American character, he writes, were "those ultimate views of the meaning of the universe and our relationship to it that are perhaps best comprehended under the word 'religion'—and religion was the key." More specifically, it was the reformed faith of Protestant Christianity.

> The beginning of the new man, therefore, may literally be traced to the beginning of the Protestant Reformation itself in 1517, when Martin Luther nailed his ninety-five theses to the church door in Wittenberg, Germany. . . . Luther was not content simply to attack the grossest abuses of the Roman Church and a decadent papacy. He struck at some of the basic dogmas of the Church. . . . And—perhaps most significant in its later effect on the New World—Luther held that *the individual was wholly responsible for his own salvation.*[84]

According to Smith, American individualism is principally a spiritual ideal, pertaining to one's relationship to God. We may well ask how this ideal comes to be extended beyond the spiritual realm to the socioeconomic and political spheres of life. What is the relationship between an individual's struggle to listen to God and his or her desire for social or material well-being or satisfaction in any of its forms? Is there a relationship at all between the call to become oneself under the eye of the Creator and the striving to be "original" or "untrammeled"?

This is not a rhetorical question. There is an important issue here of understanding the deep dynamics of spiritual individualism and how it can manifest without institutional "religion," as it seems to do in the character of Lincoln. At the same time, we need to discriminate between the nonreligious but deeply authentic individualism of the American soul and the possible degeneration of the ideal of individualism into self-indulgence or self-righteous moralism.

Following Page Smith further:

> Luther and Calvin, by postulating a single person entirely responsible for the state of his own soul, plucked a new human type out of [the] traditional protective context, and put him down naked, a reformed man in a reformed world. Both Luther and Calvin insisted that the most crucial aspect of the individual was his responsibility for his own spiritual state. This doctrine of the "priesthood of all believers"— each man his own priest—meant of course new burdens for the individual psyche, but it also meant remarkable new opportunities as well. Reformed congregations . . . established their own churches, managed their own affairs, chose their own ministers. There were no popes or bishops—no church hierarchy. The importance of this transformation was that it produced not only an individual, but a highly introspective, aggressive individual, who was able to function remarkably well outside these older structures that had defined people's roles and given them whatever power they possessed. To put it another way, Luther and Calvin invented the individual, and it was just such individuals—secure in their relationship to God and confident of their own powers—who dared stand up for their rights as Americans when they felt that the mother country was infringing on those rights.[85]

We cannot emphasize too strongly that at its origin American individualism is a spiritual ideal; it is not primarily social nor economic nor—in the familiar sense—psychological. But to say it is a spiritual ideal is not enough. One tends to hear that word, "spiritual," and associate it with what we are generally familiar with as religion—belief systems, theology, allegiance to doctrine or forms of behavior. But to believe in a religious doctrine in itself implies little or nothing about the state of the soul. It all depends on how the belief is held. Inwardly, one can believe in a religious doctrine in such a way that the doctrine serves the ego. Conversely, it is possible to turn away from all religious doctrine, yet inwardly be freer and more open to experiential contact with the actuality that is called God. Spirituality is not necessarily the same thing as religiosity. The former has to do with the state of the soul; the latter often refers mainly to beliefs, opinions or behavioral patterns. It may seem paradoxical, but the study of the great teachers and guides of the world often reveals an individual's spiritual force manifesting as a rejection of "religion."

The face of Lincoln draws us to ponder this meaning of spirituality as the main heritage of American individualism. If Luther's struggle turned into Lutheranism, very well, that is how religions form, and perhaps it is very good. If George Fox's raw experience of God's presence turns into Quakerism, also very good, and in the same sense. If the presence in the person of Socrates becomes Platonism; if the being of the remarkable manual laborer of late antiquity, Ammonius Saccas, becomes eventually the Neoplatonic religion, systematized through the writings of his pupil Plotinus; if the Zen master's pupils create Zen Buddhism; well, it is the way all religions, rituals and forms of human life appear for all the good and bad that these forms support. But at the heart, at the origin of all these religions or schools, there is the experience of individual presence—the conscious presence that is as yet uncaptured by forms of thought, language or social organization. That there should exist at the center of the American culture the ideal of such a man, such a human being, is not unusual in the history of nations and cultures. That this man should have been the most politically powerful man in the nation—*that* is remarkable. The central icon of our culture is a man of individual presence who is also immensely effective and engaged in all the outer forces of life—war, power, money, action, calculation, love and hate, negotiation, compromise—the whole world of the senses and the ego. The most powerful man in the United States and therefore, by then, already one of the most powerful men in the world: that this should have been a man of individual presence—*that* is remarkable.

I do not know how to measure Lincoln against figures and legends such as Luther, Socrates, Moses. We can only say, with some degree of certainty, that his face calls us to the whole question of individuality as a conscious presence that transcends the ordinary meanings of the word "individualism."

It has become fashionable to criticize American individualism as narcissistic in relation to the social demand to act for the common good. There is the materialistic narcissism of consumerism; there is the psychological narcissism of New Age self-development; there is the narcissism of political and social apathy. Against such "narcissism" is placed the duty to participate in the governance and needs of the community. The figure of Abraham Lincoln entirely eclipses this familiar dichotomy between individualism and social responsibility. It does so, in part, by making us question our individual consciousness in the very social actions we feel obliged to perform. Of what real value are actions undertaken blindly and imitatively? Or, worse, violently, self-righteously, perversely, hypocritically? Yet act we must, now and here in just this world and at just this time. The face of Lincoln is not the face of a solitary or a recluse. Or perhaps we should say that yes, it is the face of a solitary, who in his time was, paradoxically, perhaps the world's greatest and chief agent of action.

BEYOND "ETHICS"

We are now standing in front of the paradox of the ideal of democracy: the juxtaposition of the obligation to act and the obligation to become a true individual. The juxtaposition of the duty to my neighbor and the duty to myself. In order to address this question we need to see more clearly why it is futile to hold up social duty as man's chief responsibility in life. We need to see that there is something higher in human life even than ethics and morality in their usual interpretation and that, in fact, without this something higher, ethics and morality themselves eventually lose their meaning and often turn into their own opposites. How often have we not witnessed those most heinous crimes of man against man being perpetrated under the name of social justice and responsibility? The figure of Lincoln allows us to open this troubling issue in a vein and in an imagery that are uniquely American and modern, without our having to have recourse to religious language that for many of us has lost its authenticity.

Speaking just after the death of Lincoln, Ralph Waldo Emerson remarks:

> How slowly . . . he came to his place. All of us remember—it is only
> a history of five or six years—the surprise and the disappointment of
> the country at his first nomination by the convention at Chicago. . . .
> And when the new and comparatively unknown name of Lincoln was
> announced . . . we heard the result coldly and sadly.

Yet

> He is the true history of the American people in his time. Step by step
> he walked before them; slow with their slowness, quickening his
> march by theirs, the true representative of this continent; an entirely
> public man.[86]

An "entirely public man"? What could that mean when his silence and inner force were so remarkable?

Here is Woodrow Wilson, speaking in 1909 on the occasion of Lincoln's one-hundredth birthday. He is placing Lincoln alongside the great figures of history born in the same year: Darwin, Poe, Chopin, Tennyson. "And then our Lincoln," says Wilson. And here we find Wilson responding to Lincoln in precisely the same way we respond to the face of Lincoln when his photograph is held next to those of his contemporaries:

> And then our Lincoln. When you read that name you are at once
> aware of something that distinguished it from all the rest. There was
> in each of those other men some special gift, but not in Lincoln. *You
> cannot pick Lincoln out for any special characteristic.* . . . He does not seem
> to belong in a list at all; he seems to stand unique and singular and
> complete in himself . . . it is as if he contained a world within him-

self. And that is the thing which marks the singular stature and nature of this great—and, we would fain believe typical American. Because when you try to describe the character of Lincoln you seem to
be trying to describe a great process of nature. Lincoln seems to have
been of general human use and not of particular and limited human
use. *There was no point at which life touched him that he did not speak back
to it instantly its meaning.*[87]

These words of Wilson could serve, in any tradition and in any culture, as a
description of the quality which we may call human presence. Only it is expressed here in the language of America and with an icon that is strictly
American. If we have found it also in the Fayum paintings, we may also find
it in countless portrayals of inwardly developing men and women of all
traditions—in graphic representations of their faces, in legendary or literal
accounts of their actions and responses to life. It does not matter to what *degree* Lincoln may have possessed this quality of simple, pure presence; it
matters only that his face and his life can communicate the idea and the possibility of it to us as Americans, as modern Western men and women.

   Continuing with Woodrow Wilson:

We wonder what the man might have done, what he might have
been, and we feel there was more promise in him when he died than
when he was born; that the force was so far from being exhausted that
it had only begun to display itself in its splendor and perfection. No
man can think of the life of Lincoln without feeling that the man was
cut off almost at his beginning. . . . There is something absolutely
endless about the lines of such a life. And you will see that that very
fact renders it difficult indeed to point out the characteristics of a man
like Lincoln.[88]

Wilson is struggling to speak of what we, with the same difficulty, have been
calling Lincoln's quality of presence. Our language, in fact, has lost the words
it may once have had for this quality, and we must resort to complex juxta-

positions of terms that in certain respects seem contradictory or unrelated to each other. Or, perhaps, we may be able to find the poetic or mythic mode of evoking this quintessential human quality of *being*. It is out of this quality that the capacity for deep moral action arises. Such is the revolutionary teaching of all the great masters, as when the prophets of Israel say from God that before all outward obedience, what is required of man is an understanding heart; and as when Jesus speaks of the complete primacy of an inner transformation of mind (*metanoia*) or as when Socrates urges man's first priority to be setting in order the *inner republic* of the soul. Again, it is not a question of ranking Lincoln at a spiritual or intellectual level with any other world figure. It is principally a matter of allowing him to serve as the American icon of this forgotten but central meaning of human individuality.

Here again is Woodrow Wilson, speaking of the relationship between virtue and being:

> We say that [Lincoln] was honest; men used to call him "Honest Abe." *But honesty is not a quality. Honesty is the manifestation of character.* Lincoln was honest because there was nothing small or petty about him, and only smallness or pettiness in a nature can produce dishonesty. Such honesty is a quality of largeness. It is that openness of nature which will not condescend to subterfuge, which is too big to conceal itself. Little men run to cover and deceive you. Big men cannot and will not run to cover, and do not deceive you. Of course, Lincoln was honest. But that was not a peculiar characteristic of him; that is a general description of him. He was not small or mean, and his honesty was not produced by any calculation, but was the genial expression of the great nature that was behind it.[89]

CHARACTER

It has been some time since our culture has spoken of the idea of character in this sense, as that force of human presence which lies at the root of all virtues. The idea of character has been dissolved into the modern psycho-logical idea of personality where all functions and manifestations are either socially conditioned or biologically inherited and where there is no room for *consciousness*, understood as a metaphysically unique and elevated force which can permeate and direct the bio-social aspects of human nature.

> Then we may also say of Lincoln that he saw things always with his own eyes. And it is very interesting that we can pick out individual men to say that of them. The opposite of the proposition is, that most men see things with other men's eyes. And that is the pity of the whole business of the world. Most men do not see things with their own eyes.

We have come full circle to the idea of individuality. How much more res-onant, metaphysically, it now sounds. To see things with one's own eyes means to see things from deep within one's own consciousness, one's own self, one's own *I*. It does not mean simply to have perhaps idiosyncratic opinions and reactions to which one holds fast regardless of what the com-munity believes. The American ideal of individualism thus links to the an-cient, timeless vision of personhood—that consciousness in a man or woman which is independent of both culture and biology. The Zen Buddhists speak of this as one's "original face." I suggest that for Americans this great idea is represented by the face of Lincoln.

LOVE AND DETACHMENT

And now, unexpectedly, a connection emerges to another of the most pro-found elements of the ancient vision of man: the idea of impersonal love, an idea represented by the word "impartiality" or the often misunderstood Oriental concept of non-attachment, an ideal which we shall try to uncover in the American love of justice.

For now, however, let us simply acknowledge that this quality of detachment is an essential component in our attraction to the figure of Lincoln. Here again is Woodrow Wilson. Speaking of Lincoln's gifts as a wit and raconteur, Wilson seems to come upon Lincoln's detachment almost by surprise. And, of course, it must be a surprise for any of us to see the *mysterious interrelationship between detachment and its seeming opposite, love.*

> But one interesting thing about Mr. Lincoln is that no matter how shrewd or penetrating his comment, he never seemed to allow a matter to grip him. *He seemed so directly in contact with it that he could define things other men could not define; and yet he was detached.* He did not look upon it as if he were part of it. And he was constantly salting all the delightful things he said, with the salt of wit and humor. I would not trust a saturnine man, but I would trust a wit; because a wit is a man who can detach himself, and not get so buried in the matter he is dealing with as to lose that sure and free movement which a man can only have when he is detached.[90]

The American historian Richard Hofstadter, whom no one ever accused of hero worship, sums up Lincoln's character and importance in the following lines, in their way as powerful and touching as anything ever written about Lincoln and expressing precisely this extraordinary blending in him of love and detachment:

> Lincoln's rage for personal success, his external and worldly ambition, was quieted when he entered the White House, and he was at last left alone to reckon with himself. To be confronted with the fruits of his victory only to find that it meant choosing between life and death for others was immensely sobering. . . . In one of his rare moments of self-revelation he is reported to have said: "Now I don't know what the soul is, but whatever it is, I know that it can humble itself." . . . *Lincoln's utter lack of personal malice during these years, his humane detachment, his tragic sense of life, have no parallel in political history.* . . . Lincoln was moved by the wounded and dying men, moved as no one

in a place of power can afford to be. . . . For him it was impossible to drift into the habitual callousness of the sort of officialdom that sees men only as pawns to be shifted here and there and "expended" at the will of others. It was a symbolic thing that his office was so constantly open, that he made himself more accessible than any other chief executive in our history. . . . Is it possible to recall anyone else in modern history who could exercise so much power and yet feel so slightly the private corruption that goes with it? *Here, perhaps, is the best measure of Lincoln's personal eminence in the human calendar—that he was chastened and not intoxicated by power.*[91]

III.

The Crimes of
America

The Angels of Eden

> So the Lord God banished him from the garden of Eden. . . . He
> drove the man out and stationed east of the garden of Eden the cher-
> ubim and the fiery ever-turning sword, to guard the way to the tree
> of life.
>
> — GENESIS 3:23–24

The crimes of America are as much a part of its meaning as its ideals, and to
embrace one without the other will lead us nowhere. We need a new and
more precise understanding both of what is possible for us and of how we
fail, a new understanding of what we ourselves actually are and of how
we actually can and must change. We do not need a moral fervor that per-
petuates human agitation; we do not need good deeds that only cover over
or reconfigure the pattern of man's injustice to man; no more than we need
a patriotism that closes our eyes to our own cruelty and fear or philosophizing that buffers the inexplicable truth that our actions monstrously betray
our ideals.

Obviously, no search for the meaning of America can turn away from
the fact that America was built on the destruction of its native peoples and
on the institution of slavery. These two massive crimes stand before us like
the angels of Eden with their flaming swords. No entry to a new understanding is possible without confronting them. To a great extent, the material success of America rests on these crimes and others like them.

The greatness of America as embodied in its Constitution and its legendary leaders stands in stark contradiction to these titanic immoralities. *But neither side of the contradiction eclipses the other.* Like unregenerate man himself, America is both good and evil at the same time. The meaning of America, like the meaning of human life itself, cannot begin to appear until these contradictory realities are seen squarely, without compromise, and with the feeling and the resolve that are due each of them. When the real feeling, the deep sensing and pondering of each side of this contradiction begin to appear in us, something entirely new may be glimpsed in our hearts and in our actions. But, for that to happen, we first need to stand in front of each side of the contradiction without impatience and without helpless reactions of guilt or pride. We need to apprehend what is good in America, but without self-inflation; and what is evil in America, but without self-flagellation. The great wisdom whispers to us from ancient times of another kind of confrontation with what is good and what is evil in ourselves; another kind of hope, compared to which that which we call optimism is dangerously naive and childish; and another kind of remorse, compared to which that which we call guilt is impotent and self-deceitful.

With the aim of allowing America to speak to us in a new way, we need now to look at both the American Indian and at slavery and racism. But is this really so difficult? Can there be any further response to the crimes and injustices of America beyond the work of correcting them through programs of social action? The American Indian has been brutally murdered, his religion desecrated and his land stolen: is there any further response to that beyond securing what land he has left and protecting his rights, his health and welfare and his culture? Black Americans have been enslaved and massively oppressed: is there any further response to this beyond working wholeheartedly to secure the civil rights and the full social and economic standing of black Americans?

We are asking about a completely new approach in our understanding of the failures of America, an approach that goes deeper than social programs which may only rearrange rather than repair man's injustice to man. But what could this be? And how even to think about it without appearing to put words in the place of deeds?

THE AMERICAN INDIAN

The Culture of the American Indian

Will we ever really know who he was? And can we ever feel what was done to him? Can we feel it in a way that goes deeper than guilt?

We can begin by looking more closely, albeit from outside, at the culture of the American Indian.

Inevitably, the first thing that strikes us is the American Indian's relationship to nature. We know now that there was nothing "primitive" about it; we are beginning to be aware of the subtlety and sophistication of American Indian religion, its symbolism, ritual and mythology which altogether embody a vision of the universal world as profound as anything offered by the Judeo-Christian tradition. And, with this awareness, we are all the more struck by the fact that this religion is immersed in the realities of the natural world. For us in modern society it is only in special moments that we directly sense meaning in nature. Experientially and psychologically, nature, virgin nature, is only part of our world. For the Indian, nature *is* the world. How is it that a people who lived directly in nature also exhibited extraordinary qualities of wisdom, generosity and deep social intelligence? Our forefathers, including many of the most enlightened among them, could not perceive this. Nor, really, can we. Our forefathers, including many of our heroes—our Washingtons, Franklins and Jeffersons—often regarded the Indian as a kind of child. Most of us are free of that sort of prejudice, but even we have great difficulty understanding how a direct relationship to nature, free of the typically modern form of discursive intellectuality, can be so inherently bound up with a greater wisdom and a clearer form of human love than our own. We do not understand the Indian's relationship to nature, perhaps because—even with all the knowledge that science brings us—we simply do not understand nature itself. Perhaps it is from the Indian that we can confront the fact that we do not understand the earth—and what the earth really needs from us.

THE MEANING OF PEACE

Of all the features that characterize the Indian's vision of nature and reality, perhaps none is more mysterious and frequently overlooked or set apart than the emphasis he puts on what we translate by the word "peace." Speaking from my own past experience, which I am sure is quite common, I was never able to grasp the importance of that word, neither as a boy enthralled by the Indian's way of living, nor as I grew older and became a student of philosophy and the world's religions. I remember looking at pictures of Indians: the dark, stone-strong face of a chief or warrior, his body dynamic and still, his costume intricately and mystically wild, his eyes direct and unwavering. This was a *man:* why should he desire "peace"? Surely, it was *power* that he represented, the power of the storm and sky; and *wisdom,* the secrets of the animal and the forest; and *freedom*—from all social artifice; and *solitude,* his mysterious capacity to be with himself and with the powers of the wild; and *courage,* his capacity to withstand pain and suffering; and *silent force,* the power to move through nature without making a mark, to disappear into the forest beyond all discovery; and *cunning,* and *fighting skill* and *physical prowess* that could often defeat the heavy-handed genius of the white man. What could "peace" mean to such a man?

For many of us, the word "peace" evokes something static or dull, or some fantasy of endless pleasure or rest or safety. On a societal scale, it often means nothing more than political conditions that permit the unhindered pursuit of material goods and psychological satisfaction, which are certainly normal human goals when understood in a normal way. But in the conditions of the modern world these goals are not understood clearly at all. They are taken as ends in themselves, as the main source of human well-being. The condition of our lives in the modern world shows us that this perception is illusory. When an individual or a community or a nation takes personal gain of one sort or another as the basis of value, the end result is despair. Such is the teaching of the ancient wisdom: man is built to serve, consciously serve a purpose beyond himself, greater, higher than himself. It is not a question of morality in its conventional sense; it is actually more precise to call it a question of our physiology, our very neurological makeup: man is *built* to serve. Our well-being and our happiness depend on our capacity to become conscious individuals who are at the same time conscious instruments of a greater universal purpose.

Seen from this point of view, our usual conceptions of peace appear puerile, and what we call peace has very little relation to what was so valued under that name by the American Indian. For the Indian, peace is hugely dynamic and includes all the forces of life—in nature and in man. It includes, it does not exclude, what we often call "evil"; it includes, it does not exclude, struggle, suffering and sorrow; it includes the whole range of error and foolishness; it includes passion, tenderness, but also anger and defeat. And, paradoxically enough, it includes even war—of a certain kind and with a certain intent.

But what is it that includes all these things, and whatever it is, why call it peace? The answer to this question will help us see more clearly an essential aspect of the American Indian culture and will help us see what our nation killed when it killed the culture of the American Indian. We may perhaps feel guilt—even unbearable guilt—when we contemplate the death and destruction that were brought upon the Indian. But something in us that is deeper than guilt may be touched when we try to understand more completely what and who the American Indian was.

THE MEANING OF JUSTICE

For the American Indian—and this idea lies at the hidden root of every great spiritual teaching of the world—to be at peace means to be at peace with one's conscience. And to be at peace within the community or to live in peace with other nations is to submit to a rule of law that is the communal expression of conscience and that provides conditions within which an individual is free to listen for that voice within himself. The establishment of such conditions, the establishment of such law, requires an intelligence of a very high order—what is called "the intelligence of the heart." And to find such intelligence requires, in turn, an effort of exceptional people working together to respect each individual's fragment of truth until an objective, all-inclusive truth descends into the community from "above," that is, from the Great Spirit. Such an objective moral truth may be linked with the word "justice."

Justice is that which sees the place of everything—in ourselves, in our relationships, in nature and in the life of society. Justice not only sees the place of everything, it *feels* the place of everything. Justice is that which knows what to do to restore things to their right place and knows when and how to do it. But such justice does not necessarily conform to man's subjective predilections concerning what is fair and right.

The question is: How to think and live in a manner that conforms to cosmic law? How to think and live according to conscience, which is the voice of the universe within each man or woman? How to think and live in a manner that allows a relationship between the greatness of the cosmos and the needs of the earth and all that lives and *happens* on earth? It is the ancient and eternal question of man as the bridge between heaven and earth, between levels of being in the universe—man, the being of two worlds, two natures, two directions. Man the contradiction and man the reconciliation. The religion and culture of the American Indian rest on this perennial concept of the meaning of human life on earth. *To live at peace is to embrace life in all its aspects, all "four directions," all "the winds," all the creatures outside and within.* This is the basis of peace and the basis of the Indian's understanding of justice in nature and society. As we shall see, it was this understanding of justice and its necessary expression in human life that brought forward the great law of the Iroquois nations, which many observers now see in certain key respects as markedly similar to the American Constitution.[92] Could it be that just as our sense of the land and nature is bone deep in us because of the Indian, so equally is our sense of freedom and justice, which we rightly think of as intrinsically American? What is going on here? What did we destroy when we destroyed the Indian? And who are we that destroyed it? To what extent did the Indian form our nature deep down even as we destroyed his culture?

The Interdependence of Good and Evil

The opposite of this sense of peace and justice is that which divides and separates parts of reality and keeps these parts away from each other. Morality becomes "moralism" when it imposes a sense of good and evil that diminishes the interconnectedness of life. Certainly, there are things that must be destroyed, killed—*but only for the purpose of allowing the whole to restore itself.* Judgment that does not allow this restoration, judgment that keeps the good and the evil away from each other, is "moralism." It is often sanctimonious, self-righteous and, all too often, frightened and violent. The great wisdom has always seen the world as a fallen place partly because of this pervasive violence that seeks to destroy what it opposes without regard to objective law and justice. Such are the conflicts that pervade our fallen lives.

This teaching about the interdependence of "good" and "evil" is not to be found in the mainstream religious and ethical doctrines of European culture. The religious and moral doctrines that are familiar to us almost without exception support the radical separation of the good (however it is understood) and the evil (that which resists the good). Our moralism compels us to destroy. More often than not, mainstream religious and ethical moralism crystallizes the separation between parts of reality—in the form of dualisms such as mind and body; spirit and matter; man and nature; life and death. It is comfortable and habitual for the ordinary mind to perceive in this dualistic way.

THE PEACE THAT PASSES UNDERSTANDING

Beneath the surface of mainstream European religious and ethical moralism, however, there has always existed another teaching about the interconnectedness of good and evil, a teaching in which what is objectively good is the wholeness of reality and what is objectively evil is that which holds the elements of life apart from one another. In this teaching, exemplified in such "esoteric" doctrines as Kabbalism, alchemy, and Hermeticism, what appear to the ordinary mind as opposition and contradiction are understood to be elements of a unity that surpasses the habitual understanding of the ordinary mind. This unity—this reconciling interconnectedness—may be called peace, the peace that passes understanding. It is this vision of peace, and the corresponding sense of justice that springs from it, that characterizes the traditional teachings of the American Indian.

THE MEANING OF MONOTHEISM

It is ironic that the European culture has been so dominated by a dualistic moralism which it has so often imposed upon native peoples throughout the world. Ironic because at the very heart of Western religious doctrine is the pith and essence of this idea of wholeness and unity as the good. It is the very essence of the Judaic idea of monotheism—*one* God; one God who created *everything;* one God who maintains everything; one God who, as it is said in the Book of Isaiah, both makes peace and creates evil.[93] Right before our eyes this idea has existed as long as our traditions have existed. But very few of us see it anymore; very early on, our great idea of monotheism was interpreted in a way that establishes a nearly unbreakable dualism in the world: a sense that a part of creation, a part of human nature seen as evil, must be destroyed, without any hope of allowing the fundamental unity to restore itself. The great fathers of the Church, notably St. Augustine, fought against this kind of dualism, but seemingly to little avail.

THE PROBLEM OF EVIL

We are thus saddled with the so-called "problem of evil"—the insoluble philosophical, theological problem of how a good and omnipotent God could allow the existence of evil. The hidden doctrine of interconnectedness does not run up this theological and philosophical blind alley. In this hidden teaching, what we call evil—meaningless, brutal, cruel, insane emptiness of unredeemed pain and fear, the wastage of life on an individual and mass scale, man's titanic injustice to man, the "weeping and gnashing of teeth" of the spiritually or socially damned among us; in other words, so much of the evil of human life and especially human life in our era—the hidden wisdom teaches that this evil arises *because* man has attempted to exclude the force of "evil" from his life and his awareness. Wisdom teaches that when evil is so far separated off from good, its force grows and destroys the good in its unnatural isolation. This is true within the individual (in the form of unconscious forces that gather their destructive power in the darkness of unawareness) and within the community and within the life of a people or a nation where the unseen, unembraced forces of fear and resentment eventually assert themselves in the horror of murderous war (a kind of war that, it seems, the Indian only learned from the white man). Surely it is here that we must look for the roots of what we call racism; and it is here that we must look for the roots of the crimes of America. And when we find these roots—in ourselves and in our nation—we will pass beyond guilt to another kind of understanding, another kind of hope and resolve, another kind of sorrow.

WHAT WAS KILLED? WHAT CANNOT BE KILLED?

How did the Indian manifest and communicate this profound doctrine of objective peace and justice? Standing on the outside of this culture, which, however, is at the same time deeply in our American bones, we catch only glimpses of the modes and forms by which this vision of wholeness permeated his world, only glimpses of his art and ways of living. We need to listen very attentively to the still reverberating echoes of his teaching—its gravity and joy, its tears and laughter, its inner power and outer helplessness before the juggernaut of American military might. In the blinking of an eye, a great civilization was crushed by American guns and cannons, by overwhelming numbers of American soldiers, by incomprehensible modes of warfare—scorched earth, sustained siege, even the intentional spread of disease. It was crushed by the American sense of manifest destiny, fueled as it was by the peoples of Europe who were pouring out of their own native lands in search of a new life away from the Old World, which was convulsing in the intellectual, political and economic cyclone of modernity. When one adds to all these forces the one element that was most decisive—namely, America's awesome treachery, its astonishing pattern of broken treaties—the fate of the American Indian was sealed. Which was harder for the Indian to fathom—the white man's guns and warfare or his lack of honor? And what was harder for the Indian to resist—the white man's amazing baubles and whiskey or his false promises?

IDEAS LIVE IN PEOPLE

The civilization of the Indian comprised hundreds of tribes, scores of languages, countless images, symbols, rituals and *stories*—myths, legends and tales—by which the teaching of dynamic peace and care for the earth was transmitted to the people. The lack of a written record of these stories is of little account. The important fact is that these stories were *told;* the ideas they communicated were passed between people in the medium of a human exchange of attention and feeling. This is the principal way ideas were transmitted in the ancient world. Ideas lived only in people and only in the dynamics of face-to-face relationship. Only when the stories are told with understanding do they live, and only when the ideas are given to those who need them are their deeper meanings revealed to those who transmit them. This is the ancient law of the transmission of wisdom. In the act of giving and in the act of asking and listening, truth descends from above and is given to man.

DREAM AND VISION

It is necessary to emphasize this point. It is not simply the content and wit or depth of the stories that are important; of even greater importance is the means by which they were transmitted. And if we then ask ourselves how the Indian received his sometimes extraordinary knowledge of nature, we discover that it came to him not so much by our scientific methods of study, but largely through what we translate as "dreams." But "dreams" is a misleading word; the better word is "vision"—a knowing and a seeing that are given when the individual—*always with the support of the tribe* (the community or group)—prepares his inner world to receive it. Thus, in large measure, the entire culture of the Indian—his art, ritual, medicine, intimate knowledge of plants and animals, his world-view, his crafts and technics— came to him in a known inner state for which he worked to prepare himself.

A Culture Based on a Different State of Consciousness

Studying the Indian culture, we can come to the conclusion that—like every community or culture that deserves the name of "theocentric," every culture whose center of gravity is a sense of the sacred—the Indian culture was a culture resting on a *different state of consciousness* than does our modern civilization. This notion may astonish us and provoke a new kind of reflection on the true nature of the Indian civilization. This does not mean that every non-modern, non-Western society has operated at a different and perhaps more refined state of consciousness than our own. It only means that what we are beginning to value and appreciate in the Indian culture may be summed up by the possibility that the higher, more balanced state of awareness was, so to say, the "default position" of his entire society.

Nor, of course, does this mean that everything the Indian did was noble; nor does it mean that the Indian civilization did not have its own crimes and sins and fatal errors—we can be certain that it did, no less than our own. It only means—and this is a major thing—that his life circled around another kind of knowing and feeling, another source of understanding, another measure of action and ethics than does our own.

What Really Was Destroyed?

Our own modernity has lost its relationship to the wisdom tradition, the seeds of which were carried in the minds and hearts of many of those who came first to these shores from Europe but were forgotten in the material expansion and success of our empire. If we are seeking to re-mythologize America, it is to capture the last drifting seeds of this wisdom and re-plant them, as it were, in a soil—our earth—that is desperate to nourish them— soon, *now*.

The question now deepens as to what was lost in the assault on the culture of the American Indian and the incomprehensible murder of men, women and children. Not only was a way of life lost, but also a way of seeing—that is, *a state of being, a state of consciousness* higher than our own. Higher than our own and perhaps in some mysterious way, *less capable of defending itself against violence, lies and treachery.* Another kind of drama begins to reveal itself, a drama we did not expect to encounter here, one with a strangely and disturbingly familiar resonance: the drama of the destruction of the higher by the lower. A drama in which that which is closer to truth is pulled down and destroyed by—by what? By whom?

The myth of America begins to deepen now. Let us allow this deepening to proceed: it is a process, this deepening, that leads to an entirely new meaning of America and an entirely new kind of hope.

THE LEGENDS

Continuing, then, to look at the culture of the Indian, we may fasten our attention on the legends and the stories, which, amid all their variety, are pervaded by the sense of a mysteriously intimate relationship between good and evil, a mysterious conjunction of opposites. We can study this theme especially well in certain legends of the creation of the world that also show us the metaphysical basis of human society and government. When we hear these ancient stories of the creation of the world, we need to remember that they are telling us of something even more fundamental than the temporal origins of the universe; they are representing the nature of life itself, reality itself. When the legends of wisdom speak of *origins,* they are not speaking, as we do, only of beginnings in linear time but of a thing's essential, defining nature. "Once upon a time" means: "down deep, at the source, in the essence of things." If the Indian speaks of the conjunction of good and evil at the origin of the world and the social order, he is saying that life itself, reality itself, *is* a mysterious and intimate relationship between opposing forces. Law—in both its cosmic and political sense—is that which preserves this relationship and thereby preserves the dynamism of life.

The Two Brothers[94]

This is the tale as I have heard it told.

Toward the beginning of the vast Iroquois story of creation, the progressive diminishing of power and light in the eternal world necessitates the activity of a creator god whose task—for the sake of the universe—is to bring into existence the earth and human beings. This creator god is named, in the language of the Onondaga, *De'haĕ"'hiyawă''kho"*, which may be translated as "He Grasps The Sky With Both Hands." He is given that name when he is sent down to earth and is tested by being asked, "Do you know from where you have come, and to what place you will go when you depart from this place?" He answers, "I know from where I come, and that is the sky . . . I will not forget that. I will continue to grasp with both hands the place from where I came." The name of the creator thus represents the power to remember one's higher identity in the midst of action in the world.

But the creator is born with a twin brother, who then speaks as follows: "I am not thinking about the place from where I came. . . . It is sufficient that my mind is satisfied in having arrived at this place. . . . This place will become exceedingly delightful and amusing to the mind. . . . I trust in the thing which my father gave me, a flint arrow, by which I have speech. This I will use perhaps to defend myself so that I will not think of that other place." This twin is then named *O'ha'a,* "He Who Is Crystal Ice, He Who Is Flint." The twin brother, from then on referred to simply as Flint, or the Winter or Ice god, represents evil in the form of forgetfulness, intentional forgetfulness of the higher identity. Flint is self-justified absorption in the outer world. Few legends of the world's traditions make it so clear that the real root of all that we call evil is primal forgetfulness of our Selves.

A great and complex drama of creation ensues, but always and in everything the drama involves the dynamism of exchange between good and evil, the question of how close together they can become and how far apart they need to be. It is of special significance that the evil twin, Flint, sees the forms of life that his brother creates and attempts on his own to imitate him. At one point, Flint gathers all the animals created by his brother and shuts them in a cave. The power of forgetfulness and untruth, manifesting here as jealous egoism, exercises itself in the darkness (the cave) of unawareness. It was then, so the story goes, that He Grasps The Sky With Both Hands, troubled by the actions of his brother, sought to separate him from himself. But he soon realizes that it is only when Flint is cut off from the good that he actually tries to imitate his brother's work of creation. Cut off from the good brother, Flint tries to create birds, flowers and fruit. And this troubles the good brother even more. He Grasps The Sky With Both Hands now rescinds the act of separating himself off from evil and returns to his brother to see what he has done.

In fact, Flint has created not birds, but flies and bats; not the sunflower but the thistle; not fruit, but thorns—all that resists and stings and frightens. Seeing this, the good brother embraces his brother's work, giving all that Flint has made their proper names (that is, assigning them their proper role in the scheme of things) and declaring, "All this shall assist me. The flies shall assist me. The thistle will be food for small animals, the thorn will be food for game animals . . ." The mind of Flint was gratified.

But Flint goes on attempting to imitate the works of creation, and He Grasps The Sky With Both Hands comes to understand that it is right that he maintain a *small distance* from his brother, while at the same time keeping his attention upon him, neither letting him drift too far from his awareness, nor letting him blend with him. The good brother understands full well that Flint will forever attempt to destroy his rule.

THE CREATION AND MEANING OF HUMAN LIFE

It is at this point that human beings are created and where we are shown most clearly how the American Indian understood the meaning of man's life on earth.

He Grasps The Sky With Both Hands now considers that it would be good to bring to the earth a source of light and warmth. He turns to his own father who in turn sends him to the being who is described as the elder brother of his grandmother, that is, a being close to the source of the source of all creation.

Through a special ritual, He Grasps The Sky With Both Hands departs from the earth to ask the elder brother of his grandmother to bring daylight to the world. The ancient one answers, "It is a long time that I have watched for you to remember me. My eyes are on you and what befalls you. So now I am fully prepared to do that which has become a difficulty for you. On the underside of the sky present here, I will attach myself, and there I will start my journey for a certain distance, and then return to where I started. Then I will rest before I start again. To all the many things that you complete on the earth below, I will provide light and warmth during my journey. And that is how it will be as long as the earth below here will endure. . . .

". . . Truly, your brother is doing things which cause anxious thought. It is known that he will attempt to make a mockery of all things by trying to do the things that you are doing. You were right to separate a small distance from your brother. It will cause him difficulties. Be it known, during the time the earth below is present, your brother will attempt to destroy your rule."

When He Grasps The Sky With Both Hands returned to his lodge he began to create human beings. As soon as he had made the flesh of the human being, he meditated, and said, "It will result in good if the human being shall have as much life as I have life." So he took a portion of his own life, and put it inside the human being. And he took a portion of his own mind and enclosed it inside the head of the human being. And he took a portion of his own power to speak and enclosed it within the throat of the human being. And then, after that, he placed his breath in the body of the human being, and the human being then came to life, and he arose, and stood upon the earth present here. And then He Grasps The Sky With Both

Hands made another in the same manner as the one just completed, and she arose, and stood upon the earth present here.

Now He Grasps The Sky With Both Hands said, "I have completed your body and now you are able to stand upon and overspread the earth. Look to all that the earth present here contains. It is I who have completed it all and I will continue to give peace to your mind."

Just then he saw the Elder Brother come up over the horizon, and it was the first day and the daylight was beautiful and agreeably warm. He Grasps The Sky With Both Hands spoke again to the human being. "Look at the orb coming up over the horizon, and see that it is beautiful in causing light to be on the earth present here. It will be for you an ever-present object of thought, and also it will continue to give pleasure to your mind in that it will continue to warm the days that will come. Thereby, all that lives on the earth present here will continue to live."

Continuing to speak to the human being, He Grasps The Sky With Both Hands said, "Now you will travel about and know the earth present here and you will do so as long as the daylight will last. When the darkness falls over the earth present here, you will rest, you will stop. And so will it be for the animals that will be food for you. And now I have completed all that will be during the time that the earth present here will continue."

The story goes on and helps us feel who the Indian really was:

FLINT TRIES TO CREATE HUMANS

Because there was daylight, Flint now became aware of what was happening. Building a bark canoe, he traveled to his brother's lodge and saw all that He Grasps The Sky With Both Hands had completed. Returning to his own lodge, he decided that he too would make a human being and so he made a human being as he thought it should be. But when Flint commanded his creation to arise and walk, it only leaped away and immersed itself in water. "I must have made a mistake. I will try again." This time when he commanded the being to stand up and walk, it rose, walked, and climbed into a tree. Flint pondered the situation. "Perhaps I have made another mistake." So he tried again. This time, when commanded to rise and walk, the being did so. Flint watched and said, "Now that I have done this thing correctly, I will make another thing, a game animal for the human being's food." And he made that thing and when it stood up and walked, he called it a Deer. And he made another thing, which he called Bear.

"THAT IS NOT A HUMAN BEING"

Now, when Flint had left his brother's lodge, he had invited him to come visit him, and just at this moment He Grasps The Sky With Both Hands arrived at Flint's lodge. Flint, being proud of his creations, offered to show them to his brother. The two brothers walked together for a time and soon came to the water wherein rested the first human being that Flint had created. He Grasps The Sky With Both Hands looked, sat near the edge of the water, and spoke to the being.

"What manner of thing are you?" he asked.

The being cried out.

He Grasps The Sky With Both Hands continued to look and said, "Do walk." The being only leaped and again immersed itself in the water. Soon, however, it poked its head out. He Grasps The Sky With Both Hands turned to Flint, saying, "That is not a human being. It will be called *Mwa'en*, the Frog."

Flint replied, "Well, I have made another human being. Come see."

So the two went on and soon found the being who sat up in the tree. He Grasps The Sky With Both Hands looked, saying, "This is not a human being. He has a tail and fur grows on his body. It will be called Monkey."

The two brothers moved on and soon found a human being, sitting. He Grasps The Sky With Both Hands saw the being sitting on the ground, and asked, "What kind of thing are you?"

The being cried out and wept.

He Grasps The Sky With Both Hands turned to his brother. "It is not a good thing that you are trying to create beings," he said. "What you have made is not correct. This one will be called an Ape."[95]

Flint answered that there were still two beings to be seen.

"This one I call a deer, and the other is bear." He Grasps The Sky With Both Hands looked, and spoke. "This one is not a deer. It will be called the Wolf. And the other is not a bear. It will be called the Grizzly Bear."

At this key juncture of the story, He Grasps The Sky With Both Hands shows Flint the real human beings that he has created by mixing into their flesh and blood portions of his own life and mind. Seeing them, Flint asked his brother, "Do you have anything against my making two lives such as these which I have now seen?" He Grasps The Sky With Both Hands replied, "If this time you will use great care, and will exactly copy the form of the body of the human being, then it is possible that human beings will also dwell upon the separated island wherein is your lodge."

Greatly pleased, Flint departed and began his work. He arrived at his island and there, at the water's edge, began to make a human being out of the foam floating on the water that washed upon his island from some distant place. So he gathered the foam and with great care fashioned the body. As soon as it was done he attempted to cause it to live, but it did not come to pass. "I will ask my brother to help me," Flint said to himself. "I will ask him to help me cause this being to come to life. Have I not done much work to bring about peace on this earth present here? And didn't he agree to let me make a human being?"

As Flint prepared to cross once again the narrow channel that separated him from his brother, he was startled to see that He Grasps The Sky With Both Hands had already crossed the water and was coming toward him. Flint greeted him, saying, "I have come to meet you because I desire your aid in causing the human being to live."

He Grasps The Sky With Both Hands agreed and went with Flint to the place where the human being was. He Grasps The Sky With Both Hands took a portion of his own life and put it inside the human being. So also he took a portion of his own mind and enclosed it in the head of the human being. And so also a portion of his own blood and enclosed it inside the flesh of the human being. And so too did he take a portion of his own power to see and enclosed it in the head of the human being. So also he took a portion of his power to speak and enclosed it in the throat of the human being. Finally, he also placed his breath in the body of the human being. Just then the human being came to life, and he arose, and stood upon the earth present here.

Turning to Flint, He Grasps The Sky With Both Hands spoke. "I now have aided you in this matter. And now, I see that *this* human being will become hostile to me. What will come to pass because of that?"

Flint quickly replied, "Since both you and I took part in completing this human being, let both you and I have control over it. In that way you will have something to say concerning these human beings who will dwell on this earth." He Grasps The Sky With Both Hands agreed to that, adding: "That human being whom I alone created, who is the first human being to become alive on this earth—we shall call him real human being. And this human being whom you and I have now created and is now alive on this earth, we shall call him the hatchet maker, the bringer of strife."

Time passed—and here the legend speaks in powerfully symbolic language of the creation of the moon and how its influence was under the sway of Flint and the forces of evil, but was finally put in the service of good by the good brother. Thereafter the two brothers departed from the earth, leaving only the influence of their separate minds. Before his first departure, He Grasps The Sky With Both Hands spoke to the two kinds of human beings and told them to recognize that two kinds of mind had come into being in the world above and on the earth present here and in human beings. "And when you human beings will be numerous, then I will return again." Then He Grasps The Sky With Both Hands and his brother Flint departed for the world above.

The human beings became numerous and, as he had said, He Grasps The Sky With Both Hands returned to the earth present here and instructed the human beings in the manner in which they should practice their ceremonies. He spoke to them, "All of you have an equal right to this which I have ordained. So then it will affect us all alike in that we will all have peace within our minds. Do not ever forget this, that in the days and nights to come a grave thing will come to pass if ever you forget peace. You will not continue to live if you forget peace. Nor will your children live. You must care and attend to one another as to your minds on this earth present here. I give all this instruction to you because my brother and I will disagree. I believe that my brother will let loose upon the earth present here that which will kill human beings. The time will come to pass when there will be great divisions between the minds of human beings, and there will be nothing but contentions, and the people will forget happiness, peace, and me."

He Grasps The Sky With Both Hands concluded, saying, "Then I will come again." And he departed for the world above. And it came to pass as He Grasps The Sky With Both Hands had said. Twice more he returned to the earth present here to instruct the human beings. These were the last words he spoke to the people:

"When you exhaust the days allotted to you, then you will depart from the earth present here and take the path that leads to the world above. If it be that you have lived your life as I have instructed you, then your path will lead to where I abide. And there you will see joy and peace and happiness. For in that place there is no illness, nor death, nor must one struggle hard for that which will allow one to live.

"But if your mind has been the mind of my brother, if you do that which is not right, and do not love each other and put peace above all things, then when you exhaust the days allotted to you, you will depart from the earth present here and your path will take you to the lodge where my brother dwells. And there you will see great suffering, and you will be famished, and you will be without liberty, and you will share the fate of my brother. I have confined him, and I have kindled a fire for him, and for this purpose I used his anger. This fire is hotter than any fire you have ever known; and this fire will burn eternally in that my brother even now desires to control all minds among human beings.

"Whichever mind you choose, you must obey it. I will not come again, for I have finished my three visits to the earth present here. Still again it may come to be that you will forget love and you will forget peace. So, the next time I will send another person who will aid you and he will aid me also. Only twice will I send this one to aid you in your mind. If a third time it comes to pass that you forget, then you will see what will come to pass. The things upon which you live will diminish so that finally nothing more will be able to grow. The earth will quake, and the monsters dwelling deep within the cavern will come forth. It will be my brother who will do all this, for he will be able to seduce the minds of all human beings and thus spoil all that I have completed.

"Now I leave the matter to you."

He Grasps The Sky With Both Hands departed and went elsewhere. Now the matter rests with all the human beings as to which mind will be manifest, and which path will be followed.

This is the legend as I have heard it told.

THE AIM OF AMERICA

We are hearing what is but one of many legends which show us the American Indian vision of human life. No less than the Judeo-Christian tradition, it speaks of man as a cosmically unique being obliged and gifted with the task of conducting the "mind of God" into the life of the earth. Here, no less than in the Judeo-Christian tradition or, for that matter, all the great spiritualities of the world, the *earth* is more than what we take it to be, more than an astronomically defined planet; the earth is the sphere within which all the forces of God's creation play themselves out, including the forces of stoppage and resistance (Ice, "The Winter God," "Flint"). And there is something necessary about these forces of resistance, as necessary as the serpent in the Garden of Eden, who was, after all, placed there by God himself. Americans who, even until quite recently, regarded the Indian as a mere "savage" or "child" did not see or could not bear to see the depth of refinement of the culture they were destroying. And perhaps even today it is hard for us to grasp that their legends, symbols and ritual practices and much of their customs and ways of life originated in minds of the same order as the minds through whom the Judaic and Christian religions were revealed and developed. Perhaps hardest of all for us to grasp is that their ways and customs directed them to a quality of experience, a state of consciousness through which alone the meaning of human life could be understood and through which alone one can experience the true impetus to live life intentionally and with the depth of feeling proper to a human being. Our own spiritual traditions were once based on the need for the same inner freedom, but over the centuries much of our religion has become automatized, and, in a certain sense, our culture actually has forgotten that human life is meaningless without practices and social conditions that support the search for interior freedom.

But . . . wasn't this the main hope in the social order created by the Founding Fathers? Strip away the chains of pride-bound religious language and forms; strip away the hollowed-out monarchies that oppressed the human body and mind; strip away the dead weight of the past and start again from zero to organize human society on principles geared to the search for truth and freedom—wasn't this the aim of America? Isn't this the American dream—and not its childish interpretation of owning many things and satisfying the desires of an uneducated body and an automatized mind? The miracle of the Constitution, the inspired structure of the American government: wasn't this once the hope of humanity just because it sought to base itself on the very laws by which God had ordered the universe? We know the answer is yes. The American government was to be a reflection on earth of cosmic principles through which men and women can live in peace in relation to a higher and all-encompassing reality. In encountering the Indian, were we in fact encountering an embodiment of our own ideals of freedom, unity and the search to live under nature's God? And, in fact, have we discovered this about the Indian only after we have all but destroyed him? What sort of response to *that* is required of us?

The Great Peace and the Iroquois Confederacy

Let us look now at the government and social order of the Indian—at how he understood law and society. We shall see in the Iroquois government many of our very own principles of liberty and democracy—principles which we may have imagined were invented solely by us. Let the legend continue to tell us who and what the Indian was.

He Grasps The Sky With Both Hands has left the earth, and the two-natured beings he created are unable to follow the good mind within them. The human beings cannot live in peace—peace understood not as a matter of external agreement, negotiation or rules of behavior, but as unity of mind and feeling, as "good thought" between nations, peace as a state of consciousness. The human beings are not able to live in a non-coercive society, in the climate of good will essential for the life of humanity. Instead of the mind of peace, there is only contention, conflict and battles between nations. There is no place, no structure, there are no conditions within which the forces of the earth and of man can confront each other in a way that allows a harmonizing, uniting and peacemaking force to act from within. We need to remember that it is just such conditions that define the ideal of the government created by our Constitution.

THE NEW MIND

True to his promise, He Grasps The Sky With Both Hands, the Creator God, sends "another person" to aid the human beings. His name is the Great Peacemaker, which is interpreted to mean "The Master of Things"—mastery through peace, understood as an energy to which all things joyously submit. Before the Great Peacemaker's birth, He Grasps The Sky With Both Hands reveals his name and mission in a dream to the Great

Peacemaker's grandmother. From the very beginning of this part of the legend, we are thus given to understand peace not as something passive, not as a mere absence of conflict, but as a force that can harmonize the actions and impulses of human life in all their multiplicity and opposition to each other. Peace—a unifying energy that paradoxically also allows each element to flourish in its individuality.

In the legend this force of peace is also called "the new mind." The Great Peacemaker is to bring the new mind to the tribes and nations, to all the human beings. The force called peace is, in the universe and in the individual, a quality of mind, *a conscious energy.* And it demands of man a new attitude within his own mind—and the legend tells us that this new attitude is joyously embraced the moment a human being has a taste within himself of the new mind. Throughout the legend, the tribes, after first doubting the message of the Peacemaker, are readily persuaded to join him.

A surface perception of this aspect of the legend is not enough; why should these proud nations and warriors so readily accept the message of peace? Not because they are afraid of war. The message is accepted not only in the hope of being freed of something negative, of being rid of fear for themselves and their people, but also because they glimpse something infinitely more honorable than war, infinitely more active and requiring a higher level of courage and sacrifice, and which shows them the real essence of their ideals of what it means to be human beings and to care for each other. This is peace as the field of life in all its vibrancy, peace as the call to serve what is far greater than oneself. Who would not agree to this "new mind," this good mind?

But the legend tells us there is one who does not accept it, a powerful wizard and chief of the Onondagas named Atotarho, without whose assent the Peacemaker's mission cannot succeed. The actual identity of Atotarho and the story of the struggle with him throw astonishing light on the meaning of the democracy created by the Iroquois Confederacy and on the mystical pragmatism that lies at the root of our own American democracy. But, as before, we need to take the time to listen as the story tells itself to us.

THE STONE CANOE

When the Great Peacemaker grew to manhood he built himself a canoe of stone and spoke to his grandmother and his mother, telling them his time had come to seek out other tribes and nations and bring the message of peace. "It is my business to stop the shedding of blood among human beings," he says. "I have built my canoe and I will now take to the rivers and lakes where the sun rises and not return to this place in this direction again."

"But the canoe is made of stone," says the grandmother. "It will not float."

"It will float," says the Peacemaker. "It will be a sign of the message that I bring."

From the very beginning, the legend thus speaks of the conjunction of incommensurables; the stone canoe glides upon the waters. Under the power of peace, matter and spirit blend.

The Great Peacemaker sets off and travels eastward, scanning the horizon for rising smoke. Day after day he sees nothing, for all the settlements are now hidden in the hills to protect themselves from the war parties plaguing the land. Finally, the figures of hunters are seen running along a barren shore in the distance. The Great Peacemaker turns toward them and, making land swiftly, he beaches his canoe and stands before them. "Go back to your settlement," says the Great Peacemaker to the hunters, "and tell your chief that a new and good message has come, the message of peace that is power."

When the tribal chief hears their news, he asks the hunters, wonderingly, "Who told you this?"

"He is called the Great Peacemaker in the world."

The chief is silent as he takes in the meaning of the name—the peace that is power in the world. Is it true? Is it possible? Can there really be such a new thing in the world? This first response of the chief is a critical element of the story, and were the tale to be told as it may have been meant to be told, one would want to take the time very carefully to portray this response, so that the listener could feel the call to an attitude of the mind toward the idea of a new kind of force that is meant to govern human life—just as, in their way, Penn and Washington and Jefferson and, yes, Franklin—and others, especially Lincoln—can be seen as embodiments of a faith in a unifying peacemaking power latent in the human mind and heart. The American Indian seems to have understood how important it is to put one's hope in just *this* kind of power, as opposed to the power of an imagined external god or, here on earth, what our Founding Fathers referred to by the term "monarchy." The Iroquois Confederacy was rooted in this deeper hope no less than our American Constitution.

Again, the chief asks the hunters, "Where did you see him?"

"On the Beautiful Great Lake [Lake Superior]," is the answer. "He came from the west and he goes toward the sunrise. His canoe is made of white stone and it moves swiftly."

The legend tells us that the chief continues to wonder, his eyes turning toward the stockades that hold his starving, quarreling people.

"How could it be?" asks the chief. "From what source will such peace come?"

The hunters reply simply: "It will come."

The hunters' strength of conviction fully opens the chief's mind to his own sense of certainty, his own sense of faith, that in the world of man there exists a force of peace that can come to the people if only they, too, will turn their minds to it. " Truly," he says, "this is a wonderful thing. This news of itself will bring the beginning of peace to our people if once they can hear it and understand it and believe it. It will begin to free their minds of the hatred that comes from fear."

The Great Peacemaker passes from settlement to settlement, and the same scene is repeated with each of the chiefs as they are quickly brought to the conviction of the power of peace and how it can act on all the peoples turning to it.

Thus ends the first part of the legend of the Great Peacemaker. The stage is now set for the deeper meaning of peace to be shown and its practical application to the common life of humanity explained. One may imagine the storyteller rising from the circle, leaving his listeners to wait until the next night's fire is lit.

A CERTAIN WOMAN ALONG THE WARRIOR'S PATH

The second phase of the tale begins with the Great Peacemaker seeking out the tent of a certain woman who, we are told, lives alone alongside the warriors' path which passed between east and west. It is through the mediation of a woman that the mission of peace takes form in the world, and in fact it is women's power of judgment that will ultimately determine the leadership of the Iroquois Confederacy. Both here and in the cosmic myth that precedes the story of the Great Peacemaker, the role of woman is as fundamental—both for good and evil—as is the role of the male sex. So intertwined and equally basic to the legends are the roles of woman and man that the hearer of the story cannot possibly think of one sex or the other when the word which is translated "human being," or sometimes simply "man," is spoken. Although the legends tell us a great deal about the nature of man and woman, what they are speaking of is mainly *human-ness,* human nature *anterior* to the division of the sexes.

That said, the character of this woman whose tent is set along the warriors' path is of great importance. Her role is to welcome the warriors on their way to and from battle and give them food. So she is one who knows very well the heart and mind of men engaged in war. She knows the power of the forces that drive them. She places food before the Great Peacemaker and, when he has eaten, she asks him his mission.

"I carry the mind of the Life God," he replies, "and my messages will bring an end to the wars between east and west."

"How?" she asks. "How will this be?" She has wished for that with all her heart, but it has not come to pass. In fact, some versions of the story have her as "the peacemaker queen," a role at which she ultimately fails, leaving "the tent of peace" empty, as it is said. But in this version of the tale, she is presented purely as a wise woman who has seen the strength of man's compulsion to make war.

The Great Peacemaker's answer is given in a way that shows both the inner and outer requirements of peace; he shows her he understands peace to be more than a pause between wars.

"The word that I bring," he said, "has three parts: Righteousness and Health and Power—*Gaiwoh, Skenon, Gashasdenshaa.* And each part has two branches . . ."

Each part has an outer and an inner dimension.

"Righteousness means justice practiced between men and between nations; but it also means the *wish* to see justice prevail." The woman knows this wish is the most important thing; it is a special kind of desire—stronger than anger and hatred. It is a desire stronger than the wish for pleasure, for renown, for comfort, for bravado. Stronger than the desire to be right. It is a kind of love—a power of love which she herself knows very well.

The Great Peacemaker goes on:

"Health means soundness of mind and body and it is such health that leads the mind toward peace. Sanity of mind and a right attention to the body are inseparable and a precondition of true peace."

And, finally, the Peacemaker speaks to her of the outer and inner meaning of Power.

"Power," he says, "means authority, the authority of law and custom, backed by the force that is necessary."

But that is only the outer half of the meaning of Power. The Great Peacemaker goes on: "But Power is also religion. Just as laws justly enforced reflect the will of the Holder of the Heavens." This concept of justice, expressed in words of this kind, is surely one of the most prevalent and dangerous truths of human history. All tyrannies as well as all beneficent governments have used such words—calling themselves representatives of God. The importance and the danger of such a concept were precisely in the minds of the Founding Fathers who called on God just as had the monarchy they were rejecting. But what kind of God? And what were the means by which the will of God was to be instituted on earth—and, of highest importance, what needed to take place within people, in their inner life, or only in their mental life, for the laws to remain just? Laws by themselves, the Founding Fathers knew, do not bring peace or justice. Without the assent—and the faith—of the heart and mind, even the best laws are powerless. Jefferson knew this, Madison knew this, Franklin knew this.

And so does the woman who lives along the warriors' path. "The message is good," she says, "but do you bring more than words?"

THE NEW SOCIETY

The Great Peacemaker answers first by describing the outer form of the new society—a longhouse, a structure in which many families live together, each with "their own fire," and yet all under one roof. "All shall live as one household under one chief mother."

The Peacemaker continues: "Hereabouts there are five nations, each with its own council fire, yet they shall live together as one household in peace. They shall be the *Kanonsionni,* the Longhouse." The structure and form of the Longhouse are of utmost significance; in general, the Indian dwelt in circular structures—the form of the circle indicating a unity and a common center. The Longhouse is the Great Peacemaker's innovation, indicating the blending of unity and plurality that was now needed because of the conflict into which the people had sunk. The circle can hold its meaning only when each nation conforms its mind to the good of all the people. The Longhouse was now necessary—and there were those among the Founding Fathers who knew a kind of "longhouse" was needed for the separate colonies in America. Over and over again, before and during the revolutionary period, the Iroquois leaders were telling the Americans to "bring their separate council fires under one roof."

As the Great Peacemaker finishes speaking of the form of the government—and one can imagine that here he begins to outline the Iroquois constitution itself, what we know as the Council of the Great Peace—the woman before him quietly waits for him to tell her of the inner meaning of power, the meaning he attaches to the word "religion."

"The people shall have one mind and live under one law," he says.

The woman continues to wait.

The Great Peacemaker also waits and then, finally, adds the decisive words:

"Thinking shall replace killing."

"That is indeed a good message," says the woman. "I take hold of it. I embrace it."

The place of women in the Longhouse is now spelled out by the Great Peacemaker. Women will choose the chiefs, because "you, my Mother, were the first truly to grasp and accept the message of the peace that is power." And he gives her a new name: *Jigonhsasee,* meaning New Face. "It is in your countenance that the New Mind is manifest." Out of the womb of the New Mind the nations will be born anew.

Then Jigonhsasee says, "I am a woman and do not make war. My work is to feed the warriors passing my door. They, too, must accept the New Mind, or there will be no end to conflict and killing. Where will you take your message?"

"I go toward the sunrise."

THE MAN WHO EATS HUMANS

"In that direction lies great danger," she says. "In that direction stands the house of a man who eats humans."

The second phase of the tale ends, setting the stage for the part of the legend that reveals the inner process by which a human being can discover the Great Mind within himself and how he can allow it to transform his life and the life of the community.

The legend has already told us of the powerful "evil chief" Atotarho, who in many versions is indeed described as an eater of human flesh. But the Great Peacemaker's first encounter with "the man who eats humans" is not this Atotarho, but none other than the man known as Hiawatha, who was to become the most beloved hero of the Five Nations.[96]

HIAWATHA

The story of Hiawatha that now unfolds represents an archetype found in many mythologies of the world. Here is a human being whose journey to greatness begins from the lowest, most helpless human level. Unlike the miraculous Peacemaker, Hiawatha is not born as an incarnate divine force. He is a weak and degraded human being—and to listen to his tale is to feel that now the legend is actually speaking about oneself. Hiawatha's journey to greatness takes him through man's actual condition, his actual suffering and loss—despair, depression, self-pity, fear and hopelessness and the understandable, all-too-human craving to give up just at the point when a renewed inner commitment to the goal is needed and possible. Taken together, the pure Peacemaker and the afflicted Hiawatha are felt to be man both as he can be and man as he is—that is, the human being in his entirety and wholeness. It is ourselves as we are in both our inner divinity and our actual vulnerability, weakness and misery. This is the human being as he was made by both Flint and He Grasps The Sky With Both Hands—this is man's cosmic definition. And it is the human being in both his aspects who is called to create the ethical, communal world, the world of law, justice and peace. It is the human being as the mysterious blending of two opposing natures who must work and care for his neighbor and for the life of the society. America, can we listen to this tale? What is the form of communal life that does justice to both the spiritual and material needs of man? Wasn't it this dream that brought the passion and hope to our Founding Fathers?

When the Great Peacemaker comes to the house of "the man who eats humans," he climbs the roof and lies flat on his chest beside the smoke hole. He waits until the man comes home carrying a human body, which he puts in his kettle on the fire.

The Great Peacemaker moves closer to the smoke hole and looks straight down.

THE NEW FACE

Just at that moment, the man in the house bends over the kettle and sees not only the body of the human being he has killed and is about to eat, but also a face looking up at him. He is amazed. It is the Great Peacemaker's face, reflected in the water, that is looking up at him, but the man thinks it is his own face! And there was in this face such wisdom and strength as he had never seen before nor ever dreamed that he possessed.

Startled, the man moves back to a corner of his house, sits down and begins to think.

"This is a wondrous thing," he says to himself. "Such a thing has never happened before as long as I have lived in this house. I did not know I was like that. It was a great man who looked at me out of the kettle."

He goes over to the kettle to look again, and there again is the face of a great man looking up at him.

"It is true," he says. "It is my own face in which I see wisdom and righteousness and strength. It is not the face of a man who eats humans." And he takes the kettle out of the house and empties it by the roots of an upturned tree.

"No more will I do this thing that I have done for so long. No longer will I kill humans and eat their flesh."

The man falls silent and then speaks again to himself. His voice is breaking with remorse.

"But that is not enough. The mind inside is more difficult to change. I cannot escape from the suffering I have caused. I cannot bring back the dead. I cannot erase the cries of the women and children."

Here we feel the scale of this legend and of the source from which it has come. For here the legend speaks of a human crime for which no ordinary action can atone. Here the story may well be heard as speaking to our own remorse as we see in a clear light what has been done to an entire people. And here the tale echoes the constitutive legend of our own culture—the crime for which no ordinary action can atone, a level of self-remorse which demands of man an action of an entirely new quality. And for this action the man needs now to turn to the greatness he has seen in himself.

The legend speaks of the man weeping over his crimes, and of his loneliness. He wanders away from his house and returns, still weeping. There the Great Peacemaker is now waiting for him. The two men enter the house together and sit down across the fire from each other. The weeping man speaks first. "I saw a face looking at me out of the kettle in this house where I live. It was my own face, but it was not the face of the man who has lived here. It was the face of a great man, but I am become miserable."

The Great Peacemaker tells him that he is now living the great truth of man and his purpose on earth. "The New Mind has come to you," he says, "and you are miserable because the New Mind does not live at ease with old memories." And the Great Peacemaker instructs him: "Now you will work with me to bring justice and peace to those places where you have done injury to man. We will work together to bring to the earth the new idea of the peace that is power. Such is the work given to man by the Creator of Life."

"It is a good message," says the man, and he speaks in the ritualized form of acceptance, words that indicate his intention always to remember what he has seen in himself and how it obliges him to act in the world. "I take hold, I grasp it," he says. And, he continues: "Now what work is there for us to do?"

The Great Peacemaker explains the new order to be brought to the nations: *Kanonsionni,* the Longhouse, and *Kayanerenhkowa,* the Great Peace, the Great Law.

ATOTARHO

The weight of the story now shifts to the inner struggle required of man. The figure of the evil wizard, Chief Atotarho, now takes center stage because in him and what he represents lies the secret of man's great resistance to the truth and the key to how he is called to overcome this resistance.

Atotarho is described as a man who kills and devours all men who approach him uninvited, and so strong that birds flying over his lodge fall dead at his feet when he waves his arms. The man listening to the Great Peacemaker is hearing his own former life described in magnified terms. He too has been an eater of human flesh, but now he has seen the greatness that calls to him from within himself.

The description of Atotarho continues:

"His body is twisted and his mind is twisted and his hair is a mass of tangled snakes. No man can bear to look at him, and the sound of his voice strikes terror throughout the land. His power is mighty, but the peace cannot be brought to the land without him."

The Great Peacemaker continues:

"You must visit this man Atotarho, for he is one of your people, the Onondagas. He is ugly, but we need him. When he asks you for your message, say to him 'my message is righteousness and health and when men take hold of it and grasp it they will stop killing one another; they will live in peace.'"

And then the Great Peacemaker speaks of that which is the mystery at the heart of human evil and of what he is really asking of the man in front of him, whose tears of remorse are not yet dry upon his face:

"He will not listen to you. He will drive you away. But you will go to him again and again and at last you will prevail—*if you do not give up.*"

The man nods in assent to his task.

A New Name

"Do not give up," whispers the Great Peacemaker and the man does not understand why this is repeated. "And now," says the Great Peacemaker, "I give you your name. You will be called Hiawatha, He Who Combs, for you will comb the snakes out of Atotarho's hair."[97]

The drama now unfolds, and the mystery and centrality of the Great Peacemaker's prediction gain immense force: *he will not listen to you.* What does this mean? Behind all of Atotarho's evil there lies again and again this notion of man's unwillingness to hear the truth in all its goodness. Why? What is it in ourselves that cannot bear to hear the life-giving truth? In no other legend of the world is this mystery more powerfully portrayed. And the immediate relevance of this issue to the question of man's common life—the question of justice in government and society—needs to be remembered.

Can there be authentic democracy without faith in the intelligence and the will of the community? The Founding Fathers understood that human passions and selfishness must be checked and balanced—that it was fatal to assume the goodwill of individual men and women. The democratic form of government they created does not pretend to impose spiritual truth upon the people—not because the Founding Fathers did not believe that spirit existed, but because they knew it could not be made to act by the agency of ordinary *individual* human effort. What they created—and for many of them this was surely explicit in their thought—was a social structure that *made room* for the appearance of spiritual power or, in their language, that made room for *Reason,* the action of a higher, independent power of mind. When Reason is needed, when the spirit is needed, it will act; but the need must be felt by the community; and the individuals in the community must feel they need each others' thought and inquiry in order for the spirit to enter the community.

A SCREAM THAT FREEZES THE BLOOD

The evil chief Atotarho strikes terror in the hearts of all who approach him not only by his murderous actions, but by the power of his voice—shouting and screaming over the waters and distances, a scream that freezes the blood and beats back all who come near:

"Hwe-do-ne-e-e-e-eh?"

What does this scream mean? The storytellers translate it for us in various ways, but each translation carries the question of the meaning of human evil.

"Hwe-do-ne-e-e-e-eh?" shouts Atotarho when Hiawatha approaches him with the message of peace. *"Hwe-do-ne-e-e-e-eh?"* he cries. "When will this be?" "It has not come yet!"

In all the workings of the evil chief—and he works great evil; he kills, lays waste—he summons the powers of nature to break the will of Hiawatha, to break his heart, to bring him to despair, to force him to *give up*. And always, at every turn, the heart-stopping scream is heard through the forest: *"Hwe-do-ne-e-e-e-eh?"* "When will this be?" "It has not come yet!"

Every great legend and wisdom tale has, as it were, its "navel," an incomprehensible center of gravity around which the whole tale revolves. Atotarho's scream is the center of gravity of this legend of peace.

Atotarho is not the figure of evil who simply opposes out of an irredeemable black heart; he does not kill, he does not destroy as a mere force, as a personification of death and destruction of the kind we find in many other legends where the center of gravity lies elsewhere (however similar the ultimate meaning might be). No, Atotarho is evil as inability—incapacity to hope, incapacity to try. The sound of the scream as it echoes through the legend is the sound of a broken heart, of man who internally yearns for the good but can see no way it will ever appear. The fact that it is Atotarho who later becomes the great leader of the peace—what does this mean? When he is defeated, he is defeated by being awakened to his own power of love and wisdom. The very intensity of his resistance is nothing less than a sign of the intensity of his goodness. Human evil is goodness acting under a wrong thought; human evil is love acting under a wrong fear, a wrong striving; human evil is the power of the spirit under the yoke of a despairing master.

Atotarho is human energy wasted and twisted. His body, as it is said in the tale, is crooked in seven places; his head is a tangle of snakes, and from his heart there only comes the blood-stopping scream: "It has not come!"

THE GREAT WORK: THE INNER WORK

Hiawatha begins the work of convincing Atotarho to accept the message of the peace that is power. Three times he sends messengers to straighten the wizard's twisted mind, and three times the wizard's evil power rushes out to meet them and destroy them, some by drowning and others by being set to murderous fighting among themselves—even they who had accepted the message of peace. Such is the power of despair.

But Hiawatha is never wounded in his body. Each time Atotarho beats him back through blows to his mind and heart, and therefore to his will to continue.

It is important to note the heroic dimension of Hiawatha—his struggle and his humanness. He stands between two pure forces of good and evil, between the divinely sent Great Peacemaker and the evil wizard Atotarho. Hiawatha is a *man;* the Great Peacemaker is a divine messenger; Atotarho is the core of human evil. Between the Great Peacemaker and Atotarho, man must work for the great peace.

One day, with no apparent occasion, Hiawatha hears Atotarho's scream crying out of the air: "Hiawatha-a-a-a-a!" and he is overcome by a sense of foreboding. Soon his three daughters fall ill and, one after another, they all die. Hiawatha is stricken by grief. "Because of the thing that has befallen me," he says, "I can no longer do the work of the Good Mind."

Seeing him lost in the emptiness of depression and sorrow, the people try to comfort him by arranging games to lift his spirits. But in the midst of the game a mysterious bird falls from the sky, and the crowd, pursuing it, tramples his wife to death.

At this, grief crushes Hiawatha entirely. Unable to remember the words of the Great Peacemaker, "Do not give up," he leaves the land of his people.

HIAWATHA'S JOURNEY

A journey that figures prominently in Iroquois legend now begins. Hiawatha becomes a wanderer, moving through the forests without direction, aimlessly searching for someone with a grief as deep as his own—someone whose need would call forth from him the words of consolation and truth. But although the smoke of his fire can be seen wherever he roams, no man is drawn to come to him. He is alone, away from his people, cut off from any human being with the same need as his own. The essence-emotion of grief has blackened his mind and emptied his heart of all hope and all sense of his sacred mission and destiny. His mind has become almost like the mind of Atotarho himself, despair turning him away from the truth. Such is man's descent into the underworld as given by the Iroquois legend: man must experience *himself* as the force that resists the good; here Hiawatha experiences the explicitly emotional reactions (in other tales they are often "monsters" or "demons") that turn one away from the call of the Self.

It is said that on the twenty-third day of his wandering, he builds himself a canoe and comes to a certain village and makes his fire nearby at the edge of the forest. That same night the Great Peacemaker, who has all along been aware of Hiawatha's wandering, goes toward the smoke of the fire. He listens to Hiawatha crying out, as he has been crying out each night. He sees him holding three shell strings (wampum) in his hand; he listens to him as he speaks out of his great yearning to find another like himself in need of help so that the consolation of truth can find its words on his lips.

Out of the darkness, the Great Peacemaker now steps forward and gently takes the wampum from Hiawatha and, adding his own wampum, speaks to him words that from then on will be used in the Iroquois ceremony of condolence:

"I wipe away the tears from your face," says the Great Peacemaker, "using the white fawn-skin of pity . . . I make it daylight for you . . . I beautify the sky. Now you will think with a quiet mind when your eyes rest on the sky, which the Maker of All Things intended should be a source of happiness to man."

Thus, by looking above himself at the beauty of the sky, Hiawatha's mind was cleared of its grief.

"Now," said the Great Peacemaker, "Reason has returned; your judgment is firm again. You are ready again to carry the New Mind to others. Let us work together now and make the laws of the Great Peace."

And so they worked together, the divine messenger and the purified man, and conceived the Great Law of Peace, fashioning a string or belt of wampum for each item in it to help them remember. Carrying these immense belts of wampum which was as a sacred book to them, they brought the Great Peace to the nations of the west—the Oneidas, Onondagas, Cayugas and Senecas.

Their work met with success among the nations, except for the Onondagas. There, as they approached, they were compelled to leave by the paralyzing cry of Atotarho, "*Hwe-do-ne-e-e-e-eh?* When will this be? It has not come yet!" Atotarho alone stood in the way of the Great Peace.

"Come," says the Great Peacemaker to Hiawatha, "you and I alone will go to the Great Wizard."

FACING ATOTARHO

Hiawatha's heart is lifted, knowing that now he will be accompanied by the power of the Great Peacemaker. But what is that power? "I shall sing the song of the Great Peace, " says the Peacemaker, "and you will explain the Words of the Law, holding the wampum in your hand."

To sing and to explain—the song from the lips of the divine messenger and the words from the man who has passed through the hell that still engulfs the evil wizard, the hell of despair which is the root of all human evil, the anger and hatred and fear that brings violence, bloodshed and war. "His mind is twisted," says the Great Peacemaker, "and there are seven crooks in his body. These must be straightened if the Peace is to endure."

The two put their canoe into the lake, and halfway across they heard the shriek of Atotarho, "It is not yet!" The wind blows and the waves crash angrily against the canoe as again Atotarho's cry rushes out to meet them; "*Asonke-ne-e-e-e-eh!* It is not yet!" So great is the resistance created by the anguish and doubt of Atotarho that the Great Peacemaker himself is nearly beaten back. But he adds all his strength to Hiawatha's efforts, and their canoe soon reaches the east shore of the lake. They beach the canoe and climb the embankment. There before them stands the evil chief Atotarho. The importance of this moment in the story cannot be overstated. Hiawatha's struggle has now brought him directly in front of evil. With his divinely sent companion at his side—that is, with his mind remembering the greatness of the truth—Hiawatha sees at the same time the actual face and form of Atotarho. And he is astonished that he feels no fear. Astonished because there before him stands a hugely powerful warrior chief, his face and towering body twisted, his eyes burning, his head writhing with spitting snakes. But Hiawatha feels only pity and compassion. He glances at the Great Peacemaker, whose calm demeanor confirms his own absence of fear.

"We two have come," says Hiawatha.

"Who are you?" demands Atotarho.

"Have you not been told," replies Hiawatha, "that there were two that would come to you?"

"I have heard," answers Atotarho, "that Hiawatha and the Great Peacemaker were on their way to me."

"It is true. And now we are here."

At this, the mystery of Atotarho deepens and lifts at the same time.

"I have been waiting for you," he says.

Atotarho has been waiting? He whose awesome power has brought death and despair to Hiawatha and whose heart-stopping screams have turned nature itself into an instrument of violence and bloodshed? What does it mean, this "waiting"?

THE ONE THING NEEDFUL

Here the tellers of the tale seem not to know what words to put in Hiawatha's mouth. Atotarho is spoken of as "impatient" where before he was described as evil, hating peace, vicious, cruel. But the tale is strong and clear. As it draws to an end, the whole meaning of Atotarho's evil power is illuminated. Atotarho represents the fact that *man has not seen real power; man has not experienced* real power. Man is a being charged with mind and energy, born to be an instrument of the Good, a servant of the Holder of the Sky. But he has not understood where power and energy come from; and without this knowledge and experience all the force within him is turned outward to violence and inward to doubt and despair. There is an indestructible energy in man that is meant to master nature in the world and in himself; it is the energy of struggle and of overcoming, and if it is not turned toward the striving to obey the Master of Life and to overcome one's own weaknesses, it will be turned to violence; if this energy is not turned to helping one's neighbor, it will be turned to killing one's neighbor. Atotarho is power without understanding; he is the desire to live without knowing the Good. And nothing can overcome this force of violence except the direct experience of the Good within oneself, an experience that turns all the energies of man around so that they serve what they are created to serve. Without this central event, all impulses toward peace and inner freedom eventually must fail.

Holding the great belts of wampum in his hand, Hiawatha speaks further to Atotarho.

"These are the words of the Great Law. On these words we shall build the House of Peace, the Longhouse, with five fires, that is yet one household. These are the words of Righteousness and Health and Power."

Atotarho sneers. "What is this foolishness about houses and righteousness and health?"

The Great Peacemaker answers him. Until now, the Great Peacemaker has given the task of speaking to Hiawatha. According to the legend, the

Great Peacemaker stuttered (in some versions his name is translated as "double-rows of teeth"); Hiawatha, however, has been blessed with the gift of oratory—it is he who is chosen to be the instrument of expression. But now the Great Peacemaker speaks with a great voice:

"The words we bring constitute the New Mind, which is the will of He Grasps The Sky With Both Hands. O Chief, here is what you must take hold of and you must grasp it. You are right to think there is no justice, but that is because of what men desire. I tell you now that there shall be righteousness when men desire justice. You are right to say there is no health in body or in mind. But that is because of what men obey. There will be Health when men obey Reason. And you are right to scoff at words of power because of your own great power. But you are misery and your power is a burden to you and to all men. There will be the power of peace when men accept the Great Law. These things shall be given form in the Longhouse, where five nations shall live in quiet as one family. At this very place, Atotarho, where the chiefs of the five nations shall assemble, I shall plant the Great Tree of Peace, and its roots shall extend to far places of the earth so that all mankind may have the shelter of the Great Law."

"What is that to me?" says Atotarho.

The Great Peacemaker holds out his hand to Atotarho. "You yourself shall tend to the council fire of the Five Nations, the Fire That Never Dies. And the smoke of that fire shall reach the sky and be seen of all men."

Atotarho shakes his head in denial, but there is no violence in his gesture. "Who will bring this about? There is no one."

The words of Atotarho have only the weight of sadness.

"You are wrong," answers the Great Peacemaker. "It is you yourself who will bring it about, *if you desire it*. You shall be the head chief of the Five Nations."

Atotarho bows his head ever so slightly. "Of course I desire this thing," he says. But then he stiffens again. Something like anger flares in his eyes. "But there is nothing in what you say. You are a dreamer, where is the power that can bring it to pass?" And Atotarho screams. "*Asonke-ne-e-e-e-eh!* It is not yet!"

At that, Hiawatha and the Great Peacemaker leave, but there is surety and strength in their steps. They return across the lake to where the chiefs of the nations are waiting for them.

"We must hurry," says the Great Peacemaker. "Now is the time!"

The chiefs of all the nations put their canoes into the lake, and with the Great Peacemaker and Hiawatha they move swiftly over the water. As they near the middle of the lake, the terrible voice of Atotarho rushes out to meet them. "*Asonke-ne-e-e-e-eh!* It is not yet!" The waves crash against the canoes, but they put all their strength into their paddles, and even before the voice has died away, they stand before Atotarho.

"Behold!" says the Great Peacemaker. "Here is power. These are the Five Nations. Their strength is greater than your strength, Atotarho. But take hold of this and grasp it: the voice you now have, the voice that terrifies and kills, will no longer be your voice. It is their voices that shall be your voice when you shall speak in council. And all men will heed you. This will be your strength in the future: the will of a united people."

He Who Combs

The Great Peacemaker gestures to Hiawatha. Hiawatha comes toward the unresisting wizard and combs the snakes out of his hair. Then, says the legend, the mind of Atotarho was made straight.

The Great Peacemaker lays his hand on Atotarho's body and says, "The work is finished. Your mind is made straight; your head is now combed; the seven crooks have been taken from your body. Now you also have a New Mind. You shall henceforth preside over the Council, and you shall strive in all ways to be the voice of the Great Law. All men will hear you and be touched by the peace that is power."

Then the Great Peacemaker placed antlers on the heads of the chiefs in sign of their authority, and gave them the words of the Law.

So ends the story of how the Holder of the Sky brought the human beings into existence for the sake of the universe and the earth, and how he taught them to fulfill their lives by struggling against the power of forget-fulness and doubt within them, and how, when they repeatedly forgot their true nature and began to do violence to themselves and to each other, he sent them a final messenger to lead them back to the becoming path, and how through one man's struggle to remember his inner God even when at the extreme of degradation and despair the Master of Life raised a heroic human being to stand for them as a symbol of their own obligatory work, and how with such a man and with the divine messenger as a guide there was created a constitution of laws known as the Great Peace to enable humanity to live as one family in a manner and in ways that would permit the power of divine peace and harmony to enter their lives, and how, to accomplish this once and for all on the earth and among men, it was necessary to go into the broken heart of human evil and comb the snakes out of man's mind and soul that had brought upon him despair and out of despair a thick coat of anger and bloodshed.

What We Must Do

As we now return to history, we need to keep in mind what this legend shows us about the actual level of the Indian civilization, so that this story can help us, as purely historical information alone cannot, feel in our bones what we lost when the Indian was destroyed. It is clear that the civilization of the American Indian was rooted in the deepest and most refined vision of reality and of the aim of human life, a metaphysics as comprehensive and subtle as any we know of in the European world from which most of us Americans have come; an ethics as compassionate and wise as any we know of from the Judeo-Christian tradition, and a form of government that was based on a powerful vision of reality and human good.

And so, the question we began with needs to return to us: how to be toward the crime that America committed in destroying this world and its people and its ideas and forms of life, with all that is of the Good within them? Personal guilt is entirely too small a response unless it repairs the broken conduit of life that the Creator of Life fashioned for the Indian. If we glimpse even a little that America killed something that was divinely ordained, not only for the Indians themselves but for all humanity and for all the earth—if we can be touched by the feeling that is a deeply organic response to such an act of human destruction—only then may we perhaps approach a true response and a true direction of recompense, not only to the Indian spirit, but to what we ourselves may recognize as the Good—why not call it God? Can we now do for man and for the earth what the culture of the Indian was designed to do? Can we help bring to the world and to ourselves the energy of the Great Peace? Although America betrayed all its ideals by slaughtering the Indian, can it—or any of us—accept that there is no recompense for this crime except to continue the work that formed the essence of the Indians' culture, the same work that we find as well at the heart of our own ideals of spiritual Reason, ideals that are shadowed forth by the mythic and deeply realistic meaning of our history and our heroes? We are obliged, by the laws of conscience, to bring to the earth what the Indians brought. Without that, all other compensation and atonement will be perilously incomplete.

SEVEN

SLAVERY AND
THE STORY OF AMERICA

THE ILLUSION OF AMERICA

One of the great lessons of history, and one that is rarely spoken about in a meaningful way, concerns the vastness of the theater of human life on earth. The more deeply one studies past civilizations, the more it is possible not only to recognize, but to *feel* that our own culture is but one of countless societies, cultures, nations and peoples that have existed and perished over the surface of our world throughout the uncharted reaches of time. And the more deeply one studies the past, the more one may see and feel the patterns of man's injustice to man, the incomprehensible suffering that human beings have inflicted upon each other out of fear, suggestibility and self-deception. Everywhere, in almost all the worlds of man, one sees behind the thin screen of religious and moral idealism the domination of hatred, the brutal exercise of power, the enormities of bloody war occasioned by paranoia, greed or the trivialities of pleasure, position, self-importance and fantastic dreams of salvation or service. We need to situate the American crime of slavery within this picture. We need to penetrate beneath the surface of America's illusory belief that simply by its existence it stands above the laws of human barbarity.

Until we can free ourselves from the illusion of our moral uniqueness, our attempts to repair our crimes may never take us where we need to go. Even the passion with which our society is now struggling with the imperative of civil rights may lead us in the end only to new barbarities under new and deceptive covers—as has so often happened in the history of the world, where revolution and reform only change the names and the trappings of ignorance, violence and rank injustice.

We can begin by stepping back for a moment and viewing America within the immense scale of world history, much as one might view the planet earth itself within the scale of our universe of stars, galaxies and the unseen infinities of space. In this universe, the earth is but a tiny speck of a world circling one of countless billions of suns and cosmic entities of unimaginable size and age. Similarly, on the stage of world history, America is hardly more than a moment, a heartbeat in the life of man on earth. Consider the greatness of Egypt—a brilliant sun that blazed for who knows how many thousands of years; consider ancient Greece, whose sciences and philosophies transformed the Western world; consider the thousand years of Rome, its empire straddling half the earth; and China in the East, dynasty upon dynasty reaching across the millennia; and only begin to scan the globe for all the nations and peoples and languages and gods that have risen and fallen, and with them man's dreams of uniqueness and intimacy with his gods: consider the worlds upon worlds of tribal cultures on the continents of America: the greatness of the Aztec, Toltec, Maya; consider the human galaxy we now call India with its past reaching farther back than our eyes can see, and consider the visions of art and spirit that it conducted onto the earth; sweep northward to Tibet and its two thousand years or more of spiritual mystery; and northward yet to the immensity of Central Asia— and then westward to the culture of Russia; and then sweep southward from there to the great worlds of ancient Mesopotamia; and then forward in time and meet the great civilization of Islam, millions of peoples, tribes, histories and ambitions under the umbrella of the religion of Mohammed; turn back again to the ancient world of Israel and consider how it lived; and only spin the globe in front of you and register in your mind the human worlds spinning before you: sub-Saharan Africa, with names upon it that only conceal the hundreds of tribal kingdoms, each with its own sacred customs and rituals; Australia with its 30,000-year-old aboriginal civilizations—then northward to the ten thousand islands and hundreds of millions of people in the Malaysian archipelago; and consider southeast Asia and the remnants of its ancient glories—the temples of Cambodia, Burma and Thailand; and northward again, to the world of Japan, its monarchs and warriors, its subtlety and its fire and energy streaking through the length of recorded history. Consider all this and more of the history of human civilization on earth and know that in all these worlds war and barbarity carved the lineaments of each nation and each people's destiny. Always and everywhere humanity has fallen prey to paranoia, hysteria and arrogance; always and everywhere, with hardly an exception, man has murdered and enslaved his fellowman. With all the evidence of the sacred, with all the monuments of spiritual truth that shimmer in the dark flood of history, humanity has been and has remained asleep to the call of conscience. And in that sleep, human beings destroy each other and degrade themselves and their own culture.

It is the human condition; and we need to accept that America lives under all the laws of human life on earth. The question is: can America offer the newness of hope for the world without deceiving itself about its own actual significance and uniqueness? If we are to re-mythologize the story of America, if America is to offer to the world something more than hypocritical and intrinsically unrealizable ideals of freedom and justice, then we must look with new eyes at the forces within ourselves that oppose these ideals, not imagining that we are literally a "chosen people" or that we are bringing something literally new and unprecedented to the world. The teachings of wisdom tell us—but can we hear them?—that in essence it has all happened before; "there is nothing new under the sun." Unless America can free itself from its illusion of uniqueness, it will be lost—as it is now being lost—to the poisonous effects of this fundamental illusion: either an arrogance that courts its own destruction at the hand of man or nature, or a suicidal cynicism, despair and self-contempt that cast to the winds the very ideals that can show it the goal toward which it must strive, free of its megalomaniac illusions; or, finally, an external moral perfectionism that fails to attend to the real inner causes of human barbarity under the illusion that the improvement of outer conditions, imperatively necessary though that may be by all the laws of conscience, by itself will end or even diminish the crimes of man against man.

To look at slavery in America and its continuing echo of racial hatred and injustice is to see more than a condition that we are obliged to repair with all the moral and social energy that we can bring; it is also to see the inner human condition. It is to see that America, too—we, too, no less than the slavemasters of Egypt and Rome, no less than the blind, murdering armies of every nation in history, no less than all those millions who have pulled deadly levers and triggers, lashed and beaten innocent bodies and even scientifically engineered the destruction and degradation of millions— we, too, are asleep to conscience. The story of America, the very story that can bring hope to the world, must include the truth of the human condition, not only as it can be, but as it is now.

And when it accepts this truth about itself, how will the story change? That is our question now. In this new story, will our heroes no longer be heroes? Our triumphs no longer triumphs? Not at all. On the contrary. Yet, at the same time, something entirely new and necessary will fill every limb and cell of the story of America—and that "something" has a very precise designation: *humility and the need to experience the taste of genuine remorse.* The heroes remain heroes, but they are now also calling us to understand what in ourselves holds us back from all that they represent. Our triumphs remain triumphs, but now they are also reminders of the inner human qualities we need in order to sustain them. The normal human pride that comes from belonging to a nobly conceived nation now points us to the real meaning of self-respect, namely, that every human being has within himself the possibility and the capacity to search for what the Founders called Reason, the real inner God of truth, love and freedom. Slavery and its omnipresent effects have the power to never let us forget that we have to become different beings as well as act according to the good laws of the land. Laws by themselves, the Constitution by itself, cannot bring justice.

Frederick Douglass Speaks

"Do You Mean, Citizens, to Mock Me?"

On July 5, 1852, Frederick Douglass was the honored speaker at Corinthian Hall in Rochester, New York. Born into slavery in 1818, Douglass had escaped to the North at the age of twenty and had become widely respected for his courage and intellect as he traveled throughout the northern states speaking about the meaning for America of slavery and its horrors. The bitter irony, on this occasion, of a black man being invited to celebrate the Fourth of July was not lost on him—and he made certain it would not be lost on his audience. "Do you mean, citizens, to mock me, asking me to speak to-day?"[98]

> What, to the American slave, is your 4th of July? I answer: a day that reveals to him more than all other days in the year, the gross injustice and cruelty to which he is the constant victim. To him, your celebration is a sham; your boasted liberty, an unholy license; your national greatness, swelling vanity; your sounds of rejoicing are empty and heartless; your denunciations of tyrants, brass fronted impudence; your shouts of liberty and equality, hollow mockery; your prayers and hymns, your sermons and thanksgivings, with all your religious parade, and solemnity, are, to him, mere bombast, fraud, deception, impiety, and hypocrisy—a thin veil to cover up crimes which would disgrace a nation of savages. There is not a nation on the earth guilty of practices, more shocking and bloody, than are the people of these United States, at this very hour.[99]

In this talk, as in many others he delivered during his long and influential life, Douglass shows his audience what the story of America looks like when seen from the perspective of the American slave. His great gift as a writer and as a speaker, and in the actions of his life, was not only to make white Americans feel the monstrosity of slavery, but also to represent to them, with unsurpassed insight and sensitivity, the meaning of the idea of America itself. He understood America and deeply embraced its ideals even as he recoiled at what America had become. We need to pay attention to this juxtaposition of understanding and outrage. It is a juxtaposition of mind and emotion that is all too rare among us. We have become accustomed to the love of America being joined only to the emotions of fervid and often blind patriotism or, on the other hand, the emotions of protest being joined to the wholesale rejection of the story of America and its heroic figures. We are accustomed, that is, to witnessing reason functioning in the service of emotional agitation. What is rare, and exceedingly precious, is to witness a calm, reflective mind joined to a breaking and angry heart. In such a man, appreciation of America is a thousand times more compelling than praise coming from the lips of the privileged or fortunate; and judgment against America is a thousand times more penetrating than the all-devouring rage and resentment of the afflicted. In such a man, one senses that he knows with both his mind and his heart and that he feels with both his heart and his mind. The life and thought of Frederick Douglass can do much to show us how the idea of America can be deepened, rather than destroyed, by looking at it through the lens of the crimes of slavery.

"Fellow citizens," says Douglass, "I shall not presume to dwell at length on the associations that cluster about this day":

> The simple story of it is that 76 years ago, the people of this country were British subjects . . . you were under the British Crown. Your fathers esteemed the English Government as the home government; and England as the fatherland. This home government . . . although a considerable distance from your home, did, in the exercise of its parental prerogatives, impose upon its colonial children, such re-

straints, burdens and limitations, as, in its mature judgment, it deemed wise, right and proper.[100]

It may be helpful to have a picture of Douglass before us—a man of great physical magnetism and personal charisma with his broad shoulders, his startling aquiline features and brilliantly lit eyes. Perhaps we can imagine what the people in the audience must be feeling as they watch him and listen to him. He is, after all, a "Negro" recounting America's own history to them in a way that reminds them that they, too, rose up out of rebellion against man's injustice to man.

> But, your fathers . . . presumed to differ from the home government. . . . They went so far . . . as to pronounce the measures of government unjust, unreasonable and oppressive, and altogether such as ought not to be quietly submitted to . . .[101]

The audience listens approvingly, even as Douglass begins to introduce another dimension of the great story:

> To say *now* that America was right, and England wrong, is exceedingly easy. Everybody can say it; the dastard not less then the noble brave, can flippantly descant on the tyranny of England toward the American Colonies. It is fashionable to do so; but there was a time when to pronounce against England, and in favor of the cause of the colonies, tried men's souls. They who did so were accounted in their day plotters of mischief, agitators and rebels, dangerous men. To side with the right against the wrong, with the weak against the strong, and with the oppressed against the oppressor! *here* lies the merit, and the one which, of all others, seems unfashionable in our day. The cause of liberty may be stabbed by the men who glory in the deeds of your fathers . . .[102]

The audience, perhaps, is already beginning to feel a bit uneasy. Yes, the fathers of the country rose up in magnificent moral action; and we take pride

in that; we celebrate that. But, but . . . have we inherited their moral passion? Do we really imagine *we* are like *them?*

Douglass takes his time:

> Oppression makes a wise man mad. Your fathers were wise men, and
> if they did not go mad, they became restive under this treatment.
> They felt themselves the victims of grievous wrongs, wholly incur-
> able in their colonial capacity. With brave men there is always a rem-
> edy for oppression. Just here, the idea of a total separation was born!
> It was a startling idea, much more so, than we, at this distance of time,
> regard it. The timid and prudent . . . of that day were . . . shocked
> and alarmed by it. . . . Fellow Citizens, [the] signers of the Declara-
> tion of Independence were brave men. They were great men too—
> great enough to give fame to a great age. It does not often happen to
> a nation to raise, at one time, such a number of truly great men. The
> point from which I am compelled to view them is not, certainly, the
> most favorable . . .[103]

At this, perhaps the audience steels itself. But Douglass continues to go
slowly, carefully allowing the development of a long, well-balanced thought.

> . . . and yet I cannot contemplate their great deeds with less than ad-
> miration. They were statesmen, patriots and heroes, and for the good
> they did, and the principles they contended for, I will unite with you
> to honor their memory.[104]

Douglass continues, gently introducing a new thought without dwelling
on it—the idea that patriotism, even at its noblest, is not man's highest calling. Wisely, he only touches this idea, resonant as it is with a more inner and
spiritual meaning of virtue, and goes on, following the momentum of his
oratory:

[Your fathers] loved their country better than their own private interests; and, though this is not the highest form of human excellence, all
will concede that it is a rare virtue, and that when it is exhibited, it
ought to command respect. He who will, intelligently, lay down his life
for his country, is a man whom it is not in human nature to despise.[105]

Did the audience—do we?—stop for a moment at the word "intelligently"?
What did Douglass mean? What kind of risk is he speaking of?

Your fathers staked their lives, their fortunes, and their sacred honor,
on the cause of their country. . . . They were peace men . . . but they
did not shrink from agitating against oppression . . . with them, nothing was "*settled*" that was not right. With them, justice, liberty and
humanity were "final"; not slavery and oppression. You may well
cherish the memory of such men. . . . Their solid manhood stands out
the more as we contrast it with these degenerate times.[106]

Having now introduced—again lightly and in passing—the word itself,
"slavery," Douglass picks up the thread of the idea of intelligence that he
had used to characterize authentic courage, risk and sacrifice:

How circumspect, exact and proportionate were all their movements!
How unlike the politicians of an hour! Their statesmanship looked
beyond the passing moment, and stretched away in strength into the
distant future. They seized upon eternal principles, and set a glorious
example in their defence. Mark them![107]

Having said this, having equated circumspection and exactitude and a sense
of proportionateness with reliance on "eternal principles" and having, by
implication, defined the great American ideal of courageous rebellion in its
light, Douglass goes on—*for just a moment more*—to let soar the oratory
of praise:

Fully appreciating the hardship to be encountered, firmly believing in the right of their cause, honorably inviting the scrutiny of an on-looking world, reverently appealing to heaven to attest their sincerity, soundly comprehending the solemn responsibility they were about to assume, wisely measuring the terrible odds against them, your fathers, the fathers of the republic, did, most deliberately, under the inspiration of a glorious patriotism, and with a sublime faith in the great principles of justice and freedom, lay deep the corner-stone of the national superstructure, which has risen and still rises in grandeur around you.[108]

THE NEW STORY OF AMERICA

Having sung these praises, having sung the American story in tones that all who heard could accept—with just one or two sharp notes that were soon to reveal that the whole song was being rewritten in another key—Douglass begins his transition. Here begins the deepening of the myth of America:

> Friends and citizens, I need not enter further into the causes which led to this anniversary. Many of you understand them better than I do. . . . They have all been taught in your common schools, narrated at your firesides, unfolded from your pulpits, and thundered from your legislative halls. . . .[109]

> I remember, also, that, as a people, Americans are remarkably familiar with all facts which make in their own favor. This is esteemed by some as a national trait—perhaps a national weakness. It is a fact, that whatever makes for the wealth or for the reputation of Americans, and can be had cheap! will be found by Americans. I shall not be charged with slandering Americans if I say I think the American side of any question may be safely left in American hands.[110]

A certain silence in the audience. What is the man saying about us? "My business," says Douglass, "is with the present. The accepted time with God and his cause is the ever-living *now.*"

> But now is the time, the important time. Your fathers have lived, died and have done their work, and have done much of it well. You live and must die, and you must do your work. You have no right to enjoy a child's share in the labor of your fathers, unless your children are to be blest by your labors. You have no right to wear out and waste the hard-earned fame of your fathers to cover your indolence. . . . It was fashionable, hundreds of years ago, for the children of Jacob to boast, we have "Abraham to our father," when they had long lost Abraham's faith and spirit. That people contented themselves under the shadow of Abraham's great name, while they repudiated the deeds which made his name great. Need I remind you that a similar thing is being done all over this country today? . . . Washington could not die until he had broken the chains of his slaves. Yet his monument is built up by the price of human blood, and traders in the bodies and the souls of men shout—"We have Washington to *our Father.*"[111]

The great voice now lowers:

> Fellow citizens, pardon me, allow me to ask, why am I called upon to speak here to-day? What have I, or those I represent, to do with your national independence? Are the great principles of political freedom and of natural justice, embodied in that Declaration of Independence, extended to us? . . . I say it with a sad sense of the disparity between us. I am not included within the pale of this glorious anniversary! Your highest independence only reveals the immeasurable distance between us. . . . The rich inheritance of justice, liberty, prosperity and independence, bequeathed by your fathers, is shared by you, not by me. The sunlight that brought life and healing to you, has brought

stripes and death to me. This Fourth of July is *yours,* not *mine.* You may rejoice, I must mourn. To drag a man in fetters into the grand illuminated temple of liberty, and call upon him to join you in joyous anthems, were inhuman mockery and sacrilegious irony. Do you mean, citizens, to mock me, by asking me to speak today?[112]

A NATION THAT HAS LOST ITS SOUL

And now Douglass comes to the *central idea* of his impassioned, yet precisely realized oration. This central idea shows America as imprisoned in man's eternal incapacity actually to will and to do what he knows to be right. The ancient warning of the Old Testament is sounded—with no trace of the tinny religiosity that so often renders recourse to the Bible powerless. The idea—the *fact*—that Douglass is bringing forth is the idea, the *fact,* that man, America, has lost its heart and its will in the contradictions it now embodies. There is no authentic unity in the so-called United States—as, of course, the coming war will soon show in blood and devastation. Like man, America imagines it is free, imagines it is one, imagines it prizes independence, liberty and justice—but in fact, like man, America swarms with contradictions held together physically rather than morally—economically and geographically, rather than through intention and purpose, as is the proper calling of man. But it is precisely because America was only yesterday conceived as an expression of humanity's greatest moral ideals that its contradictions and failure of will call out most clearly and most sadly. Other nations, other people, yes they too are only fallen, weak, oppressed and oppressing. But America swept into the world by rising in force and self-sacrifice above that all-too-human condition and sounded the eternal striving for freedom and compassion and the search for God within. It is America's greatness that makes its evil so clear and so shocking. Douglass is thus, in effect, calling upon America to become the most *morally shocked,* the most *metaphysically shocked* people on earth, the people who see and suffer most acutely man's failure to be man.

AMERICA MUST REMEMBER ITSELF

Of course, America must end slavery! Of course, it must repair this crime! And of course, today America must do everything it can to repair the consequences of this original crime. But America must also see and feel and sense, deeply in its heart and guts, that it is not what it thought it was; America must bow its head at the human condition it represents. Then, and only then, can a man, a people or a community really begin to repair its crimes; because only then through this process of remembering what it is and what it was meant to be, only then does it allow into itself the process by which it can repair its own spiritual and moral contradictions. *America must remember itself.* And it is the slave, the black man, living in chains, physically or otherwise, who is the instrument of remembering.

"I can today," says Douglass, "take up the plaintive lament of a peeled and woe-smitten people." And he recites the first verses of the 137th Psalm, the Psalm of the great Remembering:

> "By the Rivers of Babylon, there we sat down. Yea! we wept when we remembered Zion. We hanged our harps upon the willows in the midst thereof. For there, they that carried us away captive, required of us a song: and they who wasted us required of us mirth, saying, sing us one of the songs of Zion. How can we sing the Lord's song in a strange land? If I forget thee, O Jerusalem, let my right hand forget her cunning. If I do not remember thee, let my tongue cleave to the roof of my mouth."[113]

Douglass reminds his listeners of the fate that befell Babylon after its conquest and enslavement of the Israelites, how the crimes of Babylon, "towering up to heaven," led it to be buried in irrecoverable ruin. "O daughter of Babylon, who art to be destroyed," sings the Psalmist, "happy shall he be that rewardeth thee as thou hast served us."

Look at yourself, says Douglass to America, look at what you are and measure it against what you imagine you are and what your fathers, that is, your conscience, tell you you must be! Be shocked, America! Be stunned, be overwhelmed by what you see, and feel at the center of your being, the purifying fire of remorse!

Douglass is calling for that rarest of movements a human being can make—a fusion of inner opening and decisive outer action. Feel the truth of what you are, America, and at the same moment *do! Act!* Risk yourself for what you know is right and true. It was what Douglass himself discovered during his own life as a slave when, as a young man of sixteen, he did the unthinkable act of physically turning against his slavemaster.

FREEDOM FROM AMERICA

Without doubt, this episode must take its place in any renewal of the story of America. The background of the episode is as follows. Born a slave in 1818 at Holmes Hill Farm on Maryland's Eastern Shore, Douglass spent his earliest years under relatively protected conditions. He had been sent to live with his grandmother, whose job on the farm was to look after some of the younger children until they were old enough to work. Although he was not allowed to see his mother more than four or five times (and that furtively in the darkness of night), and had heard only vague whispers about the identity of his father (the manager of the plantation), Douglass did not think of himself as a slave during the first years of his life. He spent his childhood playing in the woods near his grandmother's cabin.

At the age of six, he began to learn that he was a slave. Saying that they were going on a journey, his grandmother abandoned the terrified child at the Plantation mansion, and from that moment on, he was fed, housed, clothed and worked like an animal among animals. One night he was awakened by a woman's screams, and peering through a crack in the wall of the kitchen, he saw the plantation manager (his rumored father) lashing the bare back of a woman who was his aunt. Trembling with fear, he forced himself to watch the entire ordeal.

Douglass' autobiographies contain page after page of powerfully objective accounts of the degradation and barbarity of the life of a slave. More and more deeply, he realizes the horror of his situation—that he is owned, that he will be forever a man in chains, without freedom, entirely at the mercy of other men who will beat him or even kill him at their whim if he provokes them in any way or seems to them to fall short of his function as a working animal.

The Awakening

At a very early age, Douglass began to *think* and to resolve, against almost everything that his world presented as possible, that one day he would be free. With hardly any concept of what freedom was or meant, he knew it was his single goal.

It was forbidden to teach slaves to read, but through luck and through his own resolute mind, he found rare opportunities to learn some letters of the alphabet and, cleverly asking, talking, secretly poring over a few scrap pages of a Bible, by the time he was eleven he was able to read and write. He began to understand that there was a world of freedom and that the condition of slavery was an abomination unto God and man. The anguish of mothers seeing their children torn from them and sold to faraway slavemasters; the brutal and unjust punishments of whipping, mutilation and even murder; the invincible physical control and power of the white man; the impossibility of protest or even questioning the tyrants to whom one belonged—when even a slight hesitation in obeying an order could mean a flogging; the continual degradation of black men and women forcing themselves to act respectfully to masters they feared and often loathed; to pretend to be happy when they were in abject misery; to act grateful for a piece of rotten food or a trough of mush; to work their bodies to exhaustion and go at night to a bed of cold earth under a scrap of cloth; or, for some, to be dressed up as circus monkeys serving at the master's mansion and, most horrible of all, taking their "privileges" as signs of their own intrinsic superiority to their comrades, when in fact they, like all of the slaves, were nothing but beaten-down, dehumanized and stunted men and women. More and more, as his miraculous self-education proceeded, Douglass grew shocked, stunned at the cloud of forgetting that enveloped the slaves, the forgetting of what it meant to be human beings; he was as repulsed by what the slaves took for their pleasure as he was by the cruelties they suffered from the masters.

And yet, at the same time, there was something else streaking through all this, something rising out of the self-forgetting and the oppression under the slavemasters—a deep, tender humanness would rise up, and suddenly the slave was seen by Douglass not only to have remembered his humanness, but to have opened himself to a nobility and purity that made the heart ache and rejoice at the same time. Douglass felt deeply the music and the religion of the slave—with its roots in both the mysticism of Africa, in which every movement of nature and the human body was sacred, and in the Christianity that they had transformed in the alembic of their own unending submission to a life of crucifixion.

EDWARD COVEY: BREAKER OF SLAVES

In 1833, at the age of fifteen, and clearly standing out for his intelligence and independent spirit, Douglass was rented out for a year as a field hand to the farmer Edward Covey, whose brutal treatment of slaves had earned him "the execrated reputation of being a first rate hand at breaking young negroes."

During the following months, Douglass was continually whipped until be began to feel that he was indeed "broken in body and soul." One hot August afternoon, he lost consciousness and collapsed in the field. Each time Covey ordered him to stand, he struggled for a moment to his feet and then collapsed again, half delirious with pain and exhaustion. While he was down, the "merciless negro breaker" took up a stick and struck him a heavy blow in the head, causing the blood to flow freely, and saying, *"If you have got a headache, I'll cure you."*

Covey finally turned away, and Douglass, bleeding and stumbling, found the strength to slip into the woods, where he finally made his way back to his former master, pleading with him to take him back and keep him from the monstrous cruelties of Mr. Covey. To no avail. Douglass was sent back to the "breaker of slaves."

On the day after his return, long before daylight, he was called up to go and feed, rub, and curry the horses.

In his despair, he had somehow brought his mind to a firm resolve "to obey every order, however unreasonable . . . and, if Mr. Covey should then undertake to beat me, to defend and protect myself to the best of my ability." Here is how Douglass describes what happened and what took place within himself:

AN AMERICAN REVOLUTION

Whilst I was obeying his order to feed and get the horses ready for the field, and when in the act of going up the stable loft . . . Covey sneaked into the stable . . . and seizing me suddenly by the leg, he brought me to the stable floor, giving my newly mended body a fearful jar. I now forgot my *roots*, and remembered my pledge to *stand up in my own defense.* The brute was endeavoring skillfully to get a slip-knot on my legs, before I could draw up my feet. As soon as I found what he was up to, I gave a sudden spring. . . . Whence came the daring spirit necessary to grapple with a man who, eight-and forty hours before, could, with his slightest word have made me tremble like a leaf in a storm, I do not know: at any rate, *I was resolved to fight,* and, what was better still, I was actually hard at it . . . and I found my strong fingers firmly attached to the throat of my cowardly tormentor; as heedless of consequences, at that moment, as though we stood as equals before the law. The very color of the man was forgotten. I felt as supple as a cat, and was ready for the snakish creature at every turn. Every blow of his was parried, though I dealt no blows in return. I was strictly on the *defensive*, preventing him from injuring me, rather than trying to injure him. I flung him to the ground several times, when he meant to hurl me there. I held him so firmly by the throat, that his blood followed my nails. He held me, and I held him.

All was fair, thus far, and the contest was about equal. My resistance was entirely unexpected, and Covey was taken all aback by it, for he trembled in every limb. "*Are you going to resist,* you scoundrel?" said he. To which, I returned a polite "*yes, sir*;" steadily gazing my interrogator in the eye. . . .

Covey at length (two hours had elapsed) gave up the contest. Letting me go, he said—puffing and blowing at a great rate—"now, you scoundrel, go to your work; I would not have whipped you half so much as I have had you not resisted."

The fact was, *he had not whipped me at all*. He had not, in all the scuffle, drawn a single drop of blood from me. I had drawn blood from him; and, even without this satisfaction, I should have been victorious, because my aim had not been to injure him, but to prevent his injuring me. . . .

 . . . this battle with Mr. Covey . . . was the turning point in my "*life as a slave.*" . . . I was *nothing* before; I WAS A MAN NOW . . . A man, without force, is without the essential dignity of humanity. Human nature is so constituted, that it cannot *honor* a helpless man, although it can *pity* him; and even this it cannot do long, if the signs of power do not arise.[114]

And now Douglass brings home the central meaning of his struggle with Covey, the meaning that illuminated his whole life and that enabled him later to illuminate for others the meaning itself of America:

> He only can understand the effects of this combat on my spirit, who has himself incurred something, hazarded something, in repelling the unjust and cruel aggressions of a tyrant. Covey was a tyrant, and a cowardly one, withal; after resisting him, I felt as I have never felt before. It was a resurrection from the dark and pestiferous tomb of slavery, to the heaven of comparative freedom. I was no longer a servile coward, trembling under the frown of a brother worm of the dust, but, my long-cowed spirit was roused to an attitude of manly independence. I had reached the point at which I was *not afraid to die.* This sprit made me a freeman in *fact,* while I remained a slave in *form.* When a slave cannot be flogged he is more than half free. He has a domain as broad as his own manly heart to defend, and he is really *"a power on earth."* . . . From this time, until that of my escape from slavery, I was never fairly whipped. . . . Bruises I did get. . . . But the case I have been describing, was the end of the brutification to which slavery had subjected me.[115]

Douglass had found—or, perhaps more precisely, was found by—the real Self within him. If this is not a spiritual fact, there is no such thing as the spirit—though, of course, there may be many degrees of it. And the risk that was required of him has absolutely no element in it of posturing or bravado or impetuosity; there is not a trace of foolhardiness or egoism about it. There is not even—if one looks closely—the element of anger or resentment in it. (The anger came before it, and it came later—but the force of Douglass' will at this moment consumes and transforms every kind of emotion that is the expression of one part of a man fighting against another part, a characteristic of ordinary anger.) Instead, what we see here is the risk one takes in those rare moments of life when the Self speaks to the self, and one wholly and instantly submits, without bargaining with what the mind "knows" or with the way the world "appears," without bargaining with the fears or with the surface prudence that in our everyday manifestations form such a thick crust over our essential nature.

It is a revolution from within that is being spoken of here—from deep within the Self. And, as the ancient wisdom teaches, there is nothing, nothing at all in the world of appearances, the world constructed within the frame of the socially conditioned personality, that can resist the uncompromising will of the Self to manifest in human action. Satan himself—so the legends tell us—bows down and submits when the real Self steps forward.

Douglass interiorized the American Revolution. The Revolution arose and came to fruition within the crucible of this same quality of risk. Its outer results in the political, economic and societal realms had spread out, and as the country grew toward becoming the richest and most powerful nation on earth, the inner meaning of the events that gave it birth was forgotten and covered over. America was becoming rich and successful, but inwardly it was already dying and drying up. But the people it had oppressed and enslaved still contained the element that had brought the original fire to the nation. The crime of slavery (in both its broad and narrow meanings) was the outward expression and echo of the deeply human sin of forgetting the inner Self that is the only real source of power and virtue in a human being or in a group or in a culture.

It is sometimes said that slavery is the shadow side of America. Although there is great truth in that, it is equally true to say that America itself had slipped into the shadows of forgetfulness. The continuation of slavery was the result of this forgetting. And Douglass' rebellion is one of a thousand echoes—most of the others are lost in historical obscurity—of the process of remembering the Self that in the past had brought about the glory of the Revolution and was destined to bring about the agony of the Civil War, and which eventually led to Lincoln's decisive redefinition of the meaning of America, which became the basis of such hope for the world: the idea of a nation founded on the intrinsic sacredness of all men and women—in Christian language, the equality of "all souls."

The Sin for Which There Is No Forgiveness

After citing Psalm 137, the Psalm of Remembering, Douglass continues:

> Fellow-citizens; above your national, tumultuous joy, I hear the mournful wail of millions! whose chains, heavy and grievous yester-day, are, to-day, rendered more intolerable by the jubilee shouts that reach them. If I do forget, if I do not faithfully remember those bleeding children of sorrow this day, "may my right hand forget her cunning, and may my tongue cleave to the roof of my mouth."[116]

What Douglass wants to say is that the whole nation must remember its origin and its higher nature. Through the perpetuation of slavery, America is forgetting what it is—and perhaps the word "forgetting" needs to be explained in a manner more explicitly consistent with its meaning in the wisdom traditions of the world: namely, to forget the Self is to deny the divine spirit within man, to deny the goodness of man, to deny the purpose of God's creation of man. In sum, although these are not Douglass' exact words, the perpetuation of slavery denies the intrinsic conscience of man. It is, symbolically, mythically, and perhaps literally as well, a manifestation of a towering and shattering idea that lies in the heart of the great wisdom. In Christian language, it is *the great and awful sin against the Holy Spirit, the one sin for which there is no forgiveness.*

Can a shadow of this idea enter into the re-mythologization of America? The words and logic of Frederick Douglass' July 5 speech—perhaps the greatest anti-slavery oration in American history—can show us the way. But we need to go slowly, for it is a long thought that is coming through Douglass, and it is necessary to meet his thought with our own need to deepen the story of America.

> I do not hesitate to declare, with all my soul, that the character and conduct of this nation never looked blacker to me than on this 4th of

July! . . . America is false to the past, false to the present, and
solemnly binds herself to be false to the future. Standing with God
and the crushed and bleeding slave on this occasion, I will, in the
name of humanity, which is outraged, in the name of liberty, which
is fettered, in the name of the Constitution and the Bible, which
are disregarded and trampled upon, dare to . . . denounce . . . everything that serves to perpetuate slavery—the great sin and shame of
America![117]

Douglass continues, pouring white-hot irony on the present America. The
form of his speech is fire and storm. "The feeling of the nation must be
quickened," he says; "the conscience of the nation must be roused." And he
continues in passionate denunciation. But although the outer form of his
speech is blazing fire, the essence of it is a sustained, slowly developing idea,
all the more penetrating and shattering because of its objective, philosophical significance. We need to let in the fire that is carrying a great and ancient idea about the real nature of evil as the denial, not only of one's
neighbor's humanness and human rights, but of one's own divinity, one's
own cosmic and moral nature as a human being created by God. To do evil
to another is, first and foremost, to deny the sacredness of man, and to deny
the sacred dignity of man is to blaspheme against the Holy Spirit. It is the
unforgivable sin—and in the ancient wisdom teachings, it is this sin, and
no other, that inevitably calls upon man the wrath of God, with its destruction of human life and of any civilization that disallows the entry of the
spirit into the life of the earth. Douglass is accusing America not only of
rank brutality and injustice toward the slave, but of denying its own reflection of the idea of the Holy Spirit; of denying its own sacredness.

Like fallen man himself, America cannot see what it has become. It
cannot see its contradictions; it cannot *feel* that it is not what it imagines itself to be. It does not feel or understand that, in the words of St. Paul, the
good that it would, it does not; and that which it hates, it does. There is a
screen, a tight network of self-deception that prevents America from being

shocked by itself; and it is a central aspect of Douglass' mission to help America free itself from these self-deceptions in order to suffer the fire of seeing its contradictions:

> Americans! . . . You boast of your love of liberty, your superior civilization, and your pure Christianity, while the whole political power of the nation . . . is solemnly pledged to support and perpetuate the enslavement of three million of your countrymen. . . . You invite to your shores fugitives of oppression from abroad . . . but the fugitives from your own land you advertise, hunt, arrest, shoot and kill. . . . You are all on fire at the mention of liberty for France or for Ireland; but are as cold as an iceberg at the thought of liberty for the enslaved of America. . . . You can bare your bosom to the storm of British artillery to throw off a threepenny tax on tea; yet wring the last hard-earned farthing from the grasp of the black laborers of your country. You profess to believe "that of one blood, God made all nations of men to dwell on the face of all the earth," and hath commanded all men everywhere to love one another; yet you notoriously hate (and glory in your hatred), all men whose skins are not colored like your own.[118]

And now Douglass sounds the note that will bring to its final form the great thought he is carrying—namely, that the nation is denying the goodness of its own "scripture," its Declaration of Independence, its Constitution. The nation is slandering itself, forgetting what it is, denying its own sacred essence:

> You declare, before the world, and are understood by the world to declare, that you "hold these truths to be self-evident, that all men are created equal; and are endowed by their Creator with certain inalienable rights; and that, among these are life, liberty and the pursuit of happiness;" and yet, you hold securely, in a bondage which, according to your own Thomas Jefferson, "is worse than ages of that which your

fathers rose in rebellion to oppose," a seventh part of the inhabitants
of your country.[119]

It is worth calling attention to more of Jefferson's words here, for the clarity
with which he saw what we have referred to as man's fatal weakness of
blindness to his own moral and existential self-contradiction. "What a stupendous, what an incomprehensible machine is man! Who can endure toil,
famine, stripes, imprisonment or death itself in vindication of his own liberty, and the next moment . . . inflict on his fellow men a bondage, one hour
of which is fraught with more misery than ages of that which he rose in rebellion to oppose."[120]

Blind to its own contradictions, America's twisted perceptions, cold-
ness of heart and brutality of deed amount to nothing less than a rejection
and forgetting of its own essential nature, its own Self. The great initiative
force that created America has met its counter-force, its principle of resistance equal and opposite to its sacred initiative. And so it has been through
all the ages. In every nation and civilization, every active thrust toward the
good has met its resisting force from within its own bosom. Every nation on
earth, every people, every institution, secular and religious—by a cosmic
law that requires great force to meet its opposing, denying principle—has
seen its destiny shaped by the manner in which it has understood this inevitable, lawful opposing force.

What we see in history as the obvious result of this clash is humanity's
repeated descent into barbarism and violence. What is harder to recognize
are the occasions in history when the opposing force is understood for what
it is and where a third principle—in Christian language, the Holy Spirit—
reconciles the two opposing forces. Such reconciliation is quiet and invisible and takes place behind the scenes in the hearts and minds of individual
men and women. We need to understand that to a significant extent, the
American Constitution was created to allow forces to confront each other in
a manner that makes room for the appearance—the "descent from above,"
if one wishes to put it that way—of the reconciling principle that preserves
and even deepens unity, union. This, continuing with Biblical language,

and echoing the same vision of peace as that of the American Indian, leads to the idea of the "peace that passes understanding," that which bridges two mutually opposing forces.

The deeper meaning of evil lies here. Evil is that which fatally obstructs the action of the inner reconciling force, which fatally obstructs the "descent of the dove," the Holy Spirit, in human life. To resist what is good is not in itself the unforgivable sin. What is unforgivable is to resist the reconciliation of the struggle between good and its antagonist.

In the ancient wisdom there exist two ideas of evil—that is, two words for the devil. One word, the Hebraic *satan,* means the "adversary," the resisting force. The other word, the word "devil," comes from the Greek *diabolos,* the "divider," and means the accuser, the slanderer, the liar. In its first form, as Satan, the devil is ultimately an instrument of God and in the end serves a holy purpose—as Christ says to Satan, "get thee behind me": that is, follow me, work for me. But in its second form, as that which divides off and denies the Holy Spirit, it is an unredeemable evil and must be destroyed. All the truly terrifying images of the devil are in one way or another rooted in the *diabolical:* that which hardens the division between good and evil and thereby compels man to forget his intimate bond with God—for example, to think of himself *only* as an animal (as in the horror story *The Exorcist*) or as a machine.

The crime of slavery, and all that it represents about America, shows us that America, like every other nation and civilization in history, is subject to the universal law that brings equal and opposite resistance to every great initiative. America, we begin to understand, must break free of the illusion that it is an exception to the laws of the universe that operate on earth in every era and in every people. With the crime of slavery—along with much else, of course—we see America slipping into barbarity on a massive scale. We see the danger of the resisting force—the force that resists love, freedom, justice—eclipsing the good and plunging the nation into the same degree of barbarism as it has witnessed in the nations of Europe with their internecine warfare and brutal oppressions. It is one thing to be a nobly conceived nation that, nevertheless, must inevitably contain within it massive currents of cor-

ruption and criminality; that cannot be avoided in the world as it is. But it
is another thing to see a nation destroyed through a widening fissure in its
very essence. This fissure was and is slavery with all its implications and results. In the new story of America, in the re-mythologization of America,
slavery appears as the deepest and most visible evil. The suffering and injustice inflicted on a whole people is a monstrosity. But it is not yet the "blas-
phemy against the Holy Ghost." The nation itself defines itself as that which
cannot abide such injustice. The Constitution itself is to be understood as
that essence of America which will allow the descent from above of the force
that will bring reconciliation of white and black. This is the myth, that is to
say, the sacred story, the sacred meaning that is echoed by the structure of the
American nation. To deny this possibility, to assert that the essential mind
and heart of America favor slavery, favor the monstrosity of evil—*that would
be the unforgivable sin,* that would be the death of America.

THE SLEEP OF AMERICA

And so Douglass continues:

> Fellow-citizens! . . . The existence of slavery in this country brands
> your republicanism as a sham, your humanity as a base pretence, and
> your Christianity as a lie. It destroys your moral power abroad; it cor-
> rupts your politicians at home. It saps the foundation of religion; it
> makes your name a hissing, and a by-word to a mocking earth. *It is the
> antagonistic force in your government,* the only thing that seriously dis-
> turbs and endangers your *Union.*[121]

This antagonistic force, says Douglass,

> fetters your progress . . . it fosters pride; it breeds insolence; it pro-
> motes vice; it shelters crime; it is a curse to the earth that supports it;
> and yet, *you cling to it as if it were the sheet anchor of all your hopes.* Oh! be

warned! be warned! a horrible reptile is coiled up in your nation's bosom; the venomous creature is nursing at the tender breast of your youthful republic; *for the love of God, tear away* and fling from you the hideous monster, and *let the weight of twenty millions crush and destroy it forever!*[122]

Lest there be any doubt as to what lies at the heart of evil, Douglass concludes by utterly condemning the view that slavery, with its attendant evils, is *sanctioned* by the Constitution. This is the unforgivable sin against that spirit which emerged and flowered in Independence Hall in the summer of 1787 and which has since defined the essence, the Selfhood, of America. Be warned, says Douglass. Do not slander, do not live in the lie about what America is and must be by its very nature. Is one to say, asks Douglass ironically, that the Fathers of the Republic "stooped, basely stooped"

> . . . and instead of being the honest men I have before declared them to be, they were the veriest imposters that ever practiced on mankind . . . But I differ from those who charge this baseness on the framers of the Constitution of the United States. *It is a slander upon their memory* . . .[123]

THE SIN OF DESPAIR; THE REBIRTH OF HOPE

Douglass' final words can now show us yet another unexpected and essential aspect of the inner story of America. The unforgivable sin, the denial of the intrinsic goodness of God and man, of God in man, manifests itself inwardly as *despair.* The devil as the liar and slanderer is that which takes away all hope, all possibility, which denies God's power, which regards evil as equal or even stronger than the spirit. The masters of wisdom—in the Christian tradition and elsewhere—spoke of this as heresy, which means, in its serious interpretation, a fatally wrong attitude of mind which obstructs the action of God in one's own individual life or in the life of a people.

Hope—not foolish hope, not childish hope, but hope based on vision and consciousness—is necessary. And is this kind of hope the real, inner meaning of the story of America?

These are Douglass' words about hope:

> Allow me to say, in conclusion, notwithstanding the dark picture I have this day presented of the state of the nation, *I do not despair of this country.* There are forces in operation, which must inevitably work the downfall of slavery. *"The arm of the Lord is not shortened,"* and the doom of slavery is certain. I, therefore, leave off where I began, with *hope.*[124]

And here Douglass points not only to the Declaration of Independence and the Constitution—these elements which define the identity of America. He points as well to the forces of modernity, the changes in the world in which he sees the possibility of divine hope entering into the life of humanity. We need to mark well what he says here because it is America that has been the chief source of the spread of modernity—the new powers of technology, commerce and communication. If America has become an empire, it is so not only because of its inspired concepts of government, but also because of forces that are far more ambiguous—the forces that trouble so many of us and that seem to carry seeds of a destruction that Douglass may not have been able to foresee. Or is he, in some sense we do not yet understand, more prophetic than it may seem? Is there a way of embracing the forces of modernity, which America has so powerfully fueled, that allows the action of the spirit to pour into the world through them? The question arises: can we live in a way that can manifest spirit in the ever-accelerating life of commerce, technology and the dazzling new instruments of communication?

Douglass has cited, and paraphrased, Isaiah 59, one of the Old Testament's most powerful evocations of the ultimate goodness and power or God or spirit:

> Behold, the Lord's hand is not shortened, that it cannot save; neither his ear heavy, that it cannot hear.[125]

And he follows this by reminding his audience that

> Nations do not now stand in the same relation to each other that they did ages ago. No nation can now shut itself up from the surrounding world. . . . Long established customs of hurtful character could formerly fence themselves in, and do their evil work with social impunity. . . . But a change has now come over the affairs of mankind. Walled cities and empires have become unfashionable. The arm of commerce has borne away the gates of the strong city. Intelligence is penetrating the darkest corners of the globe . . . wind, steam and lightening are its chartered agents. Oceans no longer divide, but link nations together . . . space is comparatively annihilated. . . . The fiat of the Almighty, "Let there be light," has not yet spent its force. No abuse, no outrage . . . can now hide itself from the all-pervading light. The iron shoe, the crippled foot of China must be seen. . . . Africa must rise and put on her yet unwoven garment.[126]

Throughout his long and illustrious life, Douglass was one of the most powerful forces in the struggle for racial equality in America. Through his words, wrathful and biting as they often were, and through his actions, he unfailingly brought a sense of hope and confidence in America's intrinsic goodness. But his place as a heroic symbol in the story of America has another dimension than that of a great warrior. He was what the ancient wisdom would call "the bringer of the question." To listen to Douglass and to be awakened in one's heart and mind to the depths of the crime of slavery is, inwardly, suddenly to stop, suddenly to come to an inner silence—even while outwardly one rightly senses the call to help, to act, to make things right in the civic and social sphere. But the bringer of the question does something else as well. He carries a force that acts in a completely interior direction: he brings us to the silence of remorse—a remorse completely beyond any plans of action, completely beyond any possibility of doing something. And yet it is there, in that condition of the encounter with conscience, that something beyond ourselves can appear, something that, were it to be more enduring, could transform the life of man, far beyond any immediate but ultimately superficial remedy. Without the experience of genuine remorse, and without the intentional effort to return again and again to that experience, injustice and barbarism change only their name and form, but not their substance in the life of man and nations. So wisdom teaches and so history shows. America cannot be the hope of the world until it returns to learn that lesson.

And thus in the very last speech of his life, a life committed so energetically to improve the social and political conditions of the Negro—in a major address on September 3, 1894, at the dedication of the Colored Industrial School at Manassas, Virginia; in the midst of his eloquent words of encouragement and his wise articulation of the central importance of education in the life of black men and women, Douglass brings forth the following evocation, for all who have ears to hear, of the path of remorse:

> [The Negro] was driven from time to eternity in the darkest ignorance, herded with the beasts of the field; without marriage, without family, without school, and without any moral training, other than that which came by the slave driver's lash. People who live now and talk of doing too much for the Negro, think nothing of these things, and those who know them, seem to desire to forget them, especially when they are made the basis of a claim for a larger measure of justice to the Negro. They forget that for these terrible wrongs there is, in truth, no redress and no adequate compensation. The enslaved and battered millions have come, suffered, died and gone with all their moral and physical wounds into Eternity. *To them no recompense can be made.* If the American people could put a school house in every valley; a church on every hill top in the South and supply them with a teacher and preacher respectively and welcome the descendants of the former slaves to all the moral and intellectual benefits of the one and the other, without money and without price, such a sacrifice would not compensate their children for the terrible wrong done to their fathers and mothers, by their enslavement and enforced degradation.[127]

There is no end to the tragedy and heroism, the horror and beauty of the history of African Americans in our country. These few glimpses of the life and thought of Frederick Douglass are offered simply as evidence that the hope of America can never be renewed without allowing the entire reality of slavery and its consequences to speak to the mind and heart together. The language of the world's wisdom teachings is there, waiting to serve, waiting to allow the fundamental crimes of America to be seen in their universal meaning so that the moral action that is needed will be rooted in a deep truth about ourselves and not only in an anxious self-condemnation, or in an unfeeling cloud of self-justification, or in the futile dream of progress that has so blinded America to what it shares of the barbarism that has stained the whole fabric of human history.

IV.

The Two Democracies

EIGHT

THE WOUND AND
THE TURNING

FROM WASHINGTON TO EPHRATA

The Lincoln Memorial was our first stop in a research trip that would take us, my wife and I, from Monticello to Philadelphia and, finally, to Ephrata, Pennsylvania, where one of America's most important and least-known communal experiments began in the eighteenth century.

I had been to the Lincoln Memorial before, of course, but the power of it still took me by surprise. Lincoln is the "ordinary" man, the extraordinary "ordinary" man, and it is startling to see "ordinary man" in the form of an immense marble statue surrounded by great columns, the face illuminated with such premeditated care that one feels America consciously knows exactly the mystery of what Lincoln represents. The great downcast head, the face full of impersonal suffering *and the sense of the man watching,* watching . . . observing with calm judgment not only all that goes on in the capital city of America, but all that goes on in human life itself.

THE LOOK AND THE WOUND

One feels, here, the Civil War as America's great wound, even though it in fact resulted in a stronger union, due to Lincoln's unwavering vision throughout. Of course, there is also something about the wound of the Civil War that has not yet healed; it still aches and oozes its poisons. At the same time, there exists ever-increasing hope that the wound of slavery will be healed in the passage of time. Hope in America. But there is another aspect of this wound that will not and should not ever heal. It has nothing to do, directly, with the suffering of the war, the 600,000 deaths; nothing directly to do with the horrors of slavery. It has to do almost entirely with the death of Lincoln himself. No other death has such power to bring tears to us. Lincoln never saw, never lived to see the results of his struggle and never lived to govern an America at peace. And yet, at this memorial, one feels—without any sentimentality—that we are being watched. One feels here the unfathomable powerlessness of the dead—together with their even more incomprehensible power to watch us, to see what we are and what we are becoming. Here, Lincoln comes to represent the deeply mysterious power of the look, of seeing. The force of this look has everything to do with the man and the way he disappeared. It teaches us, this monument, not so much that the dead hero sees us, but that there is a seeing that is like death itself—invisible, all-pervasive, without any capacity or even wish to act or do, yet with an irresistible power to penetrate and influence that which is seen. The monument completes the image of the living Lincoln. The living Lincoln is the mystery of presence; the dead Lincoln is the manner of seeing that emanates from pure presence. All without words, without conceptualization, without manipulation.

And yet, there, engraved on the walls of the monument are the words. At first, one passes by the Gettysburg Address. Even in the presence of the colossal stone figure, these words are at first too familiar to draw one's interest. The eye goes, instead, to the adjoining wall, upon which is carved the full text of the Second Inaugural Address. One notes the date: March 4, 1865.

Lincoln is beginning his second term of office. In little more than a month, on April 9, Lee will surrender at Appomattox. The war is over. Six days later, Lincoln is dead. The Gettysburg Address, as Garry Wills has observed, established America as one people. Here Lincoln defined the suffering of the Civil War as redemptive in giving birth to the unity of the people. The Second Inaugural is quite different. It calls us, instead, to contemplate the collective crimes of the unified nation which, under God's universal justice, have brought about the agony of the war. "In the Gettysburg Address, the people was consecrated as a whole. . . . Now we see that it *sins* in solidarity as well."[128] But, as Wills goes on to observe, the wound of the war is interpreted as *washing away* the sins of the people. The war and the suffering it has inflicted have opened the path to a second chance, a new birth. This sense of a humbled and remorseful new beginning, of a resolve that is made with bowed head—the resolve of a powerful people who have acted wrongly, but who now may go forward under the guidance of the Good—this redeemable sorrow is surely one of the chief meanings of both the Civil War and the figure of Lincoln.

THE SECOND INAUGURAL ADDRESS

Fellow Countrymen: At this second appearing to take the oath of the presidential office, there is less occasion for an extended address than there was at the first. Then a statement, somewhat in detail, of a course to be pursued, seemed fitting and proper. Now, at the expiration of four years, during which public declarations have been constantly called forth on every point and phase of the great contest which still absorbs the attention, and engrosses the energies of the nation, little that is new could be presented. The progress of our arms, upon which all else chiefly depends, is as well known to the public as to myself; and it is, I trust, reasonably satisfactory and encouraging to all. With high hope for the future, no prediction about it is ventured. On the occasion corresponding to this four years ago, all thoughts were anxiously directed to an impending civil war. All dreaded it—all sought to avert it. While the inaugural address was being deliv-

ered from this place, devoted altogether to saving the Union without war, insurgent agents were in the city seeking to destroy it without
war—seeking to dissolve the Union, and divide effects, by negotiation. Both parties deprecated war; but one of them would make
war rather than let the nation survive; and the other would accept war
rather than let it perish. And the war came.

One eighth of the whole population were colored slaves, not distributed generally over the Union, but localized in the Southern part of
it. These slaves constituted a peculiar and powerful interest. All knew
that this interest was, somehow, the cause of the war. To strengthen,
perpetuate, and extend this interest was the object for which the in-
surgents would rend the Union, even by war; while the government
claimed no right to do more than to restrict the territorial enlarge-
ment of it. Neither party expected for the war, the magnitude or the
duration, which it has already attained. Neither anticipated that the
cause of the conflict might cease with, or even before, the conflict itself should cease.

Each looked for an easier triumph, and a result less fundamental and
astounding. Both read the same Bible, and pray to the same God; and
each invokes His aid against the other. It may seem strange that any
men should dare to ask a just God's assistance in wringing their bread
from the sweat of other men's faces; but let us judge not that we be
not judged. The prayers of both could not be answered; that of neither has been answered fully. The Almighty has His own purposes.
"Woe unto the world because of offences! for it must needs be that offences come but woe to that man by whom the offence cometh!" If we
shall suppose that American Slavery is one of those offences which, in
the providence of God, must needs come, but which, having continued through His appointed time, He now wills to remove, and that
He gives to both North and South, this terrible war, as the woe due
to those by whom the offence came, shall we discern therein any de-

parture from those divine attributes which the believers in a Living God always ascribe to Him? Fondly do we hope—fervently do we pray—that this mighty scourge of war may speedily pass away. Yet, if God wills that it continue, until all the wealth piled by the bond-man's two hundred and fifty years of unrequited toil shall be sunk, and until every drop of blood drawn with the lash, shall be paid by another drawn with the sword, as was said three thousand years ago, so still it must be said "the judgments of the Lord, are true and righteous altogether." With malice toward none; with charity for all; with firmness in the right, as God gives us to see the right, let us strive on to finish the work we are in; to bind up the nation's wounds; to care for him who shall have borne the battle, and for his widow, and his orphan—to do all which may achieve and cherish a just, and a lasting peace, among ourselves, and with all nations.

March 4, 1865

Almost reluctantly, because filled with the sense of communion with Lincoln and with the haunting feeling that his message was, somehow, not for the past, nor for us in the present, but for the future, I turned to the wall upon which was inscribed the Gettysburg Address. I read it as a matter of obligation, nothing more; but as I read it, its force nearly knocked me down.

Four score and seven years ago our fathers brought forth on this continent, a new nation, conceived in Liberty, and dedicated to the proposition that all men are created equal. Now we are engaged in a great civil war, testing whether that nation, or any nation so conceived and so dedicated, can long endure. We are met on a great battlefield of that war. We have come to dedicate a portion of that field, as a final resting place for those who here gave their lives that that nation might live. It is altogether fitting and proper that we should do this. But, in a larger sense, we can not dedicate—we can not consecrate—we can not hallow—this ground. The brave men, living and dead, who struggled here, have consecrated it, far above our poor power to add or detract. The world will little note, nor long remember what we say here, but it can never forget what they did here. It is for us the living, rather, to be dedicated here to the unfinished work which they who fought here have thus far so nobly advanced. It is rather for us to be here dedicated to the great task remaining before us—that from these honored dead we take increased devotion to that cause for which they gave the last full measure of devotion—that we here highly resolve that these dead shall not have died in vain—that this nation, under God, shall have a new birth of freedom—and that government of the people, by the people, for the people, shall not perish from the earth.

November 19, 1863

VIETNAM

It was actually an accident, more or less. We intended to visit the Jefferson Memorial next, but on the way back to our car, we passed groups of people and individuals that attracted my attention in a strange way. They seemed to have a certain look, a certain feeling about them—men and women, younger and older, people of all kinds and backgrounds. Thinking back on it, perhaps what drew me most was the sameness of feeling in all these dozens and dozens of people. When you pass people on the street some are happy, some are sad, some are bored, some are distracted, some are tense, some smile, some frown, some seem lost in dreams, some are scowling. . . . But here, everyone seemed the same—quiet, sober, yet with eyes glistening and bodies moving with full, vibrant strides. Semi-consciously, not really aware of what was drawing us, we simply walked past the car and onto a broad lawn. The sober, vibrant people kept coming and coming. We soon found ourselves in front of Frederick Hart's statue of the Three Soldiers and we realized we were at the Vietnam Veterans Memorial. It was a cloudy, windy spring day and the astonishingly realistic soldiers seemed suddenly to materialize out of the moist wind and the thin, warm mist. As though out of another dimension of time. For a startling instant, I actually thought they were real soldiers and was momentarily alarmed by their automatic weapons. I realized it was a statue the same moment I was struck by the young vulnerability of their faces. They seemed eternally lost and frightened, listening and looking for danger—simultaneously ready to kill and to cry.

Of course, I had heard a great deal about the Vietnam Memorial—how in 1981 a design chosen from over a thousand entries turned out to be the work of Maya Ying Lin, a twenty-one-year-old design student at Yale. I had mentally appreciated the idea of her design from the pictures of it: a polished black granite wall, V-shaped and half-buried in the ground, inscribed with the 58,000 names of the dead, and reflecting the faces of the viewers as they passed by. Well before one begins down the path that runs alongside the black granite wall, one is struck by the impression of a monument that does not soar. It is the only such monument in Washington, and perhaps in all of America. It does not soar or rise upward; it is not positive. It recedes, it opens downward, it is an absence, like a permanent wound. Off to one side is the towering obelisk of the Washington Monument and to the other the Lincoln Memorial. Compared to the Vietnam Memorial, even the statue of Lincoln in all its somber majesty represents a positive statement, a hope, an affirmation rooted in the experience of remorse and sorrow. Not so the Vietnam Memorial. One begins walking past the black stone with the engraved names at ankle height. There at one's feet are death and grief and error, while at the same time one's eyes and ears and breathing take in the wide green lawn, the air, the trees and milling people, the traffic passing back and forth.

As one walks, one descends. Gradually. Something is entering into the psyche. But from below. Nearly unnoticed. One's head is still in the living and doing world, the world of action and decision. But something is entering more and more from below. In one's consciousness, one is aware of the names of the dead. One has thoughts of sorrow and sympathy, or perhaps anger, or fear. One sees the flowers placed at the foot of the wall by loving relatives. One sees people taking rubbings of a name here and there. The names themselves begin to take on lives of their own—suddenly they all seem to be the names of one being, one person—like the million names of God. These are the million names of mortal man.

Having such thoughts, one walks, and is moved by this profoundly conceived memorial. Yet the most important thing is happening under the surface of one's consciousness, from below. The black wall rises and rises. One hardly notices the wall rising, the names growing—until, suddenly, I see myself in the wall, my face and body on the other side, as it were, of the names of the dead; myself in the land of the dead. Yet I am alive, and from the land of the dead I am seeing myself, here and now, walking. I am being watched by some presence in the land of the dead; and the presence watching myself is: myself!

The wall is now higher than my head. The world is now only this black granite mirror, the thousands of names like thousands of eyes. What has been entering from below has now filled me completely and has softly displaced my thoughts and images of death and war. I am only darkness and the seeing of these names that are eyes; I am only a black, stone mirror. Although I continue walking, I no longer feel myself as moving; time has stopped. I see my image and the image of my wife with me, in the black wall, through the names that are eyes. In that black mirror is the world where all color is true and black at the same time.

And suddenly, something brilliant enters my eyes, painfully brilliant. The living and breathing world! Real, green grass; beams of sunlight; real people moving around; trees; air, light, buildings! I am in the world again, alive. I had started walking up the incline, without noticing it. The wall had been growing lower again, without my noticing it. And now, at eye level, the three-dimensional, affirming world returns to me; my head is above the wall, then my shoulders, then my waist. And in that progression, the black anti-world of the Vietnam War retreats from my awareness. But not entirely: this absence, this negation, this reality remains perhaps stronger than ever, but inside me, like a pillar of emptiness and darkness within the center of my body, like a counter-spine. And it is very clear: this nation, this people, America, has not "recovered" from this war. And may it never recover. If America ever fully "recovers" from this war, it is doomed. Spiritually doomed—which means, materially doomed as well. The earth cannot support a dominant civilization that has no empty center, no negative movement, no soft breathing and renunciation at its heart. There must be an inner as well as an outer, a stepping back as well as a thrust forward, a prayer as well as an affirmation. Such were my thoughts, the beginning of my thought, as I walked away from the Vietnam Memorial. This horrific, degrading war broke everything in our nation that had become breakable and mortal; and things become breakable only when they are first separated from their roots in the depth of reality.

The Civil War did not break America's heart, but Vietnam did. It is said, "When the heart weeps for what it has lost, the spirit laughs for what it has found." Another old saying has it that "The body is the temple of God but the throne of God is built in the ruins of the heart." Could it be that a healing drop of deep psychological "ruin" has entered the bloodstream of America? After two hundred years of its accelerating outward motion, is America again ready to make room for the dark mirror of conscience with its attendant sorrow and its all-embracing light?

THE ILLUSION AND THE VISION

But was my feeling about Vietnam, a war I did not serve in, out of bounds? Who was I to stand back and view this war as a metaphor? There were hundreds of thousands of Americans whose lives were literally and completely destroyed by this war. Not my life.

At the same time, the war destroyed the meaning of America for millions of the rest of us. And it was because the war destroyed the meaning of America that its devastation was also so much greater for the individuals who were wounded or who lost loved ones in the war. Far greater than in a war such as the Second World War, which at least seemed honorable and meaningful.

But was it the meaning of America that had been lost—or the illusion of America?

Wasn't Vietnam the wound that finally destroyed the illusion of America? What is the response to such a wound? For an individual seeking understanding, the response through the ages has been to acknowledge that suddenly a channel has been opened between oneself and Truth. Can this be so also for a whole nation?

A WHOLE NATION

As we entered the street again, passing the people, the cars, the government buildings, questions of the inner world suddenly seemed small and irrelevant, perhaps even self-indulgent.

We walked aimlessly down Constitution Avenue, the Supreme Court building to our right, the great dome of the Capitol just behind our shoulders. Who was I kidding? What did philosophy—and spiritual philosophy at that—have to do with what went on in all these buildings; laws that affected millions, life and death, war, justice, poverty, the life of the family, the economic foundations of the world, the whole swirling realm of the forces of planetary life—survival, safety, dignity, and, and . . .

But could it be that these massive material buildings, these massive material institutions, these powerful, outward-directed forces at work in this city and in this nation—could it be that behind them, at their source, there could still be found the hidden roots of the quest for Truth and Being?

The Supreme Court: freedom, liberty, individual rights, the powers of self-determination, privacy, the need of men and women to inhabit their own inner world, to be able to hear their own conscience—this classic colonnaded building manifesting, in heavy stone, ideals of the social structure that are as light as a thought or as the fleeting image of an invisible world, the world of the inner life, that so many of our ancestors sought to hold on to by coming to America.

And the Capitol: the arena of the experiment called representative democracy—the ideal of individuals struggling together to hear the voice that speaks to the community at the same time that it speaks from within themselves. The most difficult and most necessary struggle of all: the work of being with others in order to receive a more impartial truth—that is, a truth that represents not just one part, but all the parts in their proper place and order. Unity as the reciprocally nourishing exchange between all the parts of a society. National unity not as a means only to material and political power, but as an echo of the unity of nature and the self.

National unity: an echo of metaphysical unity, organic unity? Well, perhaps this *was* a fantasy. Perhaps, or, rather, surely, such a unity can only be found among human beings on an infinitely smaller scale and under the guidance of an immeasurably purer aim than the aims of massive, colonnaded, national power or well-being. Nevertheless, even though metaphysical unity—the unity of the great self within, or the unity of a community of saints—cannot honestly be the aim of a huge collectivity such as a modern nation, nevertheless the ideal of unity must retain its metaphysical dimension, if only as a standard by which to measure what we are as a species and what we are doing.

If, inside that Capitol, there can exist only the raw clay of self-interest, cunning and deception mixed with rare specks of honesty and conscience, then so be it. No doubt it has always been this way—even at Independence Hall in 1787 as the Constitution itself was created. A material symbol can never be as pure as what it symbolizes—but only let it retain the tiny seed of truth and meaning from which the sensitive mind can draw inspiration and direction. If the government of the United States of America has lost its way, let the way itself be remembered and seen even as we collectively fall so far from it. Let the forms we have, the words we use, degraded though they may have become, sound again their ideal meaning so that we can know again and with renewed clarity what it is we are searching for, what we wish for and why:

FREEDOM: not just lack of external restraint, but freedom to discover, to create, to know—and above all, freedom understood as submission to the inner moral law. And the creation of external conditions and internal attitudes that protect and support the struggle for that inner submission.

INDIVIDUALITY: not just the license to believe in and follow whatever thought or impulse passes through the mind, but the movement in ourselves toward what Emerson called "that overpowering reality which confutes our tricks and talents, and constrains every one to pass for what he is, and to speak from his character, and not from his tongue, and which evermore tends to pass into our thought and hand and become wisdom, and power, and beauty."

DEMOCRACY: not the cacophonous leveling that strips human community of all that is intrinsically aristocratic, psychologically noble, original and private; not that bastardization of the ideal of democratic equality which Plato condemned as a cacophony of subjective values and preferences, but rather a social order whose basis is not the lowest, but the highest common denominator in us.

Again, in the words of Emerson:

Persons themselves acquaint us with the impersonal. In all conversation between two persons, tacit reference is made to a third party, to a common nature. That third party or common nature is not social; it is impersonal; is God. And so in groups where debate is earnest, and especially on high questions, the company becomes aware that the thought rises to an equal level in all bosoms, that all have a spiritual property in what was said, as well as the sayer. They all become wiser than they were. It arches over them like a temple, this unity of thought, in which every heart beats with nobler sense of power and duty, and thinks and acts with unusual solemnity. All are conscious of attaining to a higher self-possession. There is a certain wisdom of humanity which is common to the greatest men with the lowest, and which our ordinary education often labors to silence and obstruct.[129]

In such a direction lies the deeper vision of democracy—a vision which our clumsy and crippled practices can still mirror for us. Although we have wandered far from its metaphysical source, the concept of democracy can still remind us of the idea of human equality, an idea that quickly rots when it falls away from its mystical source and, like some fruit of hell, retains its outer luster while, inside, it nourishes a community, not of saints, nor of ordinary men and women seeking understanding, but of ruined animals desiring only their own immediate pleasure and security, unable to see or hear themselves and each other as common children of the One.

My desire to visit the physical remains of the enigmatic Ephrata community in Pennsylvania was now stronger than ever. From all I had read, Ephrata had been one of America's most serious experiments in the mystical meaning of democracy—just at the time when the new nation was coming to birth and when there was still a real choice to make as to the whole destiny of the United States.

ON THE WAY TO EPHRATA: MONTICELLO

But it was surely Jefferson who understood that choice, that possibility of holding the new nation to the interior dimension of human life even as it grew into the most powerful nation on earth. I was glad that we had put Monticello in our itinerary before Ephrata. In the first place, I was half afraid I would find at Ephrata the remains of an experiment in community that was merely a failed European transplant, and therefore of no importance in understanding the roots of the American destiny. I knew I could rely on encountering America through encountering Jefferson in any aspect at all of his life and thought. But on the way to Monticello I had a similar kind of fear. I was also afraid Monticello would disappoint me. I expected to be impressed by the building and by the visible evidence of Jefferson's fertile mind. But right under the surface I still had the gnawing suspicion that Jefferson, for all that he means to America and all that he did for America, was somehow not exactly a spirit of the first order, certainly not anything like what his admirers imagined him to be.

My first impression of Monticello, seen from some distance, relieved me immensely. It was smaller and more compact than I had expected from the photographs, but it immediately struck me as a structure of exceptional concentration and intelligence. I felt in it a certain hard-to-define unity within complexity, like an unusually cut precious stone. My first glance assured me that I would not be disappointed.

I was not so foolish as to imagine it would be anything like a cathedral or a Taj Mahal or a tranquil Quaker meetinghouse. I had been able to set aside all such preconceptions. In fact, my impression of Monticello was that it was completely unlike any building I'd ever seen.

We walked around the outside of the house before joining the long line of tourists waiting to be escorted inside. As we did so, my initial impression began to alternate with quite a different feeling—a sense of nearly banal familiarity. These two impressions continuously alternated, sometimes one of them—the building's integrity and intelligence or, on the contrary, its ordinariness—lasting for a relatively long time, and sometimes just for a moment or two. But the alternation was unceasing the whole time. This double sense of a great building was unlike any experience I'd ever had of a material object. I tried to understand it even as it was taking place. Whatever the reason, this successively double impression began to produce a strangely familiar inner "taste," or state, that came upon me gradually and subtly.

Perhaps it was that I had, after all, been brought up in Philadelphia, among all sorts of colonial and neocolonial buildings and styles. Much of my childhood and adolescence, with all its boredom and its ordinary hopes and fears, had taken place against the background of this general kind of "colonial" building, these red brick walls and white-sashed windows. And having spent my university years at Harvard and Yale, I took even the best examples of American neoclassical or federal architecture for granted. In fact, I grew up fairly blind to architecture as an art form, as an incarnation of ideas.

At the same time, I was actually seeing this building in a way I had never seen a building before. In my travels I had, of course, marveled and wondered at cathedrals and ancient churches and great ruins. But that was expected. They were time honored and officially sacred buildings.

But Monticello? In Virginia? I kept telling myself that however excellent this structure might be, it was after all only American, and only the product of an individual American mind, however brilliant. It was Jefferson's invention, Jefferson's ideas piled side by side in stone; his ideas about man, about reason and—in its setting atop a great hill, with its inspiring views, a very impractical place to set a great house in the eighteenth century, away from docks and roads—his hopes in the perfectibility of human nature, his dreams of the power that can come to human reason when it consciously re-blends with nature.

Our appointed time to tour the interior of the building was approaching, and we joined the long line of tourists stretching down the hill around the perimeter of the house. Thoughts about Jefferson's vision of man in nature continued as we slowly moved with the line at the edge of the orchard, now replanted with the varieties of fruit trees that Jefferson had originally chosen.

It was midafternoon; the Virginia sun was warm, the scent of grass and blossoms was intoxicating. I had read a great deal about Jefferson's views on the importance of agriculture in the new nation, on the need for individuals to live and work in contact with the land and the earth . . . and, therefore, with the physical body. This stance of Jefferson toward agriculture has been interpreted by scholars, and with some justice, as mainly of economic and political significance—as Jefferson's sense of how the growing nation could retain its political autonomy in the face of the forces and powers emanating from Europe.

ENTER HAMILTON

And it is these economic and political factors that are taken as the main context for Jefferson's great struggle with Alexander Hamilton, whose vision of

America's well-being was diametrically opposed to his own. Hamilton, America's first secretary of the Treasury, conceived of the nation as centralizing in the cities, intensifying manufacturing rather than agriculture and, above all, creating a sophisticated and powerful system of banking and finance. Through the manipulation and extension of the money device—promissory credit, instruments of investment and the accumulation of capital—the forces of the world would centralize in America and would bring the new nation the power and self-sufficiency that were its proper destiny.

Very early in his presidency, Jefferson seems to have realized that Hamilton had won. By the time Jefferson took office, it was already too late to see America as rooted fundamentally in agriculture. On the contrary, America was to be rooted in . . . money. And Jefferson himself was soon taking steps, necessary steps, to increase manufacturing in the young nation.

Hamilton's course led America straight into the main currents of the emerging industrial society and helped bring America its ultimately overwhelming material dominance. In his profound and boldly prophetic understanding of the meaning and nature of money in the life of modern man, Hamilton captured for America the most powerful energies of the emerging world order. Did this mean, as Jefferson seemed to fear, that America was selling its soul to the devil?

And was Jefferson's view in any way preferable? His ideal of man-in-nature working directly with the land could not survive even the first waves of the industrial revolution that was sweeping the world. And as for the ascendancy of reason, scientific reason, which Jefferson so highly valued, could he foresee how science by itself, cut off from the governance of conscience, could serve the same kind of devil as he feared Hamilton was loosing upon the nation?

In any case, here we are, two hundred years later, in a world dominated by both the power of money and the juggernaut of continually advancing scientific technology. Could either Hamilton or Jefferson have foreseen the fusion of capitalism and the applications of scientific reason that now defines the tensions of our global culture?

The line moved. Every twenty minutes Monticello released a batch of visitors, and the line moved forward.

Was it really possible to return to a simple, direct hope in the ideals of America? A simple and direct feeling for America—completely untinged by politics, by "religion," by agendas—and, one might say, in a positive sense, completely untinged by the "facts" of history or the snarled complexity of present-day America. Present-day America—which includes in its giant belly almost all of human life with all its mass, all its anger and brutality, all its billions and billions of actions, dreams, crimes, loves, betrayals, conquests and chaos.

A simple hope. America as a beginning. Free from "Europe"—which meant, mythically as well as literally, free from the patterns of the past, free even from the achievements of the past—the great art, and awesome cathedrals, the unsurpassed depth of Europe's music, its philosophy, its poetry, all of it unable to influence for the good the impulses of fear, greed and hatred that have ravaged human life—Europe, as Jefferson saw it, the land of eternal war and tyranny. This Europe—outside of us and inside of us, the old patterns of the human passions unrelated to our perceptions of the good—our interior art and music. Europe—whose art and music serve perhaps too much as dreams in which the unregenerate two-natured being man indulges while his demons grow and do their work of destruction. America as a new beginning, a declaration of independence bringing us toward the land, toward the life of nature within and around us. Our art may not be as "great," but perhaps it is or can be really ours—that is, in relation to the whole of us and therefore not a dream into which we escape while our own demons work their work.

Yet there was this Alexander Hamilton. It was a remarkable coincidence that thoughts of Hamilton kept up with my reflections about Jefferson and Monticello. Remarkable because the moment I finally stood in the entrance hall of Monticello the first thing I noticed was the bust of Hamilton placed opposite the bust of Jefferson.

AT THE HEART OF DEMOCRACY

Knowing a little of the history, of the bitterness between the two men, it did not occur to me that Jefferson had placed these statues there himself. Yet when I wryly remarked to the guide about how things happen after a man's death, I was told that it was Jefferson himself who placed Hamilton there—right across from him.

As I later learned, even during Jefferson's lifetime, visitors to Monticello were no less astonished than I to encounter these two figures, and to see them so prominently placed. "Opposed in death as in life," Jefferson once remarked to one of his perplexed guests.[130]

The impression made on me by these two statues colored everything else that I saw during the tour. I felt a little foolish attributing so much importance to this one thing even as I was shown so many historically important elements of Jefferson's genius and life—his sense of architectural form; his mechanical inventiveness; his great erudition and the breadth of his interests and abilities in science, music and the arts; his capacity constantly to experiment and rebuild, continually searching, searching; his hands-on involvement in all aspects of the life of Monticello—from the vast gardens to the wine cellar to the kitchen and the preparation of food, to the mechanics of the hand-plow and the very design of the iron nails used in the ongoing construction of the buildings; to the expression in space and line of a philosophy that elevated the light of human reason in its correspondence with the warmth of an educated heart and a humanly engaged physical body working directly with all its strength on the land and the natural world that gave it life.

Amidst all this, it was Jefferson's placement of the bust of Hamilton that most drew my admiration and that, in fact, gave weight and reality to everything else I had learned and was learning about him.

Is this at the heart of democracy?—this valuing of the other even when he opposes me?

Or am I dreaming?

Was this what happened at crucial moments during the framing of the Constitution? Perhaps. Perhaps not. But can the form of American democracy serve to point us toward the need for a deeper kind of communal attention? I believe it can. I believe there is another democracy waiting to be born within the heart of the flawed, but resonantly symbolic democracy within which we all now live and move.

The question is: can the ideals of democracy remind us that we need to become what John Dewey called *democratic individuals:* men and women who are *inwardly* democratic, who are able to step back from the personal emotions in order to allow the other to think and speak and live. Democracy, in this sense, refers not only to an outer form of government, but to a power within the self.

In our time it was surely Vietnam that showed us—through the wound that it inflicted on our national psyche—that our outer form of America by itself is only another instrument in the blind play of historical forces. In that sense, Vietnam was perhaps, and paradoxically, a wound that can heal us by exposing to us the illusion of purely external politics, the illusion of history, the illusion of taking America literally, externally, as some divinely "chosen" nation.

Yet this wounded, exposed America—and the wound continues to bleed its moral confusion—this wounded nation can look inside itself and see the traces of the ancient vision of what men and women can become within themselves and with each other. The forms of our government can still serve as symbols of the individual struggle that can bring conscious, moral life into our world.

What kind of communal life is needed in order for that? What democracy-within-democracy is needed?

NINE

EPHRATA: IN SEARCH OF THE SECOND DEMOCRACY

I s this America? These high-gabled, wooden structures are as pure and original and as beautiful as they are strange. Not just meetinghouses or dormitories or churches or barns, they correspond to no familiar American image.

Yet they are here in rural Pennsylvania, sixty miles west of Philadelphia. They constitute the reconstructed remains of the Ephrata Cloister, founded in 1728 by Conrad Beissel, one of the most remarkable men in American history and one of the least recognized or understood. The community he created when the American giant was only an embryo can now help us to remember the deeper possibilities of what we call democracy.

A Small Thing

It was a small thing, this community, and fragile. It existed for a few decades and was then swept away as the American nation came to birth in the mud and fire and blood of the Revolutionary War. A fragile thing, a wisp of smoke, like the fragility of the truth that is always being pushed aside in our lives, and yet without which the earth and all its human "glories" might have long ago disappeared in violence and destruction. The great teachers of mankind have all spoken in whispers, and their messages have always begun by being submerged in the floodwaters of time and the barbarism of history. Nevertheless, these nearly inaudible teachings, these actions that lead to no outward triumphs, have brought to mankind the ideals of moral and spiritual life that have given hope to the world. And, on a level we cannot see, the mysterious "weakness" and "defeats" of these teachings may have conducted influences into human life that have made it possible for civilization to go on at all.

In order to have a sense of what Ephrata was and what it could mean to us, we can begin by looking at an occurrence that took place in the winter of 1777, in the darkest hour of the American Revolution.

A Certain Michael Widman

We are at Valley Forge with Washington and the cold, hungry Continental Army. Twenty miles away, the British, under General William Howe, occupy Philadelphia with its salons, its ladies, its warm houses and its bounty of food and drink. Here we turn to a narration by nineteenth-century historian Julius Friedrich Sachse.[131]

Washington's strength and his depth of purpose are everywhere apparent as he struggles with his anger at Congress for neglecting his troops and for its unjustified criticism of his leadership; and with his anxiety concerning the future of the army as its number dwindles through disease and desertion. "I could not keep my eyes from that imposing countenance," wrote one French officer, "grave, yet not severe; affable without familiarity. Its predominant expression was calm dignity, through which you could trace the strong feelings of the patriot, and discern the father, as well as the commander of his soldiers. I have never seen a picture that represents him to me as I saw him at Valley Forge."[132]

At the moment in question, Washington was in the command tent with General Charles Lee and several other staff officers. He had just approved, and dispatched by courier, the finding of a court-martial held at Turk's Head (now West Chester) in which a certain Michael Widman had been summarily convicted of treason and sentenced to be hanged.

Michael Widman ran a tavern a short distance from the Ephrata settlement. He had served with seemingly great dedication as the head of the Lancaster County Committee of Safety, one of many such organizations constituted throughout the colonies to support the revolution.

Widman felt nothing but contempt for the Ephrata community and its leadership, being himself a prominent member of the German Reformed Church (Lutheran), which sharply resented the Ephrata settlement. The charisma of its founder, Conrad Beissel, had attracted many outstanding members of the Church toward the mystical community on the nearby Cocalico River. Chief among those who had been drawn away by Beissel some forty years earlier in 1735 was the brilliant young Lutheran minister Peter Miller, who had become one of Beissel's most devoted followers and who had assumed the leadership of the Ephrata community on Beissel's death in 1768. Living in close proximity to the community, Michael Widman apparently lost no opportunity to show his hatred for Miller, on one occasion physically assaulting him and on another occasion actually spitting in the venerable old man's face.

Not long after Howe and the British had taken possession of Philadelphia, two men rode up to Widman's tavern and asked for lodgings. In fact, they were British scouts who had come incognito to reconnoiter the Ephrata establishment, where Washington had sent the wounded after the defeat at the Battle of Brandywine.

The two men were seated at supper, conversing with Widman, who was

standing with his back to an open window. After a few commonplace remarks, Widman blusteringly asked them how things were in Philadelphia
and how that wretched scoundrel General Howe was getting along.

Instantly flushed with anger at Widman's remark, one of the men shot
back:

"What, Sir, would you think if you were to see General Howe standing
here before you?"

"Think?" Widman replied, just as impulsively, "I think I would be seeing as damned a scoundrel as ever walked the earth!"

In an instant the stranger sprang to his feet, drawing a pistol from his
coat. Placing the gun at Widman's chest, he shouted, "You damned rebel,
you are a dead man."

Without a second's hesitation, Widman threw himself backward out of
the window. The two strangers jumped out after him. But the night was
dark and Widman succeeded in eluding them. Fearing a disturbance in the
neighborhood, the two British scouts immediately left the area.

Widman first ran to an adjoining cornfield and then to the rocky banks
of the Cocalico River, but soon realized that, come daybreak, he might easily be detected by someone sympathetic to the British. If he fell into their
hands, his life would be over. In his desperation, he sought a place where no
one would think of looking for him and found his way to the Brothers'
House in Ephrata—just that community that he had so reviled and perse-
cuted over the years.

The houses at Ephrata were never locked at night. Widman entered the
long narrow passages of the Brothers' House and quietly made his way to an
upper unoccupied loft, being careful not to awaken any of the brethren.
There he stayed, hiding behind a stack of chimneys, three days and three
nights without food or drink.

Pondering the gravity of his situation, he decided to take what seemed
to him the only course possible. He would go to Philadelphia and try to
conciliate General Howe. Late on the fourth night, he found his way out
again, hastening to his wife to tell her his plan and to supply himself with
money and clothing for the journey. He set out at once, before sunrise.

He arrived in Philadelphia the following evening and at General Howe's quarters told the guard he had matters of great urgency to communicate to the General. But when ushered into the General's presence, Widman found, suddenly, that his throat was constricted with fear and embarrassment. He could only stammer, without uttering a single word. Howe looked at him, puzzled by the meaningless silence. "With whom am I in communication?" the General asked.

Widman finally stammered out something like the following:

"May I, Sir, be assured that forgiveness might be granted to one who had embraced the American cause from the onset, and who had, in his misplaced zeal, been discourteous to the royal cause and its adherents? If such assurance is granted, I am prepared to add to the royal cause considerable important information of stores and ammunition concealed for the rebels."

While Widman was making his treasonous declaration, two officers were thumbing through a book of entry on record before them, and before General Howe replied to Widman, the officers directed his attention to the page before them. As he read the short paragraph, the General glanced up several times. "Ah!" he exclaimed, "you, sir, are Michael Widman!"

As though struck by lightning, Widman fell to his knees and pleaded for mercy, adding that he would perform any service asked of him against the Americans.

With hardly a pause, General Howe replied that, although it was the policy of the British officers to encourage disaffection in the rebel ranks, yet "an individual who occupied such a position in the confidence of his countrymen as you, sir, and who could yet prove treacherous to them on so slight a pretext—such a cowardly, contemptible pretext—such a person could never be trusted in the royal cause."

Widman remained on his knees, speechless as before.

"You may leave," said General Howe, and to his officers he added, "Be sure he is conducted safely beyond our outposts."

Not long after Widman had left for Philadelphia, his wife had spread the news about his intentions, and dispatches had been sent to all the American stations to be on the alert for him. At the first American outpost, Widman was discovered and arrested, and taken to the Block House at Turk's Head, where a court-martial quickly sentenced him to be hanged as a traitor.

Everywhere throughout the region Widman was denounced for his treachery. There was only one person who refused to speak against him: Peter Miller, the much-abused Prior of Ephrata. On hearing of Widman's arrest, the aged Prior immediately set out on foot for the camp at Valley Forge—sixty miles in the dead of winter.

THE GENERAL AND THE MONK

On hearing who was waiting to see him, Washington readily received Miller. The manner in which the Ephrata Community had sacrificed itself to care for the wounded and dying after the Battle of Brandywine had made a deep impression on Washington, and he had heard much of the sincerity of this particular man, Peter Miller, who was now waiting to see him on some urgent business or other.

The old man was ushered into the tent and stood there, facing Washington and members of the command staff. Washington requested him to be seated, but Miller replied that his business with him would not admit of a moment's delay—that it required immediate despatch; and he instantly proceeded to plead most forcibly, most eloquently for mercy toward Michael Widman.

Peter Miller, we are told, was a tall, slender man who held himself gracefully in his long, gray tunic, secured by a single belt around his waist. The monk's cowl was thrown back, his exuberant snowy, white hair and beard flowing in waves over his shoulders and covering his chest. The officers present, it is said, were profoundly moved by the intelligence and love in Miller's face as he sued for the life of Michael Widman.

When Miller finished speaking, all those present turned to Washington, fully expecting him to exercise his prerogative of mercy. But as Washington spoke, seated regally at the command table covered with maps and battle plans, his officers were made to recall the Commander-in-Chief's station and its responsibilities.

"Friend Miller," said Washington, "there is scarcely anything in this world that I would deny to you. But such is the gravity of our condition that it would be fatal to our cause not to be stringent, inexorable, in such matters, and make examples of renegades to the cause of liberty. Otherwise, I would cheerfully release your friend."

We are told that for a moment Miller simply stood unmoving with his eyes closed.

Finally opening his eyes, he replied, his voice breaking: "Friend? You cannot speak of Michael Widman as my friend. He is my worst enemy, my incessant reviler. For a friend, I might not come to you and importune you in this way. But Widman being, and having been for years, my worst foe, my malignant, persecuting enemy, my religion teaches me to 'pray for those who despitefully use me.'"

A very long silence followed. The Commander-in-Chief stood up and walked around the table to stand face to face with Miller. It must have been an unforgettable sight: the broad-shouldered general in the blue uniform of war that he wore with such presence—the powdered hair, the clean-shaven, majestically stern face; and, in front of him, not more than a foot away, the slender monk in his plain, gray habit with his untrammeled white hair, his old face and eyes imploring mercy.

What worlds, what destinies, were facing each other in that moment?

We are told that Washington wept. He took Miller by the hand. "My dear friend," he said, "I thank you for this lesson of Christian charity. I cannot resist such a manifestation of our divine religion. The pardon is granted— on one condition: that you be the bearer of it yourself, and hand it to the commanding officer at Turk's Head in Widman's presence."

THE PARDON

Miller accepted the condition. The pardon was quickly prepared and handed to him. The old monk set out immediately and reached Turk's Head on foot late that night, a distance of some twenty miles.

The story has the old Prior rising early the next morning after a sleepless night and finding the front of the Block House surrounded by a few soldiers drawn up in a hollow square, with a gibbet in the center. There, in the center, Widman stands on the step, with a rope around his neck, addressing those present. He acknowledges his treachery and the justice of his reward. Just as he is beseeching mercy from above, Peter Miller steps forward and hands the commanding officer a package, whispering that it was from the Commander-in-Chief in reference to the matter before them.

While this is transacting, Widman sees Miller and becomes greatly agitated. He interrupts his prayers and calls out from the scaffold:

"Peter Miller, hear me: Whatever has prompted your presence at this place, I acknowledge to you my great and multiplied abuse and persecution with which I have followed you for years past, and I take it as the kindest providence that I have the opportunity to retract my numerous vilifications and outrages upon you and I crave your forgiveness. Although I have no right to look for forgiveness for such wanton maltreatment, yet I trust that I may find pardon from above . . ."

The commanding officer interrupted Widman at this point by announcing to him that the Commander-in-Chief had granted a pardon for his crime and, presenting Peter Miller, added, "Here is your deliverer."

OUTER AND INNER DEMOCRACY

That moment when the monk and the Commander-in-Chief stood face to face, when two worlds faced each other, may serve as a symbol of the outer and the inner meaning of American democracy.

The General yielded to the monk and allowed another influence to enter the war of revolution. A similar kind of influence needs now to re-enter the life of America, calling us back to the "vertical" meaning of our ideals of independence, liberty and the democratic community. We need to understand democracy not only as an outer, political form, but as an inner, human ideal.

For this, we need to appreciate the important role that innovative religious communities played in the formation of our country—remembering that, for many of the Founding Fathers, America itself was envisioned as a new land, a new community defined not only politically but also spiritually. To a significant extent, America came into being as an experiment in joining mysticism and pragmatism, in joining the part of man that seeks union with God and the part that must act in the outer world of social responsibility and material necessity.

It is in the life and destiny of the Ephrata community that we can see the importance and the difficulty of such an experiment. That is, a communal experiment such as Ephrata can show us that the origins of the American nation lie in the struggle between the mystical and the pragmatic impulses in human nature. And by enabling us to see that this struggle lies at the root of America's value structure, it can help us to understand more precisely where that structure has become distorted and in what direction we actually need to turn to call back the hope for humanity that was reflected in our origins.

The Ephrata Story

Ephrata began, as to a great extent America itself began, with the flight from religious and worldly persecution toward a free space for the mind in search of truth.

Johann Conrad Beissel was born in 1691 in Eberbach, in what is now the German state of Baden-Württemberg. The Thirty Years' War and its aftermath had made this region of the Rhine corridor a bleeding land of violence, poverty, and religious oppression. This was the world of Conrad Beissel's childhood.

Orphaned at an early age, Beissel made his way by native wit, by his talented hand as a baker and itinerant musician, and by the force of his personal charisma. As a young man, he came under the influence of one of Western civilization's deepest currents of intellectual and spiritual energy, as it was embodied at that time principally in the teachings of Meister Eckhart (1260–1327) and Jakob Böhme (1575–1624). It was in this same devastated region of the Rhine corridor that these teachings flowed most strongly, also drawing upon the vision of the women generally known as the Beguines and including Hildegard of Bingen, Marguerite Porete, Hadewijch of Brabant and others.

Conrad Beissel

The central thrust of this school was the notion that within the psyche of every man and woman there slumbers an untapped capacity to love and to understand. In the awakening of these capacities and in their expression for the good of others lies the chief meaning of human life. By and large, the men and women whose names are associated with this school were considered suspect by leaders of the established religion—the Catholic Church in the Middle Ages and the Lutheran and Reformed churches during the period of the Reformation. Among other reasons, the representatives of this school refused to submit solely to outer ecclesiastical authority, but instead worked to discover within themselves the action of the highest principle, God. Once this inner discovery was made and repeatedly confirmed alone and in the company of others, it was impossible for them to bend their minds and hearts solely to outer doctrine and to sometimes rigid formalism, especially with the admixture of self-serving political factors that inevitably move in and out of all human institutions.

Respect for all men and women—the very heart of the democratic principle—was for such visionaries rooted in what they had discovered of the human essence within themselves. Touched by this vision, Conrad Beissel became a man filled with something like spiritual light. Although he was formally untutored, his electrified intellect and intuitiveness brought him considerable depth of religious understanding, and his strong instinctive energy, joined at times to a natural urge to serve what is greater than oneself, eventually impelled him to seek out the inner, solitary life.

Numerous adventures and some narrow escapes prompted by his fiery spiritual and sensuous emotional nature led him to leave Germany for America in 1720 at the age of thirty. He at first joined with other groups who had recently emigrated from Germany to practice their religion in the immediate environment of Philadelphia. But, unable to accept the arguments and rivalries of the many religious sects in Germantown, he soon struck out with one or two companions to pursue a hermit's life in the midst of an unclaimed forest in what is now Lancaster County, some fifty miles northeast of Philadelphia.

But his energy attracted others to his side and, without his choosing it, he was soon at the center of a small community along the banks of Cocalico Creek. At first named simply the Camp of the Solitary, it was organized by Beissel into three "orders"—a celibate Sisterhood called the Spiritual Virgins, a celibate "Brotherhood of Angels," and a third order of married Householders, who were not required to give up property and family. His peasant's shrewdness in handling people was manifested in the creation of this resilient triadic structure, which was one of the chief factors that enabled the improvised community to withstand the shocks from within and without that assailed it in the ensuing decades.

It was not until several years later that the community assumed the name Ephrata, the pre-Israelite name for Bethlehem, indicative of Beissel's aim, like that of many of America's first settlers, of building a new Christian Israel in a new world. The community grew rapidly, to about 150 householders and about 70 in the celibate orders before 1740. Beissel proved himself to be an effective force in keeping the community together as it continued to grow, and he spoke out boldly on the questions of the day, such as the keeping of the sabbath, baptism and peace with the marauding Indians.

Considerable, even fierce, austerities were practiced, and visitors to Ephrata can still see and obtain replicas of the wooden pillows that were used for sleeping on the narrow cots in the dormitories. A feature was the Night Watch service at midnight, which lasted up to four hours, when the hymns composed by Beissel were sung.

Concerning Beissel's gifts as a composer and choirmaster, Thomas Mann speculates that his hymns demonstrate the power of the art of music at any moment to begin "at the beginning, [to discover] itself afresh out of nothing, bare of all knowledge of its past . . ." Mann continues: "The music of Ephrata . . . was too unusual, too amazing and arbitrary, to be taken over by the world outside. . . . But a faint legend had persisted down the years, sufficient in fact to make known how utterly [strange] and moving it had been. . . . Beissel's [music] rang deep down into the soul and was nothing more nor less than a foretaste of heaven."[133] Visitors remarked on the impression given, when the Ephrata men and women sang these hymns, that their ethereal voices seemed to come down from above. Such reports, among others, caused the French philosopher Voltaire to characterize Ephrata as the most important social experiment in the world of his day. The secret of this hymn-singing has been lost. It was based on a system of harmony and voice control so perfect that Beissel claimed "the angels themselves, when they sang at the birth of Christ, had to make use of our rules." Even more to the point, it was based on the inner struggle of the singers to purify their attention by freeing themselves from emotional, mental and bodily associations and impulses. The voice, Beissel taught, reflected one's interior harmony and disharmony with great precision. The study of the role of the voice in other esoteric traditions of the world supports Beissel's personal discoveries in this area.

The Second Democracy

Contrary to the practice of the Shakers, where there was strict segregation of the sexes, there was as unrestrained a life in the Ephrata settlement as though all were of the same sex. In this respect, where others went out of the way of danger in the celibate's life, Beissel plunged his followers into the midst of danger. There has been speculation and difference of opinion among historians about Beissel's own morals, particularly in his later years. But certainly there was nothing at Ephrata like the free love at Oneida, and in nearly a century of Ephrata's existence no major scandal was reported, in spite of many rumors and innuendoes.

As the community settled down, the farm, lumber mill and bakery prospered, and, along with the strict adherence to devotional practices, the material wealth of the brethren increased and in its turn made increasing demands on them. A time arrived when the Prior, Israel Eckerling, who had successfully guided these undertakings, challenged the authority of Beissel, and Beissel had to step down as "Overseer." Under the new leadership, the brothers and sisters enjoyed luxuries of diet and clothing. Colorful robes were worn at the rituals.

Here Ephrata's history mirrors on a small scale what was taking place all around in Pennsylvania, and indeed in America, and what is now taking place in the developing countries of the world as the influence of America spreads over the earth. Immigrants who had left Europe in order to be free to practice their chosen form of religion found themselves caught up instead in the formation of the culture and industry of their new homeland. This demanded unusual external efforts, but produced unexpectedly great material benefits.

And it is here, too, that the fate and drama of Ephrata take on mythic dimensions. We can speak of this drama as a mythic expansion of the idea of the second democracy, and see it as offering a glimpse of the deeper meaning of American democracy in its origins and its present crisis. And we can see that without the second democracy, the first democracy is bound to fail—that is, without the inner meaning of democracy, the outer forms will not withstand the forces of subjectivity, fear and suggestibility that spin our world again and again into false hope and eventual violence and despair. It will become more understandable that attempts to imitate or follow the model of American democracy by other nations and communities may not lead toward the resonant hope that was and still is implied in the American vision—precisely because the sense of the second democracy is not seen or embraced.

To respect all people—to give each individual his or her own rights and voice—requires that we have an adequate understanding of what it is that really does define the nature of human beings, what it is that all men and women really have in common by virtue of being human. We need to see what a human being is—the human being independent of all distinctions of sex, race, ethnic background, wealth and physical or mental prowess. We need to see what a human being is and what the real possibilities of man really are—as well as what his real failings may be. *It is at this level that people can be really united. The deeper meaning of democracy can be seen only by understanding the deeper structure of the human self.*

The idea of the second democracy shows us that what all men and women have in common are the possibility and the necessity of a specific kind of struggle with themselves. It is the struggle between the two natures of man that we all share. And it is this possibility which must be respected. The Ephrata story, as it played itself out at the very root of the creation of America, shows us this and thereby throws an entirely new light on the meaning of America. In this light we can be taught anew by the ideas of the Founding Fathers and by their struggle. The material for a new story of America that repositions all that we deeply value of our history may now begin to emerge.

THE CROSSROADS

We need to look a little more closely at the story of Ephrata as it enters its period of deepest crisis.

This crisis took the outer form of a conflict between two exceptional individuals: Conrad Beissel and Israel Eckerling, the former the creator and spiritual father of the Ephrata community, and the latter a man so trusted by Beissel that he appointed him as Prior, to serve immediately under him in the spiritual and material administration of the community.

Under Beissel's vision, the life of the community was to be a search for an inner opening to the power of God. In this respect, Beissel's vision of the meaning of the community was comparable to the stated aims of many mystics and many spiritual communities through the ages. But for Beissel, this search for an openness to God involved as well the practice of allowing the reality of God to enter into the social and material actions and relationships of the community. Here, too, what Beissel envisioned was comparable to the aims of many monastic communities, Christian and otherwise, through the ages: the aim, namely, of men and women acting in the world as the instrument of a higher power within themselves.

But such an enterprise was being tried not in the pre-established structure of a European monastery, where society and civilization of one sort or another flourished all around, however degenerate they may have been, and however riddled with violence and danger. Here in the Pennsylvania wilderness, there was only nature with its beauty and danger, and the only civilization surrounding the new community was one that the members of the community could hardly recognize as such, the Native American culture that had itself become so embattled that it often had to act against the newcomers for its own survival.

Furthermore, this new community, being founded by a Protestant mystic and visionary, began its life with no assumption of the necessity of obedience, no assumption of the importance of hierarchy or priesthood. All that, all sense of communal administration and governance, all sense of the necessary obedience had to be, as it were, made up on the spot; that is, obedience was to be to the spiritually advanced individual not because of any established social form, but because the individual manifested something that *attracted* obedience. This voluntary wilderness community, struggling to its feet in the midst of a colonial social and legal order, had in itself no "enforcement," no legality, no physical punitive measures. It was a voluntary community in a sense and to a degree that probably had not existed since the time of the origins of Western monasticism itself, although in this it probably corresponded to some extent to earlier experiments, such as the fourteenth-century Brethren of the Common Life and other "proto-Reformation" movements in Europe. But in Europe, not in the wilderness of a New World.

So here was a little America being born. Wherever America was being born, it was "little." What has now become large, immense, was itself once very small. This little Ephrata was trying to exist at the same time that everything in our now vast America was little: in Puritan New England, in the enterprising colonies of Virginia and the South and, a continent away, in the Southwest under the influence of the Spanish missionaries.

Although Ephrata was small, the forces playing in it were of fundamental, universal significance. Here was a group of men and women under the powerful and experimental leadership of a man with an individual, mystical vision seeking to create a communal order in which the primary values were contact with and obedience to God while at the same time the outer world of material necessity and social uncertainty made unprecedented demands on their human energies. Nature alone made conditions stringent; living closely with others made these conditions emotionally stringent; the contrast with the prevalent European mores, weakened though they may have been, also made life stringent. Add to that Beissel's rules of community discipline—work, sleep, prayer, outer and inner sincerity: there was nothing protected about this "sequestered" life. Ephrata had to survive in the wilderness and in the social upheaval of prerevolutionary America. All of America had to so survive. And much of America was trying to survive while at the same time trying to submit its will and actions to God. It was only with experiments such as Ephrata, however, that this was being tried in the specially created *commune.* The confrontation of the forces of mysticism and pragmatism was developing in many parts of America, but nowhere with more concentration than at Ephrata.

With this in mind, it is astonishing to see that Beissel keeps showing his community that the aim of simultaneously opening to God and acting in the world is *impossible.* It cannot be done. Yet it *must* be done. How are we to understand this? The Eckerling episode can show us what this means.

Israel Eckerling was Prior at Ephrata for three years, from 1742 to 1745. These three years and their aftermath are crucial to understanding Ephrata's importance in the metaphysical history of America. But we must step carefully as we examine this period.

One historian has characterized the Eckerling years as "the self-destruction of a materialistic work ethic."[134] Put this way, however, it is only a half-truth. It is true that the Prior was responsible for many initiatives that brought material prosperity to the community. The facts and historical context are complex and somewhat obscure, but what is clear is that in late 1741 and early 1742 Eckerling, with those whom he had enlisted, began reconstituting the marginal economy at Ephrata, which until then had been based on communal property and voluntary labor in the fields and craft houses—all labor being intended only for the necessities of survival and to support the inner work of submitting oneself to God.

Under Eckerling, "an intensive agricultural effort extended the production of wheat, flax for oil and linen, millet for hay and seed, pasturage for livestock, hemp for fiber making."[135] Wider water rights were obtained to power the new mills, and a new gristmill was constructed, as well as a sawmill, a linseed oil mill, a fulling mill and a paper mill, the latter being in fact one of the first paper mills in the colonies. As E. G. Alderfer tellingly writes,

> What resulted was an entirely new kind of industrial and market-oriented commune under extreme pressure to produce, very different from anything visualized by Conrad Beissel. Shortly the markets for Ephrata produce extended to Philadelphia and Wilmington, and a substantial trading system, with outside agents, developed. Ephrata's products became known for their excellence, and the community's treasury, now discreetly removed from Beissel's control, grew fat. No longer [was there a] need to depend on voluntary contributions of the Householders. Ephrata was becoming an economic force to be reckoned with.[136]

THE MEANING OF MATERIALISM

Ephrata was "moving out"—just as America was moving out toward material power and activity. The founder of Ephrata had held that money, property and commerce were intrinsically dangerous, even if their benefits were shared. Yet he took no repressive measures to keep the community away from this "danger"—in this, his behavior was comparable to his treatment of sexual relationships. He had set the tone for chastity and poverty in the structure of the community, but he had allowed the forces of everyday life, the forces of the world, to enter in without building walls of protection, without suppressing the forces that he took to be so fraught with danger.

The issue here needs to be carefully stated. The issue is not describable merely by the word "materialism" or "the world" or by any term like "sexual liberty" or by a word like "disobedience" in its usual sense. We must not see what happened at Ephrata in conventional terms of religiosity or moralism. Historians may see it that way, and often with considerable insight. But probably only a man or woman who has existed under the conditions of a teacher like Beissel can grasp what really is at issue here. An entirely new understanding of the meaning of materialism is at stake—and with it a new understanding of what it is in ourselves that draws us toward a life of materialism. And with that, in turn, we face a new question of what in a human being can be free of materialism—and, also, free of fanatical or dreamy religiosity: what in us stands above both materialism and religionism, the tyranny of the body over the mind on the one side, and the tyranny of dogma over the mind on the other side.

The American ideal of independence cannot mean, and never did mean for the most thoughtful of the Founding Fathers, "freedom" from duty to God, nor did it mean the illusion of autonomy that results from manipulating nature solely to gratify the desires of the ego and its undisciplined body. Nor did the ideal of democratic community imply the obligation to honor the "rights" of man's passing fears and cravings, listening to them and letting them rule the body politic just as, in unregenerate man, they rule the individual psyche. The ideal of democratic community implied, on the contrary, the obligation above all to respect each individual's conscience, each man's or woman's *effort* to listen to conscience by means of the cultivation of a mature quality of reason and moral sensibility. Beissel's community sought nothing more nor less than this quality of contact with conscience, the God within. And what they were asked to respect in each other was their neighbor's possibility of speaking and acting from the search for conscience.

The upsurge of materialism and obsessive, driven labor under the administration of Eckerling must be understood in these terms. Eckerling turned away from the struggle to submit to conscience. This turning-away manifested itself in an unbalanced faith in his own individual ability to master the external environment and the social structure of the community. It was *not* materialism in its conventional meaning. It was not love of power in the usual sense of these words. It was not the desire for physical comfort or bodily pleasure. These are factors that enter into superficial religions or moralistic explanations of the human condition. Such explanations have little weight; they do not go to the heart of the matter. The crisis of Ephrata was the crisis of man believing too much in the primacy of the surface self over the deep self within, through which alone the energies of a higher world are meant to enter the world we live in.

It is this crisis that comprises the drama of Ephrata and the drama of America and of the modern world itself. Like America, Ephrata fell under the sway not so much of the love of comfort or the craving for wealth and importance or the obsessive compulsion toward joyless work. It was not the crisis of a man seeking sex or personal power over others. It was the crisis of cutting one's inner life off from a universal force that the human self is intended to receive and manifest in action.

The Ephrata story is a uniquely American story. The ideals of Ephrata were the ideals of the great spiritual teachings of the world, yet they were being sown in the American wilderness and in the company of Enlightenment ideals about the freedom of the mind and the virtues of democracy. If we are to find a new and deeper meaning to the democratic ideal, we can search for it in Ephrata; and if we are to find a deeper understanding of what may fatally deflect the hope of America, we may search for that also in the Ephrata story.

Let us recall our overall aim. We have sought to provide material for rebuilding the mythic meaning of America. The ideals of the Founding Fathers and the drama of the creation of the Constitution present to us the elements of a moral and spiritual vision in a language whose deeper meaning has become lost. The ideas and symbols that shaped America no longer call us to search for the truth about the purpose of our lives. Words like "freedom," "independence," "reason," "democracy" are understood too easily and have become fatally mixed with our all-too-human impulses heedlessly to manipulate nature, society, and ourselves.

This fatal mixing is vividly and deeply seen at Ephrata. What Ephrata contributes to the new mythic meaning of America is a uniquely American story of the Fall—the ancient, eternal story of the Fall, acted out a mere 250 years ago on our own virgin soil. At Ephrata the ideal of independence began as the freedom of a man or woman to submit the will to the God within; having begun as that in the teaching of Conrad Beissel, it became, under Eckerling, the freedom to obey one's own subjective understanding and impose it on others in the name of God. When this deflected concept of human independence enters into a society, the ideal of democracy itself alters its meaning. What men and women then call freedom is not actually the freedom of the heart and soul that the wisdom teachings of the world have told us is our birthright—a birthright whose actualization we are obliged to work and struggle for. Under this altered concept of freedom, we create a society based on the metaphysical illusion that our apparent freedom of the intellect is actually the deep freedom of the soul. It is not so.

It is not so—and the Founding Fathers, consciously or instinctively, knew it was not so. They constructed a government based on the assumption not that we are already metaphysically free beings but only that we are free to search for God, to search for conscience, to search for what many of them called Reason. Jefferson's Reason and, I believe, Franklin's Reason, and certainly Lincoln's Reason, is not merely the reason that calculates how to impose its will on others or how simply to manipulate nature.

In 1745, just a few years after his appointment as Prior, Eckerling's innovations were rejected by the community as a betrayal of its spiritual objectives. Beissel's authority was reinstated, and the community sought to return to its initial mode of life.

It is important to regard what came about under Eckerling as a portent of what would soon define the fate of America and tempt it away from the deeper meaning of its own ideals. Pragmatic materialism overran the pursuit of inner truth, but this pragmatic materialism continued to call itself by names that had originally referred to the process of the inner search. It was not the pursuit of material gain that defined the crisis of Ephrata; *it was the pursuit of material gain pretending to be the inner struggle.* It was the outer aspects of the self pretending to be the inner functions; it was, so to say, the servant trying to do the work of the master. Fervid accumulation of wealth and property, the emphasis on producing goods and services, the reliance on principles of business organization—these developments at Ephrata are like a sudden flash of the future appearing in a crystal ball. These passions and "interests" are what would soon define the essence of the American nation and, eventually, the essence of modern culture itself. Such things as wealth, material goods and commerce themselves are by no means the evil that a pious, religious critic may think they are. What was dangerous about them was the attitude toward them that led to and reinforced the illusion that the impulse to "do," to manipulate, to innovate was the highest part of human nature. Through this illusion, man loses sight of the fact that genuine individuality and the power to understand and create are given to man only to the degree that deep down he steps down and submits himself to the higher reality called God.

In order to understand what is at issue here, and why it deserves so much attention in any attempt to reestablish the story of America, we may compare the way the historian looks at these events with the way they were perceived by Peter Miller himself, that very Peter Miller who walked through the snow to Valley Forge to sue for the life of his own bitter enemy.

We have already seen how the historian E. G. Alderfer characterizes Ephrata under Eckerling as having suddenly become a "market oriented commune" and "an economic force to be reckoned with." He goes on to speak of how "a new and demanding division of labor increased the tempo of their lives to just this side of the breaking point." "The Brothers," he writes, "were organized into specialized cadres that worked fixed, long hours at hard tasks under the supervision of watchful, hard-driving foremen. . . . There was little time or energy left for nursing religious experience and mystical speculation. The 'saints' were turned into work slaves as the harsh, Puritan work ethic, which soon lost its 'voluntary' character, took over."[137] And concerning Eckerling's motives, he concludes (based on apparently overwhelming evidence) that he had become prey to overweening ambition, "base political treachery" and a desire to control the economic resources of the members of the community.

Understood in this way, the crisis that threatened Ephrata could be treated simply as one among many indications of what was to come with the onset of the Industrial Revolution. Vast capital, submitted to the hard-driving Protestant work ethic, flourished under the bold and brilliant monetary and financial innovations of Alexander Hamilton. With the continuing opening of the frontier, the culture "emphasized individualism at the expense of community and do-it-yourself free enterprise at the expense of the older and gentler forms of agrarian cooperation."

But Peter Miller saw it in quite another way. His assessment was published in 1786, some twenty years after the death of Beissel, during which time he himself had been obliged to take on the role of spiritual father to the community. During that period he had seen how America was led by Washington through the trials of the Revolution toward its triumphant birth. The revered teacher observed the new nation accelerating toward its outer destiny as the strongest country in the world. But of Eckerling's attempt to reorganize the tiny Ephrata community on more "efficient" worldly principles, Miller said of him and those he influenced only that their "intelligence," which had been "widened" by their spiritual experience, was now being employed to setting up mechanical trades that brought in great profits: "Yes," he writes; "it is likely that if God had not destroyed this economy, the Brethren would by this time have ships upon the sea."[138]

In Peter Miller's eyes, Eckerling used the spiritual energy that was given through inner work for purposes that were directed toward outer accomplishment rather than inward toward further understanding of oneself and the inner needs of the community. Spiritual energy was spent in material pursuits. This is practically the definition of what the wisdom teachings of the world speak of as the sin of self-will.

And it is this that the Ephrata community can teach us, two hundred years after Miller's death and the fading of the community itself. The second democracy—the democracy within democracy—deepens our moral values by showing them to be rooted in a great inner struggle that must be undertaken in the company of others; in a community whose primary aims are interior freedom and service to God.

The second democracy is a community devoted solely and entirely to truth. It does not accumulate wealth. It does not put "ships upon the sea." It does not make war. It is not "strong"; it is not an "economic force" in the world. It does not have an army. It does not make treaties. It does not devise financial innovations.

Then how can it exist? In this world of force and violence, where morality is only a word, where brute power, fantasy and paranoia govern peoples and nations, where there are always winners and losers in the sense that all are eventually losers, where all promises are illusions and where nothing calls itself by its proper name—how can the second democracy actually exist?

The answer is that in our time and in our culture it can only exist when protected by the first democracy, the democracy that now takes the name of the United States—though who knows what name it will take in the future or where it will be on the face of the earth? The second democracy is the soul of the first democracy—our democracy, our world.

The second democracy—the community based on the equality of all men and women who search for conscience—requires the political and social freedom and external tolerance that are provided by the kind of democratic society Americans now live in and whose principles were so carefully crafted in Philadelphia in the summer of 1787. All the ideals of the Founding Fathers—and all the ideals of individual freedom and liberty that were brought to America by the religiously earnest and physically courageous settlers of New England and the Atlantic coast—all these ideals were based on protecting and supporting the search for inner freedom. Outer liberty had inner liberty as its main goal and its main justification. But in many respects it was intensive, mystical communities such as that of the Pennsylvania Germans that sought to create special social conditions that blended the rigor of monastic life with the task and work of maintaining a creative and powerful outer life. The great Protestant ideal had always been defined under the notion of "the world as a monastery." But it remained for the mystical communities of America—and none more than the Ephrata community—to create specially defined communal organizations for the pursuit of spiritual transformation. Beissel's vision of Ephrata was of precise principles of living that enabled the inner search to proceed in relation to the forces of everyday life—the forces of work, and money, sex and love, the material world with all that it demanded of man for his survival and his seemly existence.

The idea of an Ephrata is of a community that offers inner and outer conditions that enable men and women to strive inwardly for the human characteristics that are implied in the democratic ideal. The outer world— the world of violence and illusion—cannot really house a true democratic or republican social organization. By itself, the world of violence and illusion (or, simply, "the world" of the Christian teaching and all the wisdom teachings of mankind) can offer only the imitation of moral discipline, only the thought of respect for others, only the dream of independence and freedom. It is the second democracy that offers the conditions and the knowledge that make it possible for these ideals to enter into the blood and bone of real human beings.

The relevance of Ephrata for us is not to incite us to enter a separated spiritual community. Such communities—perhaps communities of great authenticity—may exist behind the scenes of our society, protected and sheltered by the wise principles of our however-flawed democracy. But the purpose of studying a community such as Ephrata is not to draw us into such communities. The purpose is to help us re-vision the story of America—which means, first, to help purge it of the illusions that surround America's democratic ideals and that have turned these ideals into clichés at best, or at worst, into lies; and second, to help us feel in a new way the great depth of these ideals.

In order to bring home more forcefully the need for such a re-visioning of the American story, and in order to demonstrate its goodness, it is time to summon America's greatest prophet.

WALT WHITMAN AND
THE MEANING OF AMERICA

The year is 1868. The murderous "war of secession" has ended. The unity of America has been preserved—and redefined—within the embrace of one man's influence: Abraham Lincoln. To Walt Whitman, who was by then emerging as America's greatest visionary poet, Lincoln incarnated the essence of American democracy: the harmonious blending of the mystical and the pragmatic within the individual soul. The harmony of these two seemingly opposed realities may now be identified as the fundamental meaning of what an American *is*—as a human ideal. On the basis of this ideal, the story of America can be deepened and renewed—metaphysically, inwardly.

Speaking of Lincoln's face—that is, of his mysterious individuality—Whitman wrote of how he once saw the President's carriage passing by him on a summer day in Washington. "They pass'd me once very close, and I saw the President in the face fully, as they were moving slowly, and his look, though abstracted, happen'd to be directed steadily in my eye."

Whitman goes on:

> He bow'd and smiled, but far beneath his smile I noticed well the ex-
> pression. . . . None of the artists or pictures has caught the deep,
> though subtle and indirect expression of this man's face. There is
> something else there . . .

Twenty years after Lincoln's death, Whitman said again:

> Though hundreds of portraits have been made, by painters and pho-
> tographers . . . I have never seen one yet that in my opinion deserv'd
> to be called a perfectly *good likeness.* . . . May I not say, too, that, as
> there is no entirely competent and emblematic likeness of Abraham
> Lincoln in picture or statue, there is not—perhaps cannot be—any
> fully appropriate literary statement or summing up of him yet in
> existence?

And further:

> [He] was quite thoroughly Western, original, essentially non-
> conventional, and had a certain sort of outdoor or prairie stamp. . . . I
> should say the invisible foundations and vertebra of his character,
> more than any man's in history, were mystical, abstract, moral and
> spiritual—While upon all of them was built, and out of all of them
> radiated, under the control of the average circumstances, what the
> vulgar call *horse-sense,* and a life often bent by temporary but most ur-
> gent materialistic and political reasons.[139]

DEMOCRATIC VISTAS

It was in the long, wide wake of Lincoln's assassination that Whitman composed *Democratic Vistas,*[140] the most powerful manifesto ever written about

the inner meaning of American democracy. Whitman's poetry has of course overshadowed this essay, which still remains largely unrecognized. But for the present need of America, and the Americanizing world, it sounds a call of merciless and merciful clarity, like a buoy ringing and ringing in the blinding storm and heaving waters.

From the very beginning of the essay, Whitman cries out for what we have been speaking of as the mythic meaning of America.

> For, I say, the true nationality of the States, the genuine union, when we come to a mortal crisis, is, and is to be, after all, neither the written law, nor, (as is generally supposed,) either self-interest, or common pecuniary or material objects—but the fervid and tremendous IDEA, melting everything else with resistless heat, and solving all lesser and definite distinctions in vast, indefinite, spiritual, emotional power.

"It may be claimed," he goes on,

> (and I admit the weight of the claim,) that common and general worldly prosperity, and a populace well-to-do, and with all life's material comforts, is the main thing, and is enough. It may be argued that our republic is, in performance, really enacting to-day the grandest arts, poems, &c., by beating up the wilderness into fertile farms, and in her railroads, ships, machinery, &c., I too hail those achievements with pride and joy: then answer that the soul of man will not with such only—nay, not with such at all—be finally satisfied; but needs what, (standing on these and on all things, as the feet stand on the ground,) is address'd to the loftiest, to itself alone.

And further:

> For my part, I would alarm and caution even the political and business reader, and to the utmost extent, against the prevailing delusion that the establishment of free political institutions, and plentiful

intellectual smartness, with general good order, physical plenty,- industry, &c., (desirable and precious advantages as they all are,) do, of themselves, determine and yield to our experiment of democracy the fruitage of success. With such advantages at present fully, or almost fully possessed . . . and with unprecedented materialistic advancement—society, in these States, is canker'd, crude, superstitious, and rotten. Political, or law-made society is, and private, or voluntary society, is also. In any vigor, the element of the moral conscience, the most important, the vertebra to State or man, seems to be either entirely lacking or seriously enfeebled or ungrown.

I say we had best look our times and our lands searchingly in the face, like a physician diagnosing some deep disease. Never was there, perhaps, more hollowness at heart than at present, and here in the United States. Genuine belief seems to have left us . . .

THE MYTHMAKER'S CALL TO CONTEMPORARY AMERICA

At this point, early on in *Democratic Vistas,* the contemporary American, searching for a way to understand the present and the future of our world, might be nodding his head with little more than lukewarm appreciation of Whitman's energy and eloquence, and waiting to see what Whitman proposes that we *do.*

What changes should be made? What actions taken? But the reader will find nothing of the kind; Whitman proposes something deeper: he proposes the work of understanding; and, in preparation for understanding, the work of *feeling* the present need and the future obligation. To feel, to be touched in the heart and guts and spine by what we have become and what we are called to be. And the first step toward this contact with feeling and seeing what we are, the first step toward this most necessary and most ignored inner action, is to let in all the facts of how far we fall from the idea of America, that is, to see that in our actual manifestations we really no longer believe in the meaning of America. Fervid nationalism or a patriotism that is only a mask for insecurity and ignorance is, of course, the opposite of be-lief in the inner meaning of America:

> The underlying principles of the States are not honestly believ'd in, (for all this hectic glow and these melo-dramatic screamings,) nor is humanity itself believ'd in. What penetrating eye does not every-where see through the mask? The spectacle is appalling. We live in an atmosphere of hypocrisy throughout. The men believe not in the women, nor the women in the men. A scornful superciliousness rules in literature. The aim of all the *littérateurs* is to find something to make fun of. A lot of churches, sects, &c., the most dismal phantasms I know, usurp the name of religion. Conversation is a mass of badi-nage. From deceit in the spirit, the mother of all false deeds, the off-spring is already incalculable. An acute and candid person, in the revenue department in Washington, who is led by the course of his employment to regularly visit the cities, north, south and west, to in-vestigate frauds, has talk'd much with me about his discoveries. The depravity of the business classes of our country is not less than has been supposed, but infinitely greater. The official services of America, national, state and municipal, in all their branches and departments, except the judiciary, are saturated in corruption, bribery, falsehood, mal-administration; and the judiciary is tainted. The great cities reek with respectable as much as non-respectable robbery and scoundrel-ism. In fashionable life, flippance, tepid amours, weak infidelism, small aims, or no aims at all, only to kill time. In business (this all-devouring modern word, business,) the one sole object is, by any means, pecuniary gain. The magician's serpent in the fable ate up all the other serpents; and money-making is our magician's serpent, re-maining today sole master of the field . . .

Who sees in these words not only the political entity called America, but a characterization of the human condition itself, reads Whitman correctly.

He goes on:

True, indeed, behind this fantastic farce, enacted on the visible stage of society, solid things and stupendous labors are to be discover'd existing crudely and going on in the background, to advance and tell themselves in time. Yet the truths are none the less terrible. I say that our New World democracy, however great a success in uplifting the masses out of their sloughs, in materialistic development, products, and in a certain highly deceptive superficial popular intellectuality, is, so far, an almost complete failure in its social aspects, and in really grand religious, moral, literary, and esthetic results. In vain do we march with unprecedented strides to empire so colossal, outvying the antique, beyond Alexander's, beyond the proudest sway of Rome. . . . It is as if we were somehow being endow'd with a vast and more and more thoroughly appointed body, and then left with little or no soul.

The Idea of America

With Whitman now at our side, we can see compactly and vividly what is entailed in searching anew for the mythic meaning of America. What is entailed is a rediscovery of the American ideas we have grown up with, but which no longer call to the depths of us—*which no longer stop us.* These American ideas, American words such as "independence," "freedom," "equality," have a completely different action upon us when they are spoken as elements in a vision that is as mystical as it is pragmatic; as pragmatic as it is mystical.

INDEPENDENCE

"The purpose of democracy," says Whitman

—supplanting old belief in the necessary absoluteness of establish'd dynastic rulership, temporal, ecclesiastical, and scholastic, as furnishing the only security against chaos, crime, and ignorance—is, through many transmigrations and amid endless ridicules, arguments, and ostensible failures, to illustrate, at all hazards, this doctrine or theory that man, *properly trained* in sanest, highest freedom, may and must become a law, and a series of laws, unto himself, surrounding and providing for, not only his own personal control, but all his relations to other individuals, and to the State; and that, while other theories, as in the past histories of nations, have proved wise enough, and indispensable perhaps for their conditions, *this,* as matters now stand in our civilized world, is the only scheme worth working from . . .

EQUALITY

I say the mission of government, henceforth, in civilized lands, is not repression alone, and not authority alone, not even of law, nor . . . the rule of the best men, the born heroes and captains of the race, (as if such ever, or one time out of a hundred, get into the big places, elective or dynastic)—but higher than the highest arbitrary rule, to train communities through all their grades, beginning with individuals and ending there again, to rule themselves.

Our idea of equality, Whitman tells us, is a trace, an echo of the ancient doctrine of inner transcendence that was brought to the world by the teachers of wisdom, Jesus no less than Buddha or the sages and saints of India and China. But for Whitman the political idea of equality is not to remain only a symbol. Such ideas (and here we have the echo of Ephrata and what it calls us to consider) are meant to open the question of the cultural and social conditions within which democracy serves its deeper purpose: to allow men and women to seek contact with their inherent transcendence. Whitman continues:

The purpose [of democracy] is not altogether direct; perhaps it is more indirect. For it is not that democracy is of exhaustive account, in itself.

Perhaps, indeed, it is (like Nature,) of no account in itself. It is that, as we see, it is the best, perhaps only, fit and full means, formulator, general caller-forth, trainer, for the million, not for grand material personalities only, but for immortal souls. To be a voter with the rest is not so much; and this, like every institute, will have its imperfections. But to become an enfranchised man, and now, impediments removed, to stand and start without humiliation, and equal with the rest; to commence, or have the road clear'd to commence, the grand experiment of development, whose end (perhaps requiring several generations,) may be the forming of a full-grown man or woman— that *is* something.

THE PEOPLE

[Democracy] . . . alone can bind, and ever seeks to bind, all nations, all men, of however various and distant lands, into a brotherhood, a family. It is the old, yet ever-modern dream of earth, out of her eldest and her youngest, her fond philosophers and poets. Not that half only, individualism, which isolates. There is another half, which is adhesiveness or love, that fuses, ties and aggregates, making the races comrades, and fraternizing all. Both are to be vitalized by religion, (sole worthiest elevator of man or State,) breathing into the proud, material tissues, the breath of life. For I say the core of democracy, finally, is the religious element. All the religions, old and new, are there . . .

Of all dangers to a nation, as things exist in our day, there can be no greater one than having certain portions of the people set off from the rest by a line drawn—they not privileged as others, but degraded, humiliated, made of no account. . . . Much quackery teems, of course, even on democracy's side, yet does not really affect the orbic quality of the matter. To work in, if we may so term it, and justify God, his divine aggregate, the People, (or, the veritable horn'd and sharp-tail'd Devil, *his* aggregate, if there be who convulsively insist upon it) this, I say, is what democracy is for; and this is what our America means, and is doing—may I not say, has done? If not, she means nothing more, and does nothing more, than any other land.

THE INDIVIDUAL

Whitman's *Democratic Vistas* presents a continuous back-and-forth movement between an emphasis on the idea of the People and on the idea of the Individual. It is the same back-and-forth we see in the logic, the actions and the being of Washington, Jefferson and Lincoln. In Whitman's text, it soon becomes clear that we are not obliged to choose between these two emphases; in fact, we are obliged not to choose. The resolution of the apparent opposition between the People as a mass and the Individual as the seat of the soul is to be found in the mysterious self-identity that lies beneath the surface self of the person and the mass-consciousness of the crowd. *The People is not the crowd. The Individual is not the ego. It is the ego and the crowd that oppose each other.* But there is another kind of self-identity, mysterious and concrete, waiting, as it were, at the horizon in the subtle light of morning. This mysterious selfhood constitutes the hidden meaning of the idea of democracy: the government "of the people, for the people and by the people."

"Assuming Democracy to be at present in its embryo condition," writes Whitman,

> and that the only large and satisfactory justification of it resides in the future, mainly through the copious production of perfect characters among the people, and through the advent of a sane and pervading religiousness, it is with regard to the atmosphere and spaciousness fit for such characters . . . that I continue the present statement . . .

There is, in sanest hours, a consciousness, a thought that rises, independent, lifted out from all else, calm, like the stars, shining eternal.
This is the thought of identity—yours for you, whoever you are, as
mine for me. Miracle of miracles, beyond statement, most spiritual
and vaguest of earth's dreams, yet hardest, basic fact, and only entrance to all facts. In such devout hours, in the midst of the significant
wonders of heaven and earth (significant only because of the Me in the
center,) creeds, conventions, fall away and become of no account before this simple idea. Like the shadowy dwarf in the fable, once liber-
ated and looked upon, it expands over the whole earth, and spreads to
the roof of heaven.

The quality of BEING, in the object's self, according to its own central
idea and purpose, and of growing therefrom and thereto—not criticism by other standards and adjustments thereto—is the lesson of
Nature. True, the full man wisely gathers, culls, absorbs; but if,
engaged disproportionately in that, he slights or overlays the precious idiosyncrasy and special nativity and intention that he is, the
man's self, the main thing, is a failure, however wide his general
cultivation . . .

THE AMERICAN RELIGION

Leaving still unspecified several sterling parts of any model fit for the
future personality of America, I must not fail, again and ever to pro-
nounce myself on one, probably the least attended to in modern
times—a hiatus, indeed, threatening its gloomiest consequences after
us. I mean the simple, unsophisticated Conscience, the primary moral
element. If I were asked to specify in what quarter lie the grounds of
darkest dread, respecting the America of our hopes, I should have to
point to this particular. I should demand the invariable application to

individuality, this day and any day, of that old ever-true plumb-rule of persons, eras, nations. Our triumphant modern civilizee, with his all-schooling and his wondrous appliances, will still show himself but an amputation while this deficiency remains. Beyond (assuming a more hopeful tone,) the vertebration of the manly and the womanly personalism of our western world, can only be, and is, indeed, to be, (I hope,) its all-penetrating Religiousness.

As to what Whitman means by "religion," it is enough to remember what we have already heard through the figures of Washington, Jefferson, Franklin and Lincoln and in the vision of William Penn and Conrad Beissel of a religion that cuts beneath all church and dogma, all passive belief and dependence on a purely external god. It is enough to remember both the human, communal process that created the Constitution in 1787 and the ideal of spiritual community that was epitomized in the Ephrata experiment decades before the "miracle in Philadelphia" took place:

> The ripeness of Religion is doubtless to be looked for in this field of individuality, and is a result that no organization or church can ever achieve. As history is poorly retain'd by what the technists call history, and is not given out from their pages, except the learner has in himself the sense of the wee-wrapt, never yet written, perhaps impossible to be written, history—so Religion, although casually arrested, and, after a fashion, preserv'd in the churches and creeds, does not depend at all upon them, but is a part of the identified soul, which, when greatest, knows not bibles in the old way, but in new ways— the identified soul, which can really confront Religion when it extricates itself entirely from the churches, and not before.

> Personalism fuses this, and favors it. I should say, indeed, that only in the perfect uncontamination and solitariness of individuality may the spirituality of religion positively come forth at all. Only here, and on such terms, the meditation, the devout ecstasy, the soaring flight.

Only here, communion with the mysteries, the eternal problems, whence? Whither? Alone, and identity, and the mood—and the soul emerges, and all statements, churches, sermons, melt away like vapors. Alone, and silent thought and awe, and aspiration—and then the interior consciousness, like a hitherto unseen inscription, in magic ink, beams out its wondrous lines to the sense. Bibles may convey, and priests expound, but it is exclusively for the noiseless operation of one's isolated self, to enter the pure ether of veneration, reach the divine levels, and commune with the unutterable.

But before Whitman sounds his final note, he steps out from the world of ideas and puts before us (and we put before ourselves) the question of pure, simple, practical participation in the political life of America. Coming as it does in the very midst of his powerful call to grasp the metaphysical meaning of America, the question of political action appears as just that—a *question.* We are obliged to act in our world, to inhabit the structure and the outer life we are given, to answer to its needs, to pay for what we have and what we are. But how? Under the light of Whitman's—and, we hope, our—search for the universal, metaphysical America, we are obliged to think and do and choose and act. What does this mean? How is it possible to be mystical and political in the same life? That is, how is it possible to seek contact and even fusion with the spirit while living responsibly in the world of desire and compromise, gain and loss, birth and death—the world of conflict and cunning, fantasy, power, the world of unjust poverty and unjust riches, the world of ordinary evil, heartbreak, betrayal, tragedy and the pathetic waste of human life; the world of illusion and creation and corruption and honor . . . ?

Addressing his words especially to young Americans, Whitman now says:

To practically enter into politics is an important part of American personalism. . . . It is the fashion among dilettantes and fops (perhaps I myself am not guiltless,) to decry the whole formulation of the active politics of America, as beyond redemption, and so to be carefully kept away from. See you do not fall into this error. America, it may be, is doing very well upon the whole, notwithstanding these antics of the parties and their leaders, these half-brain'd nominees, the many ignorant ballots, and many elected failures and blatherers. It is the dilettantes, and all who shirk their duty, who are not doing well. As for you, I advise you to enter more strongly yet into politics. . . . Always inform yourself; always do the best you can; always vote . . .

And now Whitman begins to turn the rudder once again toward the inner world, toward the inner qualities of mind and heart that define the American democratic soul:

Disengage yourself from parties. They have been useful, and to some extent remain so; but the floating, uncommitted electors . . . watching aloof, inclining victory this side or that side—such are the ones most needed, present and future. For America, if eligible at all to downfall and ruin, is eligible within herself, not without; for I see clearly that the combined foreign world could not beat her down. But these savage, wolfish parties alarm me. . . . It behooves you to convey yourself implicitly to no party, nor submit blindly to their dictators, but steadily hold yourself judge and master over all of them . . .

Continuing to bend the direction of his thought toward the definition of the American democratic, individual and communal soul and toward the need for a mythology that embodies it, Whitman (as he does with great frequency and passion) calls for a new understanding of man and woman:

Of course, in these States, for both man and woman, we must entirely recast the types of highest personality from what the oriental, feudal, ecclesiastical worlds bequeath us. . . . Of course, the old undying elements remain. The task is, to successfully adjust them to new combinations, our own days. Nor is this so incredible. I can conceive a community, to-day and here, in which, on a sufficient scale, the perfect personalities without noise meet . . . where a couple of hundred best men and women, of ordinary worldly status, have by luck been drawn together, with nothing extra of genius or wealth, but virtuous, chaste, industrious, cheerful, resolute, friendly and devout.

Do we now hear the echo of Ephrata and the inner meaning of the American community?

Whitman continues:

I can conceive such a community organized in running order, powers judiciously delegated—farming, building, trade, courts, mails, schools, elections, all attended to; and then the rest of life, the main thing, freely branching and blossoming in each individual, and bearing golden fruit. I can see there in every young and old man, after his kind, and in every woman after hers, a true personality, develop'd, exercised proportionately in body, mind and spirit . . . perhaps, unsung, undramatized, unput in essays or biographies—perhaps even some such community already exists . . .

Or *could* exist.

Conclusion:
The America of
Our Hopes

ELEVEN

THE GUARDIAN AT
THE DOOR

Y ou don't know what you have here."

Whenever I think of that summer night a quarter of a century ago, I ask myself why those challenging words so lifted my spirits and renewed my hope in America. Did I imagine that the American people would somehow, someday, lift themselves en masse above our ordinary level of human confusion and discover a shared sense of purpose? Did I hope that a new sense of community would appear from some great source higher than self-interest, fear and resentment? Did I really hope for such a thing?

Certainly not. America is not a monastery or spiritual brotherhood, not an Ephrata or anything remotely like it. America is what the ancient wisdom called "the world" in the form of a vast nation, "the world" with all its noise and violence, its ideals betrayed at every turn, seducing itself by noble words it can neither understand nor obey, and which only mask its actual fragmentation and deadly momentum. In the room called "the world" men have always spoken passionately of justice and the common good right before and after—and even while in the act of—cutting a throat or stealing a purse or salting a wound.

WHAT AMERICA IS AND WHAT AMERICA MEANS

And yet America still means hope. Within the "world" that is America as it actually is, there waits another America, another world. Within, behind what America *is* there lies what America *means*. We are naive only when we confuse the two, when our feeling of hope is directed toward the outer America that we perceive with the senses, rather than the America we grasp with the mind and the heart. Because this other America seems powerless or elusive does not mean it is not real. Because America betrays its ideals is no reason to reject the ideals themselves. We do not live in correspondence with the great life hidden within us; but that is no reason to deny that this hidden life exists and calls to us.

AN AMERICAN PLACE

America—the physical, actual America that we see and live in—this America needs to be understood not as in itself sacred but as a privileged, temporary corner of "the world" where men and women are granted the liberty to search for truth and the life within. Behind all the political and economic machinations of the Founders of this country, there existed in their minds and hearts the passion to create "an American place" in the midst of the world, where the Good can be sought and lived. They believed there existed the Good—some called it God, others called it Reason—and that the Good could enter human life. Of course, political freedom exists now in many countries of the world, often due to the influence of American ideas, but we will never "know what we have here" if we do not understand that the founding basis of this country was not land or tribe, but the call for people to assemble together and work together for the Good. Perhaps America's people no longer come together for this purpose; perhaps political liberty and the great rule of law serve now only to protect the cravings for meaningless comfort and meaningless power; perhaps the nation's physical strength seduces us into imagining that physical strength is true strength, that physical safety is true safety, that external freedom is true freedom, external democracy the true equality of people. If so, if we believe that the outer America is the real America, we are deceived by ourselves, and as the prophets of Israel warned, we are certain to perish—first inwardly and then outwardly.

The laws of America, the political structure of American government, the respect for the Constitution, the rituals and symbols of the American republic—all of this external America bears traces, some brilliant and others faint and shadowy, but traces of a great vision of truth and wisdom that have nourished the soul of mankind throughout history.

We need to find our way back to the other America, the inner America, which is to say that the modern world itself needs to find its way back to the fundamental reality of the inner world, what the ancients called "the world of the soul." Set aside the usual associations with the word "soul"—associations which for many of us have made of it something superstitious or something dull and ordinary. Set aside the religious and philosophical clichés surrounding the word and recognize that what it refers to is a deep, hidden power of consciousness and moral power within every human being, a force, an intensity of feeling and knowing that defines us as human beings, that defines our place in nature, on earth and with each other.

The teachings of wisdom bring to us the idea that it is through this inner power of intelligence and conscience that the Good can enter the world of man and, through humanity, the world of the earth. Wisdom teaches that the world has become what it has become, human life has become what it has become because man has lost contact with this consciousness and power of understanding within himself. What is sometimes called God, so the teachings tell us, acts in the world to help the world—yes, but not as some fairy-tale father figure with a white beard moving the chess pieces of history, but through the authentic consciousness of man. It is that consciousness—mortally asleep in us though it be—through which the helping powers operate. Through us, and into the earth, and from the earth back to the Source as man's genuine help for the Creator. The Founders of America were passionately oriented to teachings that in some distinct and significant measure reflected these ideas.

THE GUARDIAN AT THE DOOR

Man's life is what it is because man is what he is. *The American plan of government was based on that truth.* Man is corrupt and needs a specific kind of government in order to restrain his corruption—yes. But man also has within him Reason (or God) and needs a specific form of government in order to allow the kind of seeking that can open the individual and his or her community to the experience and the action of that Reason, that God, that Good.

The inspired form of the Constitution and the institutions of the American government may sometimes tempt us to imagine that the Founders believed, or should have believed, that it is external laws and principles of legal process that can improve human life and keep it safe. Nothing could be further from the truth. They understood, implicitly through the philosophy or religion they adhered to, and many times surely explicitly, that it is through the perfection of the self that human life on earth can become what it is meant to become. Government was there to protect *that* process, to allow *that* process; government was there to stand guard at the door to the room where men and women actually seek, rather than just speak about, truth, justice and the common good.

THE AMERICAN ILLUSION

Because of the material prosperity of our country and because it seemed, and actually was, after the fact, so intimately connected with market capitalism and its successes, the illusion was embraced that man's life can be morally and materially perfected mainly through external changes involving, among other things, external forms of government and social order. This illusion was our illusion, and some time ago it became the whole world's illusion.

It was this illusion that fueled the successes of Marxist communism and ultimately brought it down, just as all illusions, sooner rather than later, come to nothing. Communism placed its entire emphasis on improving the external lot of mankind. It placed its faith in external change, in the redistribution of wealth and the means of production, in the correcting of hierarchical inequities. It is not that such aims were wrong; it is only that in the absence of attending to the inner world of man, such aims could only perpetuate the crimes of society under new and newly deceptive names. Give all of mankind an equal share of material goods today, and tomorrow there will exist the old inequities. Why? Obviously, because injustice emanates from man, not from circumstances; or, to be more precise, circumstances and the laws that support them emanate from the mind and heart of man. When the mind and heart are undeveloped or corrupt, no laws or economic system, however wisely conceived, can bring about the Good.

But do we not suffer from the same kind of illusion? What do "free markets" have to do with real human freedom unless they provide for the material needs of a people seeking the inner freedom that is the essence of the developing human soul? Without this inner aim, economics turns us into consumers, rather than creators.

What does political liberty have to do with personal liberty if it means only the right to satisfy one's own subjective desires, whatever they may be, without real reference to the moral law within? At the root of the American ideal of liberty is the right of every individual to search for and attend to the dictates of conscience. The individual is free, within reason, to make his external life support that search; he is free to seek wealth and property and climb to his vocation and create his family and even, if it so happens, a dynasty of sorts. It is all right, all of it; but it is not and cannot be the aim of life. Without the development of the soul, it is an illusion, and as such, it will, as the psalm says, simply "come to nothing."[141]

WHAT IS CHARACTER?

The life of society, family, work and status, the respect from others that we all need, the love from others that we need, the simple, obvious duties toward loved ones and our neighbor that we all yearn to fulfill—all of this takes its real power and meaning as expressions of and supports to the development of the soul—or, to place this specific meaning on the word: the development of "character." The American Revolution itself, if we may make this proposition, can symbolize the inner revolution by which the individual soul, perfected—the authentic character of man, developing and developed—rightfully takes its place as the inner sovereign, displacing the false king, "the brute of Britain," and all the false kings of myth and legend. "We think our civilization near its meridian," writes our greatest philosopher, Ralph Waldo Emerson, "but we are yet only at the cock-crowing and morning star. In our barbarous society the influence of character is in its infancy. As a political power, as the rightful lord who is to tumble all rulers from their chairs, its presence is hardly yet suspected."[142]

Consider, further, the American ideal of independence. Historically and intrinsically, the outer, political meaning of this ideal echoes a deeply internal and metaphysical meaning. Self-determination as an inner ideal means the voluntary submission of the physically and socially conditioned aspects of man to the interior power of conscious selfhood. It is in this interior power that there resides both the uniqueness of every human being and his or her fundamental independence from socially conditioned personality. Paradoxically, then, authentic individuality means freedom from "individualism." To put it in language that more closely resembles the language of the perennial teachings: the true *I Am* is independent of the small self, the ego.

If we think carefully about this distinction between the authentic self and the socially conditioned self, we can see into the deeper meaning of the word "character." A man or woman has character to the extent that the socially conditioned self, or personality, is obedient to the vision and moral feeling (conscience) of the authentic self. A man or woman of character is not a ghost of a human being; he or she is both a flesh-and-blood individual and an instrument of impersonal greatness; both a personality and a soul. But for this to be, the soul must occupy its place within, and this does not happen by itself, automatically. It requires the help and the struggle that the great wisdom teachings speak of and which, behind the scenes of what we call history, they offer—if only in the form of ideas that serve as pointers leading toward the great search for truth.

Beyond Personal Freedom

But what, in fact, has become of this idea of man's fundamental independence? In its purely external and political meaning, it now often signifies little more than an ideological affirmation of personal idiosyncrasy. We need to re-discover the meaning of the American idea of independence as an invitation to the individual and the community to love and serve the common good under freely chosen obedience to a higher law.

"The tendencies of the times," writes Emerson, "favor the idea of self-government, and leave the individual . . . to the rewards and penalties of his own constitution. . . . The movement in this direction has been very marked in modern history. Much has been blind and discredited, but the nature of the revolution is not affected by the vices of the revolters; for this is purely a moral force. . . ."

But, Emerson continues, speaking of the "invisibility" and powerlessness of this ideal: "It was never adopted by any *party* in history, *neither can be.*" Is he perhaps telling us that the American ideal of independence and the right and power of the individual to search for conscience in his life and actions cannot be embodied in government, that it can only be *protected* by government? "This ideal," he says, "separates the individual from all party, and unites him at the same time, to the [human] race." It is our personal freedom, yet at the same time "it promises a recognition of higher rights than personal freedom, or security of property."

Higher rights than personal freedom? What could that mean? "A man," says Emerson, "has a right to be employed, to be trusted, to be loved, to be revered. The power of love, as the basis of a state, has never been tried." What is he talking about? Does he actually imagine that love could be the basis of a nation existing in what we called "the world," with all its fear and violence? Or is Emerson to be understood quite differently—as offering the vision of a transformed State within a State, an America within America? Is that how we must interpret the following words, astonishing either in their idealism or in their prophetic vision of what the outer America, with all its physical power, its wise laws and its triumphant/tragic heroic/crime-ridden story, is meant to protect and foreshadow:

> We must not imagine that all things are lapsing into confusion, if
> every tender protestant be not compelled to bear his part in certain
> social conventions; nor doubt that roads can be built, letters carried,
> and the fruits of labor secured, when the government of force is at an
> end. . . . Could not a nation of friends even devise better ways? On
> the other hand, let not the most conservative and timid fear anything
> from a premature surrender of the bayonet and system of force.

Again, what is Emerson imagining? Is he taking us away from the world as it actually is, the real "world" of human passions and violence? Or is he opening the doors of our perception to a possible world within the world— the America of our hopes—within the flawed but littered-with-divine markings and not-yet-ashen ideals that at this moment in history comprise the America that we know, but of which we can rightfully say, "We don't know what we have here."

Emerson is no foolish optimist: "For," he continues, "according to the law of nature, which is quite superior to our will, it stands thus: there will always be a government of force, where men are selfish." But "when they are pure enough to abjure the code of force, they will be wise enough to see how these public ends of the post-office, of the highway, of commerce, and the exchange of property, of museums and libraries, of institutions, of art and science, can be answered." But for now, he says, "we live in a very low state of the world, and pay unwilling tribute to governments founded on force. . . ."[143]

THE SECRET OF AMERICA: TIME AND THE FUTURE

Emerson sees the American future as a culture founded on love. But even in such an extravagant idea, maybe especially in it, he is no foolish optimist. He knows what the world is really like. We are therefore obliged to listen to him as we are obliged to listen to every great prophet in history. When a true prophet speaks of the future, he is not descending to mere predictions of events. We are obliged to hear Emerson and to attend to America—that is to say, to the future of the earth—as *that which is possible,* never as that which is inevitable. To the prophetic mind and in the prophetic voice, the idea of the future is the idea of what can be and what will be—*depending always on the state of man's being.*

Here lies the secret of America—that it still has the future, that it offers mankind a future. The remnants of other nations and cultures may strike the sense of wonder in us with the greatness of their art and beauty and customs. But in these places we are looking into the past. In America, we are looking into the future—maybe an increasingly threatening future, but still a real one. America's spaces still exist, its vast stretches of nature— mountains, deserts, forests. America is still raw, still unplumbed, undeveloped. Spatially and temporally, America is still unfinished—as man, the unfinished animal, is still and ever not yet what he can become.

It is what man is now and what he can become that is the real, inner meaning of time and the future as the prophet understands these words. If we take America "literally," if we see around us conformity, corruption, rank injustice, materialism, superficiality and vulgarity, metaphysical squalor and blind attachment to physical comfort—if we see only that, we see the death of America and the end of its future. But if we look more deeply, we may still see a nation and a people granted for a brief moment the material and spiritual conditions enabling them to step into the real future of man, that is the future of the developing soul.

The future is another word for the soul. And the only hope for man is in the growth of the soul: such, uncompromisingly and without any possibility of bargaining, is the message of the teachings of wisdom, those very teachings whose reflection, however faint, gave original light to the ideals of the American nation.

We still have the future. America has the future in its grasp, though that grasp is weakening. Other nations and peoples have the past—and, flowing through the past to this continent, our continent, a new world was born: in pain, in sorrow, in greed, in corruption, in injustice, in the enslavement and murder of masses—but it was born; and nowhere on earth have worlds been born independently of the crimes of man—except for the inner worlds, the second history of the earth that flows within and amid the violent, confused first history of the earth. America was born and with it, the flame of the future—the flame of hope—was transmitted.

But without a specific effort on the part of man, without will and struggle, our future will disappear, hope will disappear—real, objective hope will disappear from our world.

TOWARD OBJECTIVE HOPE

But, what *is* hope when we stand in front of the anguish of our time, the afflictions visited upon us by our successes, by the very things in which we passively placed our hope: mental knowledge, technology, laws, the flag, short-term conquests in the sciences drawing in their train long-term terrors; the abandonment of traditional customs for the sake of comfort, pleasure and superficial "liberty"; the heavy influences we allow into the minds and bodies of our children—influences of violent imagery, egoism, drugs and sham ideals of fame and sexual titillation—all of which, combined with the lethal absence of metaphysical confidence in the adult world, poisons the seeds of innocent wonder, which is the root of all that is truly intellectual and moral in man, in that it is the germ of character, the germ of the developing soul, the first threads that connect man to what is higher in himself and in the universe.

We have placed our hope in *things,* and it is especially poignant to consider how many of us, and how many in the world, have placed their hope in external America—in its military power, its laws, its Constitution, its ideals. Such hope is purely passive in that it expects something outside of the inner world of man to bring to the world safety, love, honor and, above all, meaning. Passive hope is only a dream, not a force, certainly not a force for the good.

Our first and last question is this: Can America, with its great armies protecting itself and the world, with its Constitution lighting the way to empowering the peoples of the world—can America become both stronger and weaker than it now is? Weaker in the sense of allowing itself and the world to remember what it stands for—namely, the vision that requires of the individual submission to a higher, invisible reality; stronger in that it begins to remember what it was created to protect and shelter: the process by which men and women seek to tend the soul.

Why Have We Become So Strong?

Can America remember that it exists in the world and—in some way we do not understand—may even have been *allowed* to become so strong, in order to protect that upon which all the great civilizations of history have been based? America means the melting pot, yes, but not only of races and people but of the wisdom by which all races and peoples have sought to live. As the instrument of the unstoppable processes of modernity which are destroying the forms of traditional cultures, can America realize that it must assume the great task of helping to bring to the earth that which the great civilizations of the world once brought to the earth: namely, the teachings of wisdom and the path that wisdom offers its children, which leads to the soul's birth within the earth's body.

America must give back to the world the main thing it is taking from the world. If America does not remember itself as the guardian of the process by which the soul of man can grow and act upon the earth, then America will surely be destroyed, not necessarily through war, but slowly and from within like a hollowed-out tree standing tall in the desert of petrified life.

If America remembers its meaning, even if only a little—even to the extent that it continues to shelter a search that its rulers may no longer understand or acknowledge (its leaders, that is, of government, business, science and education)—then, as the nations and cultures of the world lose their own wisdom and ways to the soul under the pressure of modernity and advancing technology, then these nations and cultures will be touched once more by America; even the ones who fear America and wish to resist it will be touched. There may appear throughout the world the strange sense that something weak and fragile and exceedingly important is possible within America. If America, outer America—that is, the forces of modernity—is taking away religious practices and customs that each culture and nation may hold dear, if the world of other, older cultures sees its children casting away its old values and turning instead to the materialism that America (that is, modernity) is projecting into the world, these other cultures may also feel, subliminally even, that another process is being sheltered by America, a process of the inner search for the soul, and that it is this process that can bring again or preserve the real meaning of their own ancient and threatened spiritual ways. It will be the same thing outwardly; the ancient customs, language and symbols may be doomed, but they were and are only the outer manifestation of the energy of the soul that the creators of tradition embodied. Who knows what carriers of truth and wisdom are waiting to work behind the scenes of the outer history of the world?—to bring to the world a continuation or renewal of its inner history, the history that brings to the earth what is truly the Good for nature and for humanity?

Is America Necessary?

Will there appear communities of men and women carrying the eternal life of the soul, seeking it in the ever-new world, the ever-changing outer world? That question lies at the heart of the future of the earth. It is the question we can put to America—the symbolic America which now exists not only on the North American continent, but in the cities of Europe, the houses and mountains of Latin America, the vast populaces of Russia, India and China and even in the dangerous air of Jerusalem—cities and nations which incline their ear and eye now toward the thing called democracy, strange to their ancient ways, menacing to their ancient customs, but yet the only political form that can allow the world of today to exist tomorrow.

The world will see that it needs this entire America, America with its soul. It does not need and will absorb, resist, imitate and dissolve an empty America. A metaphysically empty America cannot endure, it will not survive; it may keep its name and armies for a while, it may keep its Constitution and its laws and forms of government, it may keep its symbolic heroes, it may remain a place where people wish to survive physically and economically; but without the inner resonance of its ideals and values, without the olive branch in its eagle claws—that is, without the primacy of the goal of peace, the peace like that of the American Indian, the peace that passes understanding—without its American soul, America is sure to go nowhere, and, if so, where will humanity go?

It is not that America is superior to the rest of the world. It is only that its newness and vitality led it to be the conduit for the forces of modernity that are now transmuting the civilization of the world. Perhaps we may even speculate that these forces needed an America, some nation or people through which they could act in the world. In this, America could very well be understood as the bringer of evil to mankind; but, like Hiawatha or even Atotarho, this same America was also the fountain of hope for the world, hope that resided in its inner ideals, its remarkable men and women, its colossal crimes that mirrored anew the horror of the sleep of the human soul, a horror whose power to shock had been dulled in the old, now-without-hope old worlds across the ocean. The reactions against America are, among other things, often the shock of the realization that even this land of hope could also be the carrier of such barbarism and injustice. But the disappointed hope in the outer America needs to be refined into hope in the developing soul. The world hoped in the outer America while subliminally feeling the resonance of the inner America. It must now be invited to begin to feel again the inner America. But first we who live here must feel it. If Americans themselves do not acknowledge the soul of America, the world may not wish to keep us.

And the world needs to keep us. The world needs to help America. It sounds strange, but America needs the goodwill of the world for its survival and for its role of sheltering the process of the inner search. This inner search can, of course, and will take place in other parts of the world—perhaps even better and more deeply than in the United States. But the preservation of a world order in which that search can take place depends for now on the success of America. Outer America has made the world safe for commerce; but in doing so, it must make the world safe for the inner America and the search for truth. It is called to sacralize this present world by keeping alive the external conditions and by protecting the inner attitudes that comprise the habitat of the growing human soul.

TWELVE

TOWARD A COMMUNITY
OF CONSCIENCE

W e have been asking for a vision of America that can help us see more clearly what we actually are and what we can work to become. And we are saying that this is the same kind of vision that we need in relation to ourselves as individuals struggling for self-knowledge and moral power. Like America itself, we need to discover how to look impartially at both the inner greatness that calls to us and the profound weaknesses that in fact determine the life we actually live—with all its self-deception, arrogance and betrayal.

With this personal aim in mind, the story of America—its heroes and triumphs as well as its crimes—takes on a new meaning and serves a purpose appropriate to our era: the search for the knowledge of how to become genuine men and women, through the nourishment of the soul. We seek neither to revile nor to romanticize the actions and actors of America's past. But the cultural hero of the present age is the *Seeker,* no longer—as it was in other times and in other cultures—the Warrior or the Savior or the Adventurer or the Lover or the Wise Man. All these mythic icons of the past take on new meaning by representing qualities needed in a search whose purity and intensity by themselves become the transforming forces that nourish the soul. The American story becomes a mythic story of what is needed in order for us to pursue that search—and of all that resists it, against which we must struggle.

OUR HEROES AND OURSELVES

Our heroes will remain heroes, but now more clearly heroes of both the inner world and the outer world of history. Or, shall we say, they will be permitted to remain heroes of the outer world of history only to the extent that we can see them as representing qualities needed in the inner world. And our attitude toward them will reflect our attitude toward ourselves. If we are bent merely on tearing down the old heroes and the old stories, emphasizing only the human weaknesses in our common past, we will be obliged to ask ourselves if we are denying our own possibilities as well; or, what is perhaps even more insidious, if we are implying that we are better than a Jefferson or a Franklin or a Washington, that we do not have in ourselves the same frailty, and even far more of it, than we believe we see in them and that we feel driven to decry and condemn. Or, at the other extreme, if we merely idolize them and therefore put them out of reach, as religion often puts its saints or saviors out of reach, are we not equally denying our own higher possibilities? Perhaps our heroes were giants, but perhaps we are giants as well—somewhere in the future along the path of the developing soul.

We need to remember that what was called the unforgivable sin is the denial of man's possible greatness, his kinship with the highest element in the universe—God, reason, love, call it what we will. To deny our possibilities is to deny the fundamental obligations and duties put before man in accordance with his structure and nature as an image of God: namely, to care for the inner divinity and through that to care for our neighbor. The First

Commandment, "Thou shalt have no other gods before me," is surely not only a commandment respecting a purely external greatness, but a commandment to attend to and care for the growing life of that greatness within ourselves; and "Love thy neighbor as thyself" surely does not mean that as we are, with all that is in us of fear and hate, we can transmit the divine power of love to our fellowman. One glance at the outer history of America, as well as at the events of almost any given day in our own lives, will show us that this cannot be what is meant by the commandment of love.

The commandment of worship and the commandment of love—the first commandment of Judaism and the defining commandment of Christianity—fuse together and illuminate the truth that the modern world, our present life, is now obliged to see as central: we are not what we are called to be; and we cannot become what we are meant to be simply by philosophizing about it and wishing for it, and surely not by pretending we are already fully man or fully woman.

We are asking to bring our own heroes and stories into the modern world—a world that no longer knows how to listen to the teachings of the great spiritual traditions and religions, and no longer knows how to care for our fellowman and treat each other as brothers and sisters; a world where the moral, religious and metaphysical truths of the past can no longer be received in the form in which they were once presented.

We are inviting, yearning for our heroes and stories to support us in this new world, this desert which we are obliged to cross. We are seekers, not knowers; we are searching for *how* to know, *how* to have faith, *how* to love, how, even, to hate—but to hate what is truly evil, not simply what we fear or do not like; and to hate in a way that does not destroy half of reality, but which preserves and maintains, while destroying only that which obstructs the wholeness of life. We are seeking, and above all we need to know how to search, how to inquire; and we need to ask our heroes to help us understand what may also be named our fundamental, practical question: what are the qualities and virtues of the seeker; who are the gods of the search for truth?

Into the space created by this fundamental, practical question there step our heroes, the few we have mentioned and so many others—Martin Luther King Jr., Harriet Tubman, Crazy Horse, to name just a few—waiting to take voice in our lives. Who are the American heroes of the search, and what do they represent?

Here is George Washington stepping back from power in order to allow the nation he has delivered to live according to its ideals. On the way to self-knowledge, what kind of stepping back, yielding, is needed? Is there a movement within oneself where it is necessary and possible, privately and without hidden psychological agendas, to let go of an important thought or a strong reaction in order simply to see what is and to be what I am? Is there a completely different order of motivation within ourselves that can be discovered only though the inward—invisible from the outside—sacrifice of what we are conditioned to imagine as power or safety or intelligence or love? And in the space created by that inner sacrifice, what actual qualities of power, understanding and love can be given us?

For example, as the Civil War progressed, those who came in touch with Lincoln were more and more astonished by his absence of malice toward the Confederacy and its leaders. Slowly, deliberately, Lincoln directed the war toward victory with a patience and will that became visible only over time, as, in the words of one observer, "those who had sought cunningly to lead him slowly found that he was leading them."[144]

No man ever sought victory with greater intensity and single-mindedness. But what kind of victory?—for whom? Or for what? Here, as at so many junctures, the legendary Lincoln meets us as a symbol of a completely different order of feeling—unmixed with any sense of ordinary personal gain—that is possible for man, a feeling that one must "earn"— though not necessarily as Lincoln earned it through the horror of war and the unimaginable burden of the vast numbers of dead and maimed, and of families and lands destroyed. But what does it evoke in us—we who may wish to become real—when, to take only one of countless examples, we hear of Lincoln visiting the sick and wounded soldiers in Virginia during the final days of the war?" In front of one of the great tents, as Carl Sandburg reports it, Lincoln was warned by a young army doctor: "Mr. President, you do not want to go in there . . . they are sick rebel prisoners." "That is just where I want to go," said Lincoln, and he strode in and shook hands from cot to cot.

> Shot-torn in both hips, lay Colonel Harry L. Benbow, who had commanded three regiments at Five Forks. And according to Colonel Benbow: "He halted beside my bed and held out his hand. I was lying on my back, my hands folded across my breast. Looking at him in the face, 'Mr. President,' I said, 'do you know to whom you offer your hand?' 'I do not,' he replied. 'Well,' said I, 'you offer it to a Confederate colonel who has fought you as hard as he could for four years.' 'Well,' said he, 'I hope a Confederate colonel will not refuse me his hand.' 'No, sir,' I replied, 'I will not,' and I clasped his hand in both of mine."[145]

This is the action of a man who, by all accounts, had ascended to the power of the presidency through an ambition not yet permeated by anything like love or humility; a man of considerable natural presence who was yet as cunning as any politician, as able to manipulate others, to persuade, to feint and dodge, to rise up in anger, to be crushed by anxiety, sorrow and disappointment, to be hurt, to be filled with regret and remorse, and yet to act more and more from a power of love and service to his nation, the people, his bedeviled wife—more and more from a wholly different quality of feeling, like a Peter Miller in front of Washington and in the manner of Washington's response to Miller seeking the life of the traitorous Michael Widman. The point is: these stories of American heroes meet us as something possible for us *not as we are, but as we can strive to become.* Lincoln is neither an unattainable saint nor a disguised self-seeking politician. He is a symbol—for the developing soul—of what to struggle *against* and what to struggle *for* in our own process of development. Neither saint nor sinner, but a symbol of the search, as are all the great warriors of myth, legend and scripture through the ages—the Islamic Ali urging the greater Holy War of self-overcoming; Arjuna of the *Bhagavad Gita* confronting the inner enemies "on the battlefield of life"; Gilgamesh and the monster Humbaba; the Arthurian knights of the Round Table—and on and on. Could Lincoln ever have so deeply willed the union of the states—in that sense saving America as a nation—without showing in himself the qualities of interior, personal unity? The ancient cultural symbols of the warrior and the statesman become redefined as aspects of the inner quest, representing that capacity in ourselves that can identify the disparate and warring parts of our own nature and, under the embrace of conscious mercy and conscious rigor, allow these parts to find their places within a greater inner unity of the self. "Out of many, one" (*e pluribus unum*) may no longer be taken solely as an external, political motto.

And as for Jefferson, recently the most beleaguered of our heroes because of his owning slaves and his alleged intimacy with one of them, it would be wise to consider to whom we are indebted for the very ethical ideals and standards by which many of us now judge him. *In large measure, we owe the formulation of these ideals to Jefferson himself.*

We need to consider how many of the great ethical and spiritual reformers of the world found their conscience when caught by and within the very milieu which they themselves rose up to challenge. The force of true moral vision always arises from the depths of conscience—the real conscience, not the socially conditioned superego that reflects mainly the moralisms of the society and compels behavior largely through fear and guilt. The real conscience almost always arises in the pain of one's own vision of one's moral betrayals. Only through seeing the crime in oneself does the power of conscience and moral reason actually take fire and become a force that can move mankind. The message of Christianity is nothing if it is not that it is through suffering one's own failure to love that the heart and mind are opened to a higher spirit. In the East the symbol of the heart and mind's awakening is the lotus flower flourishing in the dark, muddy waters. If we were to take moral contradiction as the standard of condemning a man, then there would exist none that are wise, none that are good, including all the saints and sages of every culture and tradition of the world.

It is not simply by behavior—our own or others'—that we must judge, if we judge at all; it is by how we face our own inner and outer manifestations; how clearly we see them, how truly we feel them, and how and to what extent we can express to ourselves and to our neighbor the ideal that defines our aim as man; and how intelligently and prudently we can help to create or at least obey conditions of life and thought that help the community to struggle with our human weaknesses and more nearly approach the life of the developing human soul.

Jefferson's political philosophy represents, among other things, the ideal of democracy as the communal self. His vision can represent for us a reflection for our time of the ancient teaching that no human being can come to the purity of the truth by his or her own unaided effort. No one can think truly, no one can come to the purity of conscience, no one can come to the capacity to break away from intellectual fear, moral cowardice or blind submission to desire, without the help of others in one form or another.

TOWARD A COMMUNITY OF CONSCIENCE

The search for truth, as well as the possibility of living in a society that provides the freedom and welfare necessary to live the life of ordinary men and women—this whole world of human life, comprising both the material and the spiritual needs of man, requires the creation of a community of conscience: requires the order, the structure of a community from within which can be generated the ideals, the knowledge and, above all, the new men and women who can bring light to the whole of society. That is what Jefferson can represent as a hope to us as seekers of truth and moral authenticity.

And, say what one will about the motivations of the men who crafted the Constitution in the oppressive summer of 1787, they became, while they were there, a community that worked at respecting and listening to one another. It was not only immediate self-interest that enabled them to step back from their agendas and their passionately held opinions. To believe that is to believe that "self-interest" is always a demeaning impulse. It is not; it depends entirely on, as it were, the nature of the "self" that one is serving. The Constitutional Convention can represent a deeply philosophical meaning if we remember well that the entire company and their proceedings were constantly under the eye and in the formidable presence of George Washington, who said little, but who *was* much. And at the other end of the room, as it were, was the mind and voice of Benjamin Franklin, constantly at the ready, articulating the search for the unique blend of practical prudence and spiritual idealism that renders him, by himself, a symbol of the inner quest in the midst of active, resourceful ordinary life.

Under the influence of Washington's presence and under the scrutiny of Franklin's intelligence, the representatives of the thirteen colonies found themselves drawn into a process of communal exchange that opened them to a wisdom that no one of them and no separate group of them could have reached alone. As a symbol of one key aspect of the kind of communal relationship that is needed in the search for truth, the Constitutional Convention stands for us at the very root of the American story.

OUR CRIMES AND OURSELVES

Turning to the crimes of America, it is imperative that we internalize them as well. By that what is meant is that it is imperative that we seek the power of deeply feeling man's inhumanity to man. While striving outwardly to eradicate injustice, it is imperative that humanity strive inwardly to feel the sorrow of its own capacity for evil. The American story contains the lightning bolt of that revelation as do few other historical narratives. Uniquely clear and astonishing is the moral contradiction of a nation founded so brilliantly on the ideals of freedom and its actions of brutality and oppression.

The point is that conscience is the only sure guide to moral action, and conscience is often heard only in a whisper and only for a moment. It often happens that a flash of deep moral feeling prompts a long train of action which soon loses its mooring in the full understanding that came originally from conscience. And in such cases, it often happens that action becomes a screen covering the truth of conscience rather than an expression and extension of it into the world. While maintaining the verbal formulation of the ideals given by a moment of moral vision, the action deviates in quality and form, and even in aim, from the original impulse, and does so without the actor's awareness. Slavery and racism are surely such deviations from the ideal of equality and freedom; the destruction of the Indian and his culture is surely just such a deviation from the vision of human rights that forms the heart and spine of the American philosophy.

A key factor in this phenomenon of deviation, and one we are obliged to study in ourselves, is that it takes place in the dark, screened from our awareness, and under the banner of the very moral ideals from which it is deviating. Our capacity to avert our awareness from the moral and metaphysical contradictions of our own nature is a fact that cannot be seen and studied without a serious commitment to truth and without help from companions and from the teachings of wisdom that call to us through the ages.

One needs to try to enter into the position not only of the victim, *but of the oppressor.* It is not hard to imagine, up to a certain point, of course, the suffering of the slave or the brutalized Indian. What is in its way much harder, but absolutely essential, is to let oneself feel what it was like to murder and brutalize wrapped in a sure sense of self-justification. And if we have worked to understand the greatness of the humanity we have destroyed and the greatness of the culture we have annihilated, and if we then can imagine ourselves as the agents of these actions, we may catch a glimpse of this deep-rooted phenomenon of moral autohypnosis, the sleep of conscience, the sorrowful capacity, of fallen man to hide from our profound betrayal of the good in our actual and potential actions.

It is imperative that the seeker confront this aspect of oneself in the midst of everyday life as well as in one's place as part of mankind's actions in the sweep of history. We need myths, symbols and stories that make us both raise our heads in the vision of authentic human dignity and lower our heads in the vision of authentic remorse—and that then prepare us to live our lives with eyes and head straight forward, stepping into the future of the new America we may discover in ourselves and of the old Earth, which is yearning for all of us to become genuine men and women of the soul.

CODA

And now, Walt Whitman, give us words for the journey.

I hail with joy the oceanic, variegated, intense practical energy, the demand for facts, even the business materialism of the current age, our states. But woe to the age and land in which these things, movements, stopping at themselves, do not tend to ideas. As fuel to flame, and flame to the heavens, so must wealth, science, materialism—even this democracy of which we make so much—unerringly feed the highest mind, the soul. . . .

To take expression, to incarnate . . . to achieve spiritual meanings, and suggest the future—these only satisfy the soul. We must not say one word against real materials; but the wise know that they do not become real till touched by emotions, the mind. . . .

As we have shown the New World including in itself the all-leveling aggregate of democracy, we show it also including the all-varied, all-permitting, all-free theorem of individuality, and erecting therefor a lofty and hitherto unoccupied framework or platform, broad enough for all, eligible to every farmer and mechanic—to the female equally with the male—a towering self-hood, not physically perfect only—not satisfied with the mere mind's and learning's stores, but religious, possessing the idea of the infinite . . . realizing, above the rest, that known humanity, in deepest sense, is fair adhesion to itself, for purposes beyond—and that, finally, the personality of mortal life is most important with reference to the immortal, the unknown, the spiritual, the only permanently real, which as the ocean waits for and receives the rivers, waits for us each and all . . .

FOR FURTHER READING

These are a few of the books that have helped me deepen the question of the meaning of America.

E. G. ALDERFER, *The Ephrata Commune: An Early American Counterculture* (Pittsburgh: University of Pittsburgh Press, 1985). A superb study of the Ephrata community and its meaning in the history and destiny of America.

CATHERINE DRINKER BOWEN, *Miracle at Philadelphia: The Story of the Constitutional Convention, May to September 1787* (Boston: Atlantic Little Brown, 1966). A gripping and comprehensive historical narrative that opens the reader to all the aspects—historical, political and purely human—of the miracle of the creation of America.

LESTER J. CAPPON (Editor), *The Adams-Jefferson Letters* (Chapel Hill: The University of North Carolina Press, 1959). The thought of these two Founding Fathers, and also of the great Abigail Adams, shows us the whole of life as seen through the lens of the idea of America. It is extraordinary evidence that this idea encompasses far more than the political and economic realm. In addition, the drama of the personal relation of the two men—from friendship to enmity and finally to profound mutual respect and love—makes this collection of letters one of the most dramatic literary and intellectual documents of the American nation.

FREDERICK DOUGLASS, *Narrative of the Life of Frederick Douglass* and *My Bondage and My Freedom* in *Autobiographies* (New York: Library of America, 1994). These books plus any number of Douglass' orations are unsurpassed for their literary power and their insight not only into the problem of American racism, but into the idea of America itself.

RALPH WALDO EMERSON: Of all Emerson's great essays, perhaps "Self-Reliance" stands out for the way it connects the American ideal of the primacy of the *individual* with the ancient wisdom teaching about the Universal Self within all human beings.

BIL GILBERT, *Westering Man: The Life of Joseph Walker* (Norman, Oklahoma, and London: University of Oklahoma Press, 1985). This biography of Joseph Walker, one of the greatest of America's frontier leaders, offers a broad picture of the human qualities that defined and created the westward growth of the American nation. Of particular interest is Walker's extraordinary ability to get people to cooperate for the common good.

DONALD A. GRINDE, JR. *The Iroquois and the Founding of the American Nation* (San Francisco: The Indian Historian Press, 1977) and BRUCE E. JOHANSEN, *Forgotten Founders: How the American Indian Helped Shape Democracy* (Boston: The Harvard Common Press, 1982). Two of the best historical discussions of the question of the parallels between the constitution of the Iroquois Confederacy and principal elements of the American Constitution—and the possibility of direct influence of the Iroquois form of government on the shaping of the Constitution.

RICHARD H. GUMMERE, *The American Colonial Mind and the Classical Tradition* (Cambridge: Harvard University Press, 1963) and CARL J. RICHARD, *The Founders and the Classics: Greece, Rome, and the American Enlightenment* (Cambridge: Harvard University Press, 1994). Few Americans today realize how seriously the Founders studied the culture of the classical world and how deeply they were influenced by the writings of classical authors. These two books are excellent discussions of this underappreciated aspect of America's roots and, as such, they greatly help us to understand the intellectual depth at the heart of the idea of America.

ALEXANDER HAMILTON, JAMES MADISON and JOHN JAY, *The Federalist Papers.* From 1787 to 1788 Hamilton, Madison and Jay wrote these essays as arguments for the general ratification of the Constitution. Together, they form the most important commentary ever written on the American system of government. Several of these essays, such as No. 10, are required reading for anyone seeking to understand the philosophical underpinnings of the Constitution.

RICHARD HOFSTADTER, *The American Political Tradition* (New York: Vintage Books, 1974). An endlessly illuminating analysis of key figures in the ongoing creation of America: Jefferson, Lincoln, Wilson, FDR and others. Solid, tough-minded and boldly intelligent, this book makes a great ally in the effort to cut through clichés and assumptions about America.

RALPH LERNER, *The Thinking Revolutionary: Principle and Practice in the New Republic* (Ithaca and London: Cornell University Press, 1979). Philosophically insightful and provocative essays about individuals and issues: commerce, race, the Supreme Court, Franklin, Jefferson, Tocqueville and others.

CARL SANDBURG, *Abraham Lincoln: The Prairie Years and The War Years* (New York: Dell Publishing Co., Laurel Edition, 1959). The author's abridgement of his monumental, six-volume biography. Among the countless biographies of Lincoln, this one, written by one of America's greatest poets, surely is unsurpassed in showing us both the historical and the legendary Lincoln in a way that simultaneously informs the mind and opens the heart.

PAGE SMITH, *A New Age Now Begins, Vol. I* and *II* (New York: Penguin Books, 1989). A lucid and dramatic history of the American Revolution, forming the first two volumes of the author's masterful series, *A People's History of the United States.* Smith's often unspoken philosophical sensitivity lends an unusually vivifying energy to accounts of the political, economic, sociocultural and military aspects of American history.

ALEXIS DE TOCQUEVILLE, *Democracy in America*. Written by a French statesmen and social philosopher in the first half of the nineteenth century, this remains one of the most comprehensive and profoundly observed analyses of American society ever written. There exist many good translations and abridgments.

BARBARA W. TUCHMAN, *The First Salute: A View of the American Revolution* (New York: Alfred A. Knopf, 1988). A luminously clear narrative of the key events and protagonists of the War of Independence, showing—but without dwelling on—the human side of Washington and others, especially as their actions are played out within the web of forces, including the huge element of luck, that shapes the destinies of all nations.

PAUL WALLACE, *White Roots of Peace: The Iroquois Book of Life* (Santa Fe: Clear Light Publishers, 1994). Probably the most comprehensive and accessible published narration of the great myth of the founding of the Iroquois Confederacy.

FRANK WATERS, *Book of the Hopi* (New York: Penguin Books, 1977). There are now a great many books available that give a sense of the depth of the American Indian traditions and way of life. This book was one of the first and remains one of the very best in portraying the profundity of the Indian teachings and culture.

PARSON M. L. WEEMS, *A History of the Life and Death, Virtues and Exploits of General George Washington* (New York: Grosset & Dunlap, 1927). Written during Washington's lifetime, this book is the source of the fictitious tale of the young Washington and the cherry tree. But to read it is to be surprised by the power of the mythic Washington that is fashioned out of a combination of Parson Weems' imagination and genuine historical material, and to understand why this book was once so meaningful to so many Americans. Although it caters to the popular taste of its time, there is an honorable idealism in it that one might wish to recover, without necessarily buying into the particular kind of myth it created.

WALT WHITMAN, *Democratic Vistas*. As characterized in the present book, this essay may justly be considered the most powerful manifesto ever written about the meaning of American democracy. It can be found in many collections of Whitman's writings.

GARRY WILLS, *Cincinnatus: George Washington and the Enlightenment* (New York: Doubleday, 1984) and *Lincoln at Gettysburg: The Words That Remade America* (New York: Simon and Schuster, 1992). All of Garry Wills' books about America bring great intellectual depth and dynamism to the study of American history and culture. These two books examine the heroic significance of Washington and of Lincoln in a philosophically scintillating and historically comprehensive way.

GORDON S. WOOD, *The Radicalism of the American Revolution: How a Revolution Transformed a Monarchical Society Into a Democratic One Unlike Any That Had Ever Existed* (New York: Alfred A. Knopf, 1992). The subtitle says it all: a masterful analysis of the energy and genius that entered the world through the American Revolution.

Notes

1. See especially Carl J. Richard, *The Founders and the Classics* (Cambridge: Harvard University Press, 1994).

2. Epictetus, *The Discourses of Epictetus,* trans. P. E. Matheson, book 2, ch. 5 (brackets mine); in Whitney Oates, ed., *The Stoic and Epicurean Philosophers* (New York: Modern Library, 1940), p. 288.

3. Marcus Aurelius, *Meditations* 5.10, trans. Pierre Hadot in Pierre Hadot, *The Inner Citadel* (Cambridge: Harvard University Press, 1998), p. 130.

4. The Gospel of Thomas, logion 5, in A. Guillaumont *et al.,* trans: *The Gospel According to Thomas* (New York: Harper & Row, 1959), p. 5.

5. *Republic* 443.

6. The "Second Democracy" seems to have existed, at least in theory and in part, in the internal social organization of Freemasonry. Its influence on the American political structure is discussed by Steven C. Bullock in *Revolutionary Brotherhood: Freemasonry and the Transformation of the American Social Order; 1730–1840* (Chapel Hill: University of North Carolina Press, 1996).

7. William Penn, *Primitive Christianity Revived,* ch. 1, par. 1, in Giles Gunn, ed., *New World Metaphysics* (New York: Oxford University Press, 1981), p. 80.

8. Deut. 6:5.

9. "Motion for Prayers in the Convention," in *Benjamin Franklin: Writings* (New York: Library of America, 1987), pp. 1138–1139.

10. Catherine Drinker Bowen, *Miracle at Philadelphia: The Story of the Constitutional Convention, May to September 1787* (Boston: Atlantic Little Brown, 1966), pp. 126–127.

11. John Adams to Thomas Jefferson, May 19, 1821, in Lester J. Cappon, ed., *The Adams-Jefferson Letters* (Chapel Hill: University of North Carolina Press, 1959), p. 573.

12. "Speech in the Convention at the Conclusion of Its Deliberations," in *Benjamin Franklin: Writings,* pp. 1139–1141.

13. Garry Wills, *Cincinnatus: George Washington and the Enlightenment* (New York: Doubleday, 1984).

14. Gordon S. Wood, *The Radicalism of the American Revolution* (New York: Knopf, 1992), pp. 205–206.

15. Ralph Waldo Emerson, journal entry of July 6, 1852. Cited in Joel Porte, ed., *Emerson in His Journals* (Cambridge: Harvard University Press, 1982), p. 435. Emphasis mine.

16. Noemie Emery, *Washington: A Biography* (New York: Putnam, 1976), pp. 7–14, 383.

17. James Thomas Flexner, *Washington: The Indispensable Man* (New York: New American Library, 1979), pp. xiv–xv, 1.

18. Ibid., pp 1, 22–24.

19. Page Smith, *A New Age Now Begins: A People's History of the American Revolution* (New York: Penguin Books, 1989), 2:995.

20. Barbara W. Tuchman, *The First Salute* (New York: Knopf, 1988), p. 183.

21. Ibid., p. 182.

22. Smith, *A New Age Now Begins,* 2:1130. Emphasis mine.

23. Ibid., 2:1133.

24. Cited in Richard Brookhiser, *Founding Father* (New York: Free Press, 1996), p. 111.

25. Flexner, *Washington,* p. 34.

26. Cited in Smith, *A New Age Now Begins,* 2:1427.

27. Flexner, *Washington,* pp. 34–35. Emphasis mine.

28. The full text may be found on the World Wide Web at http://www.history.org/life/manners/rules2.html.

29. Benjamin Franklin, *The Autobiography of Benjamin Franklin,* in Franklin, *Writings,* p. 1382. (Emphasis mine.)

30. Ibid., p. 1396.

31. Ibid., p. 1395.

32. Ibid., pp. 1384–1385.

33. George Washington, *Circular to the States,* in *The Writings of George Washington from the Original Manuscript Sources,* edited by John C. Fitzpatrick, 39 vols. (Washington D.C.: Government Printing Office, 1931–44). Accessed as *The Founders' Constitution,* vol. 1, chap. 7, doc. 5, at http://press-pubs.uchicago.edu/founders/documents/v1ch7s5.html.

34. Ibid.

35. Ibid.

36. Ibid. Emphasis mine.

37. Ibid.

38. Gia-Fu Feng and Jane English, trans., *Lao Tsu, Tao Te Ching* (New York: Vintage Books, 1989), verse 66.

39. Ibid., verse 9.

40. George Washington, *Farewell Address,* in Fitzpatrick, *The Writings of George Washington,* http://press-pubs.uchicago.edu/founders/documents/v1ch18s29.html.

41. Ibid.

42. Ibid.

43. Ibid.

44. *Republic* 444; adapted from Jowett trans.

45. George Washington, *Farewell Address.*

46. The phrase "foreign entanglements" is often attributed to Washington but was not actually used by him. Jefferson, in his first inaugural address, emphasized the impor-

tance of establishing "honest friendship with all nations, entangling alliances with none."

47. Isaiah 31:1.

48. George Washington, *Farewell Address.*

49. Ibid.

50. The section title is from James Thomas Flexner, *George Washington: The Forge of Experience (1732–1775)* (Boston: Little Brown, 1965).

51. George Washington, *Farewell Address.*

52. Ibid.

53. Ibid. Emphasis mine.

54. Ibid.

55. *Republic,* book 7.

56. George Washington, *Farewell Address.*

57. *Republic* 577C.

58. George Washington, *Farewell Address.*

59. William Nisbet Chambers, *Political Parties in a New Nation* (New York: Oxford University Press, 1963), pp. 2–3.

60. Flexner, *Washington,* p. 326.

61. George Washington, *Farewell Address.* Emphasis mine.

62. Ibid.

63. Ibid. Emphasis mine.

64. Ibid.

65. Ibid.

66. Ibid.

67. Ibid.

68. Letter to J. Taylor, 1798; cited in Saul K. Padover, ed., *Thomas Jefferson on Democracy* (New York: New American Library, 1946), pp. 42–43.

69. To Abigail Adams, 1804, ibid., p. 44. Emphasis mine.

70. To Judge Johnson, 1823, ibid., p. 45.

71. To____?, New York Public Library, MS, 4, 193; ibid., p. 13. *Opinion . . . whether the seat of government shall be transferred to the Potomac,* July 15, 1790, ibid., p. 15.

72. To T. Law, 1814, ibid., p. 17.

73. To Monroe, 1782, ibid., p. 14.

74. To P. Fitzhugh, 1798, ibid., p. 52.

75. Richard Hofstadter, *The American Political Tradition* (New York: Vintage Books, 1974), pp. 3–4.

76. Ibid., p. 8.

77. Ibid.

78. This and all subsequent references to Madison are from *The Federalist* No. 10, in *The Federalist Papers by Alexander Hamilton, James Madison and John Jay,* with an introduction and commentary by Garry Wills (New York: Bantam Books, 1982). Emphases mine.

79. *The Federalist* No. 84.

80. Ibid.

81. Charles Hamilton and Lloyd Ostendorf, *Lincoln in Photographs* (Norman, Okla.: University of Oklahoma Press, 1963).

82. Philip B. Kunhardt Jr., et al., *Lincoln: An Illustrated Biography* (New York: Knopf, 1992), pp. 221, 258.

83. Hamilton and Ostendorf, *Lincoln in Photographs,* p. 348.

84. Smith, *A New Age Now Begins,* 1:153. Emphasis mine.

85. Ibid., p. 154.

86. Ralph Waldo Emerson, "Abraham Lincoln: Remarks at the Funeral Services Held in Concord, April 19, 1865," in *Miscellanies* by Ralph Waldo Emerson (Boston: Houghton Mifflin and Company, 1883), p. 308.

87. Woodrow Wilson, *Selected Literary and Political Papers and Addresses of Woodrow Wilson* (New York: Grosset and Dunlap, 1925), 1:224. Quoted from Wilson's address, "Abraham Lincoln: A Man of the People." Emphasis mine.

88. Ibid., p. 226.

89. Ibid., pp. 226–227. Emphasis mine.

90. Ibid., p. 230. Emphasis mine.

91. Hofstadter, *American Political Tradition,* pp. 171–172.

92. A substantial body of literature now exists dealing with the historical and conceptual relationship between the Iroquois principles of government and the formation of the American Constitution. See Bruce E. Johansen, *Forgotten Founders: How the American Indian Helped Shape Democracy* (Boston: Harvard Common Press, 1982), for a thoughtful treatment. An excellent bibliography is appended. See also: http://www.ratical.com/many_worlds/6Nations/NAPSnEoD7586.html.

93. Isaiah 45:7.

94. My source for the creation story is principally a retelling of the Onondaga story of creation in an unpublished manuscript by Maril Rianna Blanchard. I am greatly indebted to her for allowing me to make extensive use of her work. I have also consulted J. N. B. Hewitt, *Iroquoian Cosmology,* second part (New York: AMS Press, 1974). The full story is a vast epic, and many elements of it have necessarily been omitted here.

    For the legend of the Iroquoian Confederacy, my main source has been Paul Wallace, *White Roots of Peace* (Santa Fe: Clear Light, 1994). I am grateful for their permission to quote liberally from the story of Deganawidah. The name *Deganawidah* has been changed throughout to "The Great Peacemaker," following a personal communication with Chief Oren Lyons concerning the sacred quality inherent in the name and the demand to refrain from writing or pronouncing it before the moment that he must be called to return to the earth and its people.

95. The translation is from Hewitt, *Iroquoian Cosmology,* p. 514. "So that shall be called the great monkey[ape]." Obviously a question arises, as these animals are not indigenous to North America. In any case, the general intent and meaning seem clear from the context: Flint is creating another "imperfect animal"—a distortion of the human essence. Here it is interesting to note one of the traditional Christian designations of the devil as "the master of imperfect animals" or "lord of the flies."

96. This is not the Hiawatha of Henry Wadsworth Longfellow's epic poem. Longfellow's inspiration was a collection of Ojibwa tales, and he used the name of the Iroquois chief for the hero of his famous Ojibwa-based story.

97. According to Barbara Graymont, the name, among the Mohawks, means "He Was Awake." *The Iroquois in the American Revolution* (Syracuse, N.Y.: Syracuse University Press, 1972), p. 14.

98. Frederick Douglass, *What to the slave is the fourth of July? An address delivered in Rochester, New York, on 5 July 1852*, in John W. Blassingame and John R. McKivigan, eds., *The Frederick Douglass Papers*, series 1, *Speeches, Debates, and Interviews*, vol. 2, 1847–54 (New Haven: Yale University Press, 1982), p. 368.

99. Ibid., p. 371.

100. Ibid., p. 361.

101. Ibid.

102. Ibid.

103. Ibid., pp. 362–364.

104. Ibid.

105. Ibid.

106. Ibid.

107. Ibid.

108. Ibid.

109. Ibid.

110. Ibid.

111. Ibid., p. 367.

112. Ibid.

113. Ibid., p. 368.

114. Frederick Douglass, *My Bondage and My Freedom* (1855), in *Frederick Douglass: Autobiographies* (New York: Library of America, 1994), p. 283 (ch. 17).

115. Ibid., p. 286.

116. *What to the slave is the fourth of July?* p. 368.

117. Ibid.

118. Ibid., pp. 382–383.

119. Ibid.

120. Letter to Jean Nicholas Démeunier, June 26, 1786, in Boyd, *Papers of Thomas Jefferson,* 10:63; cited in Blassingame, *The Frederick Douglass Papers,* 2:383.

121. *What to the slave is the fourth of July?* p. 383.

122. Ibid.

123. Ibid., p. 384.

124. Ibid., p. 386.

125. Isaiah 59:1.

126. *What to the slave is the fourth of July?* p. 387.

127. *The Blessings of Liberty and Education: An Address Delivered in Manassas, Virginia, on 3 September 1894,* in Blassingame and McKivigan, *The Frederick Douglass Papers,* 5:624.

128. Garry Wills, *Lincoln at Gettysburg: The Words That Remade America* (New York: Simon and Schuster, 1992), p. 186.

129. Ralph Waldo Emerson, "The Over-Soul" in *Emerson: Essays and Lectures,* ed. by Joel Porte (New York: Library of America, 1983), pp. 383–400.

130. Susan R. Stein, *The Worlds of Thomas Jefferson at Monticello* (Monticello, Va.: Abrams, 1993), p. 219.

131. The following narration is drawn from the account in Julius Friedrich Sachse, *The German Sectarians of Pennsylvania* (New York: AMS Press; reprinted from the edition of 1899–1900, Philadelphia), 2:427–432.

132. Etienne Duponceau, cited in Smith, *A New Age Begins,* 2:1000.

133. Thomas Mann, *Doctor Faustus,* trans. by H. T. Lowe-Porter (New York: Knopf, 1948), pp. 63, 66–67.

134. E. G. Alderfer, *The Ephrata Commune: An Early American Counterculture* (Pittsburgh: University of Pittsburgh Press, 1985), pp. 86–106.

135. Ibid., p. 90.

136. Ibid.

137. Ibid., p. 93.

138. *Chronicon Ephratense: A History of the Community of the Seventh Day Baptists at Ephrata . . .* Trans. J. Max Hark. Lancaster, 1889. Reprint. (New York: Burt Franklin, 1972), p. 139.

139. From "Abraham Lincoln" in *November Boughs,* in *Walt Whitman: Collected Poetry and Collected Prose* (New York: Library of America, 1982), pp. 1196–1198.

140. All citations from *Democratic Vistas* are from *Democratic Vistas and Other Papers by Walt Whitman* (London: Walter Scott [n.d.]; republished St. Clair Shores, Mich.: Scholarly Press, 1970). All subsequent passages from Whitman are from *Democratic Vistas.*

141. Psalm 1. The King James translation reads: "The way of the wicked shall perish." The Hebrew is simple and concrete and could even be rendered as "The way of the wicked will *peter out,*" that is, the actions of the unrighteous go against the laws of the universe and, as such, can give no real results.

142. "Politics,"*Essays,* 2nd series (New York: Library of America, 1983), p. 338.

143. Ibid.

144. Carl Sandburg, *Abraham Lincoln: The Prairie Years and the War Years* (New York: Dell), 3:808.

145. Ibid., p. 802.

INDEX

ABOUT THE AUTHOR

The author of *Money and the Meaning of Life; The Heart of Philosophy; The New Religions; Time and the Soul;* and *Lost Christianity,* among other books, Jacob Needleman is Professor of Philosophy at San Francisco State University and former Director of the Center for the Study of New Religions at the Graduate Theological Union, Berkeley, California. He was educated at Harvard, Yale and the University of Freiburg, Germany. He has also served as Research Associate at the Rockefeller Institute for Medical Research and was a Research Fellow at Union Theological Seminary. In addition to his teaching and writing he serves as a consultant in the fields of psychology, education, medical ethics, philanthropy and business. He has also been featured on Bill Moyers's acclaimed PBS television series *A World of Ideas.* He lives with his wife, Gail, in Oakland, California.